DANTE GABRIEL ROSSETTI:
PAINTER POET OF HEAVEN
IN EARTH

WILLIAM BELL SCOTT, JOHN RUSKIN, DANTE ROSSETTI, IN 1864,
IN ROSSETTI'S GARDEN AT 16 CHEYNE WALK, CHELSEA, THE LARGE
HOUSE HE LEASED AFTER HIS WIFE'S DEATH IN 1862

DANTE GABRIEL ROSSETTI

PAINTER POET OF HEAVEN
IN EARTH

BY

R. L. MÉGROZ

*

LONDON

Faber & Gwyer

FIRST PUBLISHED IN MCMXXVIII
BY FABER & GWYER LIMITED
24 RUSSELL SQUARE LONDON W.C.I
PRINTED IN GREAT BRITAIN
AT THE CHISWICK PRESS LONDON
ALL RIGHTS RESERVED

PREFATORY NOTE

THE MATERIAL of this book enforced a totally different plan of composition from that of my previous study on Francis Thompson and poetic mysticism. If I should be fortunate enough to have some sympathetic readers of both studies, they will realize that there are threads of thought which connect the two. For this reason at least a word about the scheme of the present study will not be out of place. Instead of spreading out gradually over more and more of the poet's traditional background, as in the case of *Francis Thompson*, the argument is repeated in slightly different aspects every few chapters. Rossetti's rich and varied work in two arts is a miracle of concentration, a series of spiral curves the ends of which meet. 'Typical' and 'characteristic' are the words which continually jump to one's pen in writing either biography or criticism about Rossetti. His life and his work are reflections of each other, and both are reflections of an extraordinarily fixed personality. I have tried to put into fourteen lines of verse the whole essential argument of this book:

Self-hunting heart, you opened to noon's desire
   Night's deep-leaved dell where dreams moon-haunted grope,
   Because unveiled Astarte crowned the slope
Of mounting manhood though Beatrice shone yet higher;
And your blood thundered into blinding fire.
   Then Beatrice vanished, leaving the One Hope
   Less clear than Dante's in Love's horoscope
To grow through virtues vain and agony dire.

Self-exiled, oracular soul, raptured you tell
   Old secrets of the vale of Proserpine
   Where ache the servant dreams whose rich-wrought sign
Glows with your beauty in the glooms of hell,
While shaken is death's hollow by the spell
   They sing there of the spirit's Palestine.

[vii]

CONTENTS

CONTENTS

PART ONE: MAINLY BIOGRAPHICAL

PART TWO: MAINLY CRITICAL

CONTENTS

APPENDIXES

[x]

ILLUSTRATIONS

PART ONE
MAINLY BIOGRAPHICAL

CHAPTER I

PARENTS

*' Such separations (i.e., from one set of circumstances to
another), if you follow them down to their logical source, start,
I suppose, at the moment you are taken away from your mother
and given to a nurse. So it continues until old age, or bad
health, reverses the order and you are no longer taken away on
every such occasion, but are always coming back to something—
are beginning to return, in fact, towards the direction from which
you originally came.'*—SACHEVERELL SITWELL.

THE ROSSETTIS were a family of humble workers
originally named Della Guardia, in the city of Vasto,
in Abruzzo Citeriore, on the Adriatic coast of what
was once known as the Kingdom of Naples or The Two
Sicilies. Some of the Della Guardias seem to have been
thatched with hair of noticeable hue, and their Vastese
friends did not lose the opportunity of nicknaming them
'the Rossetti', 'the Little Reds', to which English school-
boys can supply several native equivalents. Burne-Jones's
mode of addressing Swinburne, 'dear little Carrots', is a
fair translation.

The Rossetti family become notable towards the end of
the eighteenth century. Nicola Rossetti, a blacksmith and
locksmith in Vasto, married Maria Francesca Pietrocola,
the daughter of a shoemaker. This humble couple had
four sons and three daughters. Andrea, the eldest son, was
preacher and became Canon of the principal church in his
native city. The second son, Domenico, was admired as a
scholar and an improvisatore; the fourth son is said also to
have shown poetic talent, although he was a barber; the
third son, Gabriele, who was born on 1st March 1783,

[15]

added to the industrious aspirations of his brothers an irrepressible self-confidence and idealism: he supplied the fire-works.

Mr. Frank Rutter ingeniously remarked that the pre-Raphaelite movement is distinctly related to the result of the battle of Waterloo. Wellington's victory (some thirty years before a few young men in London simultaneously began to paint and to have ideas about painting) indirectly caused the restoration to the throne of Naples of the Bourbon tyrant, Ferdinand I. Ferdinand's return meant the speedy exit, for life-saving purposes, of one Gabriele Pasquale Giuseppe Rossetti, the people's political poet.[1]

Gabriele, like his famous son, started early to write verse and to draw. Writing to his brother Domenico, he speaks of a self-portrait done in 1804: ' A miniature portrait of myself, the work of my own hand when I exercised myself much in the fine art which imitates visible truths. I was at that time fresher-looking, and perhaps rather plumper, and slightly paler; before the sanguine-choleric temperament obtained the mastery in me with that vigour which it now displays '.[2] The change in physical constitution was not unlike the process in the case of Gabriele's son; what has been solely attributed to chloral may have been in part a temperamental inheritance: the quickly irritable nervous organization and disorders of the circulatory system.

Gabriele Rossetti's local reputation as a poet caused his services to be used by the San Carlo Theatre of Naples, though the youthful librettist earned more glory than cash. In the heavy literal blank verse translation of his Autobiography by his son William, the unintentionally humorous but very likable Gabriele tells us:

> And I was made, without soliciting,
> The Poet for San Carlo's Theatre.

---

[1] Chap. I, *Dante Gabriel Rossetti : Painter and Man of Letters*, by Frank Rutter.

[2] Quoted by W. M. Rossetti, *Gabriele Rossetti : a Versified Autobiography*, p. 11, footnote.

I wrote some dramas there, and every one
Of my attempts was followed by success:
First Julius Sabinus' mournful fate,
Then Hannibal's light loves in Capua,
And finally the Birth of Hercules,
Were greeted with unanimous applause.
How much I joyed that on that stately stage
My mind was thus allowed to spatiate !
' In this arena of glory ', I would say,
' If I have genius, I can show it forth ';
And dreamed of mingling in one dulcet draught
Alfieri's style with Metastatio's.
But my illusions waned ; for various thwarts,
And fetters both direct and indirect,
And the composers and the Managers,
And Prime Donne, plots, and etiquettes,
And then protectors and aught stranger still,
Frequently shuffled all my hand of cards.
Incensed I cried: ' I'll leave the Theatre,
For here I'm nothing but a slave of slaves '.

So Gabriele sped to Monsignor Capecelatro, the
Minister for Neapolitan Home-affairs, ' expounding first
the facts: " The madhouse is not where I want to go " '.
The result of his interview was a post as Assistant Curator
in the Naples Museum, for which he received a salary of
about £30 a year, rising to £60 later. But the young man
amid the antique bronzes and marbles which were his
special charge, continued to educate himself, reading,
talking (he already showed an unusual gift for making
friends of interesting men), and writing verse, much of
which became part of the popular stock of balladry. He
also developed an ability above that of the average—which
was high among the Neapolitan poets—of extempore
composition, a facility which, though rarely tested, he still
possessed when he resided at peace some twenty years
later in North London, a married man and a father. His
Museum post was succeeded by a secretaryship in the
Arts section of the Ministry of Public Instruction, and
during this period, which ended in 1815 with the downfall
of the Napoleonic regime, he included King Murat among

his friends. But the odes and proclamations composed by Gabriele Rossetti at the time of the Naples ' revolution ', which Shelley sang in his ' Ode to Naples ', caused him to be a marked man when Ferdinand returned with an Austrian army in the following year and revoked the Constitution he had sworn to uphold. One lyric in particular, expressive of the patriotic rage at the treachery of *il Rè Nasone*, suggesting the possibility of him being knifed if he came back, was enough to put Rossetti's life in peril. To what extent the future pre-Raphaelite movement depended upon the escape of Gabriele Rossetti to England and the consequent birth of his children in London instead of Naples is one of those questions more interesting than any possible answer. At any rate, the proscribed patriot once more seems to have triumphed by personality. He was smuggled on board the flagship of Sir Graham Moore,[1] the Admiral of the British fleet then in the bay of Naples. This was owing to the enthusiastic intercession of Lady Moore, who had already been impressed by his political songs.

From Naples Gabriele Rossetti was conveyed to Malta, and there, virtually an exile, he stayed from 1821 until early in 1825. He had in this period established what was to be a lifelong friendship with John Hookham Frere, the governor of the island, who furnished him with useful introductions when he decided to make a fresh start in London. It was an adventurous change for the refugee, even though he had a certain celebrity as a writer and some solid attainments as a man of culture. But his personality had enlisted the cordial sympathy and practical help of Frere; moreover, when he reached London he found a society of Italians, many of them political exiles like himself, who readily accorded him the respect which he was always ready to claim for himself. No doubt the work of tutor, particularly the teaching of Italian, on which he depended for a livelihood, was not conducive to the acquisition of wealth, and there must have been many

[1] The brother of Sir John Moore, the hero of Corunna.

teachers of Italian (including young Englishwomen) to
compete with just then. A Miss Pierce had been teaching
Italian until she met the Tuscan Dr. Gaetano Polidori and
married him. Polidori was a man of mark in the Italian
community as a former secretary to Count Alfieri, the
dramatist, a translator of Milton and father of Dr. John
Polidori, the physician who accompanied Byron to Geneva
in 1816.

In this household of the Polidoris the quondam laureate
of Naples became a welcome familiar. As he tells us:

> Upon the day when I returned his call,
> And saw him 'mid his well-bred family,
> I twice and thrice fixed my admiring eyes
> Upon the second daughter's comeliness.
> A single moment regulates a life:
> My heart became the lodestone, she the pole.
> And every hour my love became more keen
> When hundred virtues and no self-conceit . . .
> I know that what I'm writing she dislikes,[1]
> But, hiding it from her, I speak it still:
> Knowing her fully, I have often said—
> Angel in soul, and angel in her looks.
> Feeling within me glow the lighted flame,
> I wrote to Polidori, and 'twas thus:
> ' If to the gracious name of friend you please
> To add the loving name of son as well
> (Pray Heaven that so it may be!) be not loth
> To give the enclosed into your Frances' hands.
> If this displease you, little though it were,
> If so it haps you disapprove my suit,
> Throw the two letters both into the fire. . . .'

Happily Polidori did not disapprove of the energetic
exiled patriot, while the maid gave him ' a most affectionate
response '. This was in December 1825. They were
married on the 8th and the 10th April 1826 in a Roman
Catholic and an English church, about a year after
Gabriele Rossetti's arrival in London, when he was forty-

[1] 'This is perfectly accurate. Mrs. Rossetti shrank from being eulogized in verse which might one day be published, and I have known her
to plead for the omission of some such matter written by my father'
(W. M. Rossetti's Note).

three and his bride (who was born at 42 Broad Street, Golden Square, London, on 27th April 1800) was twenty-six. Her name was Frances Mary Lavinia, and though she had not her husband's executive talents in drawing and in literature, she was a cultured and intellectually earnest young woman, in whom seriousness blended with cheerful good sense and immense patience. This

> 'blooming graft
> Of English mother and of Tuscan sire'

Gabriele wrote:

> . . . both speaks and writes three high-prized tongues . . .
> And, when their authors she was studying,
> She culled the flower of the three literatures.

She was also exceptionally religious in temperament, and

> Thus she presents, perfect on every side,
> The steadfast woman of the sacred page.
> From living pattern oh what strength the love
> Of ethical instructions must receive !
> Wherefore to her more than myself is due
> Our children's educating discipline ;
> For of each rule she utters with her lips
> They see in her the breathing prototype.

The lovable Gabriele concludes an eulogy with:

> And you, beloved children, thank you me,
> That such a mother I chose to give you breath.
> Others perhaps will say that every bird
> (An ancient saw) approves his proper nest.
> Maria, Christina, William, Gabriel,
> My children, *you*'ll reply, and that's enough.

The Rossetti children's maternal grandmother, Anna Maria Pierce, the governess who had married Gaetano Polidori, came apparently of an old English stock. Her grandfather was Richard Pierce, a schoolmaster in London. His son William, born in 1736, was a writing-master of the old school—'A curiously well-preserved specimen of the old school', says William Rossetti.[1] Among his grandchildren 'he had a special predilection for my mother;

[1] *Memoir*, 3.

[20]

though like a good British Tory as he was, he thought it 'very odd' that, after his daughter Anna Maria had married one foreigner, his granddaughter Frances should marry another foreigner. 'It looked like flying in the face of the blessed shades of a Chatham, Wolfe, Nelson, and George III, and truckling to the far from blessed shades of a Voltaire, a Mirabeau, and a Bonaparte, not to speak of the Pope of Rome.'[1] William Pierce died in 1829, aged ninety-three, and William Michael Rossetti was named after him.

The children of Gabriele Rossetti and Frances Mary Lavinia (Polidori) were born in the four years following their marriage: Maria Francesca in February 1827; Gabriele Charles Dante (or, as he afterwards named himself, Dante Gabriel) 12th May 1828; William Michael in September 1829; and Christina Georgina in December 1830. Some acquaintance with them in their home is necessary to an understanding of Dante Gabriel's childhood and his later personality, but before giving attention to the children, there are still a few facts of sufficient importance and interest to detail about the parents. They have both been drawn by their son, and several contemporaries have described visits to the household. F. G. Stephens, the pre-Raphaelite painter who became a critic, recalled the patriarchal Professor of Italian as 'a man of striking character and aspect' in 1848, 'and his grand climacteric was past, and (as with most Italians) a life of studies told upon him heavily, I could not but be struck with the noble energy of his face and by the high culture his expression attested while a sort of eager, almost passionate revolution seemed to glow in all he said and did. To a youngster, such as I was then, he seemed much older than his years; and, while seated reading at a table with two candles behind him, and, because his sight was failing, with a wide shade over his eyes, he looked a very Rembrandt come to life'. William Bell Scott, another of Rossetti's friends,

[1] *Ibid.*

[21]

also remembered the ' old gentleman sitting by the fire in a great chair, the table drawn close to his chair, with a thick MS. book open before him, and the largest snuff-box I ever saw beside it conveniently open. He had a black cap on his head furnished with a great peak or shade for the eyes. . . .'¹ Mrs. Rossetti, according to Stephens, on the occasion of his visit, sat just ' beyond the radiant circle of the candles—her erect, comely, and very English form and face remarkable for its noble and beautiful matronhood . . .'; while her elder son, too, ' leaning his elbows upon the table and holding his face between hands so that the long curling masses of his dark brown hair fell forward, sat on the other side, his attenuated features outlined by the candle's light '.

As we depend upon his son's early drawings for a visual impression of Gabriele Rossetti, it is appropriate to recall that the son in later life thought the drawings, or at least some of them, were bad portraits. Writing to his publisher, F. S. Ellis, in 1871, Dante Gabriel thanks him ' for kindly sending me those dreadful portraits of my father. I knew them but too well before. I assure you he wasn't an idiot, and without being one he couldn't be like those portraits '.²

The drawings of his mother, and there were many, extending over the greater part of her life, show that her children were all more Italian looking than herself. This is particularly true of Frances, the eldest, who seems to have inherited most strongly the religious temperament of her mother, and William Michael, who certainly had the greatest share of her kindness and retiring disposition, the self-effacing patience and loyalty which marked her life not less than her practical energy and her intellectual ambition for husband and children.

Gabriele Rossetti and his wife set up housekeeping at

¹ *Autobiographical Notes.*
² Letter 63 in *The Letters of Dante Gabriel Rossetti to his publisher,* *F. S. Ellis* (edited by O. Doughty).

38 Charlotte Street (re-named Hallam Street), Portland Place, near Regent's Park, London. This was within a few minutes' walk of Park Village East, the street to which the Polidori family moved later. It was a rather dingy quarter, and the house was hardly big enough for an active family of six; for this family's income ranked it, according to the standards of those days, as among the 'lower middle classes'.

Gabriele Rossetti was not unsuccessful in his adventurous settlement in London, though the livelihood he gained by teaching was modest enough. He was made Professor of Italian Literature at King's College School (then part of King's College) in 1831, a post which he retained until his failing eyesight and generally failing health compelled him to relinquish it in 1845. But this professorship added very little to his income, which, until the breakdown of his career through ill-health, averaged about £250 a year. He, however, received gifts of money from time to time from his good friend Frere in Malta; but even if he had not distributed money pretty freely to Italian refugees who visited him, he would not have been able to meet the cost of producing the commentaries on Dante which became his chief interest as the political excitements of his early manhood faded. His political hatreds were not softened, and they could still make him rhetorical when, in 1850, he wrote the autobiography in Italian rhymed sextets which William Michael, his younger son, piously translated with verbal faithfulness into blank verse half a century later. But he introduced his political passion into the study of literature, by developing with erudition and great ingenuity theories of concealed motives and meanings in Dante's works, theories which up to a certain point have engaged the serious attention of many intelligent scholars, but which became his over-ridden hobby-horse. He belonged to the secret society of the Carbonari, and one of his most firmly held beliefs was that Dante's poetry concealed allegorically the precepts and purposes of freemasonry, and an implacable hostility to the Papacy. Such hostility was a passion with Gabriele Rossetti himself.

During the first year of his marriage he printed an edition of Dante's *Inferno*, accompanied by a *Comento Analitico*. This was only the first instalment of the complete *Divina Commedia*, of which he decided to publish one part at a time on account of the cost. But although the 'analytic commentary' for the *Purgatorio* was mostly written, ready to follow the publication of the *Inferno*, it was never printed, and that for the *Paradiso* was not written. His theories gradually extended from the local politics of Empire and Ghibellinism as against Papacy and Guelfism, to include a widespread secret society to which Dante, Petrarch, and others belonged. In 1832 he printed his book on the anti-papal spirit 'which produced the Reformation'—*Lo Spirito che produsse la Riforma*, of which an English translation also was published. This and his subsequent books were financed by another generous friend, Charles Lyell, the father of the geologist, Sir Charles Lyell. Charles Lyell, being godfather to his elder son, gave the boy his only English name, which the boy abandoned at the threshold of manhood when he chose to be called Dante Gabriel instead of Gabriele Charles Dante. Lyell was keenly interested in Gabriele Rossetti's systematic interpretation of the works of Dante: the correspondence between the two men, as well as the funds supplied for the printing of the books, shows how he was taken up with the ideas of the buoyant and eloquent Neapolitan. In 1833 Gabriele's most important poetic work was published in a volume entitled *Iddio e l'Uomo Salterio* ('God and Man, a Psaltery'). In 1843 this was republished, with alterations, under the title *Il Tempo* ('Time'). Dante Gabriel was then fifteen years old, so that the family's literary tradition was a familiar idea of his youth.

In 1840 a long work in five volumes was printed; but on the strong advice of Lyell and Frere it was not published in England, though a few copies were put on sale on the

Continent, and no doubt others were given to individuals in England. This was *Il Mistero dell' Amor Platonico del Medio Evo derivato dai Misteri Antichi* ('The Mystery of the Platonic Love of the Middle Ages derived from the Ancient Mysteries'). The author's friends declared the book far too audacious for publication in England, but it is worth realizing that Coleridge, though he disagreed, was interested by Gabriele Rossetti's speculations, Isaac Disraeli convinced by them, Joseph Mendelssohn lectured on them in Berlin and afterwards published his lectures, and Arthur Hallam, Schlegel, and Panizzi wrote in opposition. *La Beatrice di Dante*, published in 1842, besides elaborating former theories, developed the well-known one that Dante's Beatrice was not a real woman, but a symbol of Wisdom. The completion of the work was never published, the printed volume being only the first part, but nowhere else does the work of Gabriele Rossetti win so much approval from his elder son.

The testimony of Dante Gabriel is available as well as that of his brother's *Memoir*, to at least the unconscious influence of the father's studies. 'No doubt', wrote William, 'our father's Dantesque studies saturated the household air with wafts and rumours of the mighty Alighieri.' Dante Gabriel wrote in the preface to the 1861 edition of *The Early Italian Poets*: 'In relinquishing this work (which, small as it is, is the only contribution I expect to make to our English knowledge of old Italy), I feel, as it were, divided from my youth. The first associations I have are connected with my father's devoted studies, which, from his own point of view, have done so much towards the general investigation of Dante's writings. Thus, in those early days, all around me partook of the influence of the great Florentine; till, from viewing it as a natural element, I also, growing older, was drawn within the circle'. There is also the sonnet, 'Dantis Tenebrae: in Memory of my Father', written in 1861, seven years after

Gabriele's death.[1] Two books of verse followed *La Beatrice*, and in 1852 *L'Arpa Evangelica* ('The Evangelical Harp') was printed, though the finished volume did not reach the author until 1853, the year before his death. Because of the date of this book, as well as the unexpected title, it is noteworthy; for the religious, though evangelical, note in it seems to show some sympathy between the father's mind and his marvellous son's best early work, which by then included the famous early pictures, 'The Girlhood of Mary Virgin' and 'Ecce Ancilla Domini', besides 'The Blessed Damozel', 'Ave', various sonnets, and other verse making poetic beauty out of the Christian religion. Many of the hymns in the father's book became a part of the hymnology of Italian Evangelical churches. The effect of the father's personality and dominant interests on the son's mind can be gauged from these facts if they are related to the other influences of the Rossetti home. Gabriele Rossetti's mind and temperament certainly tended to freethought and against dogmatic authority. His Vastese parents, according to William Rossetti, were religious Catholics of the usual Italian type, and as his bringing-up was religious this influence in his childhood no doubt revived in his last period of life. He always reverenced the personality and valued the teachings of Christ, but with the spirit of an Evangelical he fought against Church dogmas and creeds.

Thus, although Gabriele Rossetti remained nominally a Roman Catholic, he had none of the orthodox devotion of his wife, who was a zealous member of the Church of England, and who gradually moved in sympathy towards the 'High' Church and the new Anglo-Catholic, or Anglican group, to which her daughters Frances and Christina, sharing her piety, adhered. This difference in religious attitude of the parents was reflected in that of the children, the girls sharing their mother's, while the boys shared their father's to the extent of holding no orthodox

[1] Quoted on p. 179 below.

[26]

beliefs and being quite indifferent to church ceremonies and dogmas. It was as typical of Gabriele Rossetti to remain a Roman Catholic and never to become naturalized as an Englishman merely from patriotic pride, as it was in his famous son to show an almost complete lack of any national or racial political feelings. In him, his mother's religious depth and his father's polemical idealism were transformed into the self-centred passion of the typical artist. Only as general ideas of universal application do political references usually occur in his poems.

Between Gabriele Rossetti and his wife there were indeed considerable differences of outlook due to early environment, as well as of temperament. Mrs. Rossetti's father, Gaetano Polidori, was (like her husband) a nominal Roman Catholic who abstained from religious observances, but without any of Gabriele Rossetti's vehement polemical spirit. Gaetano Polidori was a natural conservative, as Gabriele Rossetti was a natural revolutionary. According to a compact the Polidori boys were brought up as Roman Catholics and the girls, like their mother, as Protestants in the English Church. The only one of the sons with an intellectual tendency was Dr. John Polidori, who killed himself in 1821, five years before his sister Frances married Rossetti. Another of the sons, Philip, was mentally deficient, while Henry, who became an unsuccessful solicitor, would have been idiomatically described as 'a little cracked'. He was, however, a very strict Roman Catholic, and when his sister Frances' girls were, in turn, brought up as Protestants he made attempts to convert them to the Church of Rome. Frances was the only one of the four daughters of Gaetano Polidori to marry, and she 'stood obviously foremost in point of mental faculty. Her religious belief was solid, her religious feeling warm; yet her tone was not exactly that of a devotee but quiet and unobtrusive, and her faith was chiefly evinced as a perpetual rule of conduct'.[1] She was, however, not incapable of

---

[1] *Some Reminiscences*, vol. i, chap. 9, by W. M. Rossetti.

something like bigotry, as is shown by her destroying, after her husband's death, all the copies she laid hands on of his *Il Mistero dell' Amor Platonico*, of which she disapproved. She gave all her children religious instruction out of the Bible, the English Prayer Book, and Church Catechism, and took them to churches of the English Establishment. It is possible that her loving care, coupled with her zealous piety, may have slightly oppressed the emotional freedom of her children.

' Neither did my father interfere with this—he never presented his own opinions to me in any concrete form, nor even advised me to ponder before adopting or professing any particular conviction. I was, however, quite aware that there was " a great gulf fixed " between his ideas on these subjects and those of the doctrinal Christians in the family. I can remember too that on one exceptional occasion he made a vigorous *sortie*, commenting upon the scriptural narrative of Abraham ordered by Jehovah to sacrifice Isaac, and saying that he himself, under the like conditions, would have responded, *Tu non sei Dio, sei il diavolo!* [1] Nothing was neglected which might have made religion persuasive to me; it was presented in a clear, unambiguous form, impressed upon me but not " forced down my throat "; and it came recommended by the tender kindness and bright example of my mother—not to speak of my sisters, whose feelings and habits always pointed to religion as the needle to the pole.' [2]

Nevertheless, neither Dante Gabriel nor William Michael ever became orthodox. They were not even confirmed, and a sort of armed truce persisted between the male and female sections of the family. Although Dante Gabriel, as the senior of the two brothers, was presumably the leader in heterodoxy, he was less alien to the Christian faith than his younger brother, no doubt because of an aesthetic and somewhat mystical approach to it. William

[1] 'Thou art not God, thou art the devil !'
[2] *Some Reminiscences*, vol. i, chap. 10, by W. M. Rossetti.

became an ardent republican and a convinced agnostic. Of Dante Gabriel he wrote: ' His fine intellect dwelt little in the region of argument, controversy, or the weighing of evidence; it was swayed by feelings, and not by demonstrations or counter-demonstrations. A thing either impressed and convinced him, or else it formed no part of his inner experiences '.[1]

A clear sign of the pervasive nature of the Polidori female influence is in a letter that the fifteen-year-old Dante Gabriel wrote to his mother in August 1843. She was away—probably with his sisters. He is denying energetically any knowledge ' as to the indecent books which you speak of ' which he is supposed to have been reading in his mother's absence. He traces the report of this matter to his Aunt Margaret. He wishes his aunt ' would refrain from circulating such falsehoods ' (a curious foreshadowing of his anxieties in mature manhood about adverse criticism of his purity of heart). The letter continues: ' on enquiry I have succeeded in eliciting that the origin of all this was my having hinted at a vague intention of purchasing at some indefinite period the works of Shelley—which I should peruse solely on account of the splendid versification, and not from any love of his atheistical sentiments '.[2]

Drawings and poems attest the degree to which elements of the family's group life became a part of Dante Gabriel's inner experiences, and that eloquent testimony becomes the most essential theme of any fresh study of his genius which can now be written. Little is there to be said in detail of his mother as compared with the necessary account of his father. She lives more than her husband as an unconscious influence in her son's life. But this almost silent figure is self-projected into momentary prominence at the time of her husband's death in 1854. Her son William preserved the memoranda of Gabriele Rossetti's

[1] *Some Reminiscences*, vol. i, chap. 10.
[2] *Family Letters*.

[29]

death which she made day by day, and from it the following may well be quoted here:

Dr. Hare confirmed Mr. Stewart's opinion. Told me my husband is suffering from an eruption of the nature of carbuncle ; and that he considers him in a highly dangerous state, on account of the accompanying debility and diabetes.—24th April. My husband so anxious to get up that I dressed him, and led him in to breakfast. On entering the room, he said, ' *Quanto ho anelato questo momento !* ' [1] Observed he supposed William was gone. On hearing the contrary, expressed his delight. Took his breakfast without assistance. Sat afterwards apparently reading, but began to droop exceedingly, and, while I was supporting his head, an alarming change took place in his countenance. Mr. Stewart advised that he should go to bed directly. Dr. Hare said he was suffering much from fever, and ended by giving me very little hope of his recovery. He passed the night in great weakness, almost total extinction of voice ; but perfect consciousness, which was evinced by his opening his eyes, and answering as well as he could to everything we said, recognizing each separately.—25th. In the afternoon he became worse, and was clearly sinking ; restless at intervals, but generally quiet, breathing with tolerable ease. So he continued all night. His eyes looked affection, and he was conscious to our call, answering to the prayers I read from an Italian translation of the Liturgy.—26th. He died without one struggle at half-past five p.m. I, his four children, my three sisters, and his cousin Teodorico Pietrocola-Rossetti, were present at the moment.—27th. The certificate stated the cause of death to be ' old age, marasmus '.—May 3rd. To Highgate Cemetery, where the service was beautifully performed, and my dear husband was buried in a very deep grave contiguous to that of Mr. Ford Madox Brown's wife. . . .

Mrs. Rossetti lived another thirty-two years, outliving her elder son by four years. But when her husband died the son had already fulfilled his parents' ambitions for him, in both painting and poetry. And that Beatrice detected by his father in Dante's poetry, that wisdom of Love, had already accepted him

to be of those that haunt
The vale of magical dark mysteries . . .

---

[1] ' How I have been longing for this moment ! '

CHAPTER II

HOME AND EDUCATION

*' For the bed is shorter than a man can stretch himself on it:
and the covering narrower than that he can wrap himself in it.'*
—*ISAIAH* (28).

THE ROSSETTIS' house, at number 38, and, after 1835,
at number 50, Charlotte Street (re-named Hallam
Street), Portland Place, Regent's Park, was the resort
of all kinds of political refugees, mostly Italian, and most
of them penurious. Indeed, it is recorded that knocks
on the front door were translated by the inmates of the
house as warnings of fresh calls on Gabriele Rossetti's
purse. But among the visitors were striking personalities
like Mazzini and Paganini, and some of a less reputable
if not less vivid character. One of these, a swarthy hero
with some legend of an assassination clinging to him, or
perhaps haloing his untidy head, fascinated the children
not a little, and is said to have provided, when recollected
imaginatively, the chief character in *A Last Confession.*
Certainly the children's ear was well accustomed to the
Italian tongue, often spoken with the excitement of political
tirade, and some of Dante Gabriel's and also Christina's
early poems were written in Italian. But Mr. Max Beer-
bohm's amusing drawing of the infant Dante Gabriel
lying on the floor busy writing verse in the midst of a
roomful of voluble politicians truthfully suggests that this
early environment was not too absorbing for the younger
generation. The elder boy seems to have been regarded
from his earliest years as a future painter of distinction by
his watchful parents; yet he was not extraordinarily precocious in this direction—not nearly as precocious as
Millais, for instance—although constantly ' drawing '. His

first achievement to have been specially noted was literary —a ' blank verse ' dramatic dialogue called ' The Slave ', which he wrote at the age of five; but nobody has ever suggested that it had any merit. Another sign of future development was the rage for collecting prints, upon which Christmas-boxes were squandered one year. Dante Gabriel and his brother William endeavoured to illustrate Scott's Waverley Novels with engravings bought separately, and Shakespeare, and later Byron, too, were also excuses for the collection of illustrations.

But the parents did not need to judge by precocious work; the personality of their eldest son very soon insisted on being recognized as something out of the ordinary. He was the best looking, most vital of the children, and difficult to manage. His brother William recalled them as they were at the time of his own birthday in September 1834, when he was five years old, Maria seven and a half, Christina three and three-quarters, and Dante Gabriel six and a half:

His [*i.e.* Dante Gabriel's] eyes were of a bluish grey, his hair a bright but not light auburn, his complexion ruddy and full-tinted. In all these respects he got darker as the years advanced, and I have heard his hair, in manhood, termed black, though it never was that. On the two junior children, Christina and myself, Maria exercised something like the function of an inspiriting Muse in a pinafore (in our household 'pincloth' was always the word) ; while Gabriel was a familiar spirit—familiar but fiery, and not lightly to be rebelled against. Apart from his mental gifts . . . the quality most innate in him appears to have been domin-ance : *Hoc volo, sic jubeo, sit pro ratione voluntas.* In anything wearing the garb of mischief he counted for all, and Maria for nothing ; he was imperative, vehement, at times angrily passionate ; but his anger was a sudden and passing impulse, and to sulk or bear a grudge was not him at all. This placable spirit abode in him through life, and even sur-vived to a great extent the hypochondriacal twist of his closing years. In childhood there was not much use in opposing him at the critical moment ; after that moment was past, things resumed their normal condition, and there was peace, with amity and warmth of heart. Even when he dictated to me, he did not bully me : leadership was in his composition, but not hectoring.[1]

---

[1] *Some Reminiscences*, section ii, vol. i.

The parents therefore were careful not to insist too far upon controlling him. There was, in any case, little corporeal punishment in the family, and that was confined to their mother's face-slapping and her rare whippings, which her best-behaved child described seventy years later as merely 'nominal'. If William was the best behaved, his brother was not the worst, it seems.

Pretty little Christina—and very pretty some people considered her in those days—was the most 'fractious' of the quartette : hardly less passionate than Gabriel, and more given to mere tantrums. This may have depended partly on the condition of her health, which was subject to greater disturbances and pains than that of the others. She had hazel eyes, bright hair, which however soon settled down into brown, a clear, good complexion, oval visage (Maria's was decidedly round), and a winning air of half-thoughtful *espieglerie*. To have a temper of her own was perhaps her right ; to be amiable and affectionate along with it was certainly her endowment.

Soon afterwards, when Dante Gabriel would have been about seven, they moved from no. 34 into the slightly bigger house, no. 50, in the same street. It was a four-floored house, with the typical kitchen-basement and 'area' bordered by iron railings. A small backyard took the place of a garden. The children spent most of their time in the two rooms on the ground floor, when they were not in bed on the third floor. The first floor had the reception rooms. One of the rooms on the second floor, which had been used as a dressing-room, was assigned to Dante Gabriel as a workroom when he became a full-fledged art student. In this room he and his brother would sit and practise writing sonnets to end-rhymes, chiefly during 1847-48, a strenuous form of amusement which their sister Christina was only rarely induced to share. Opposite the front of the house was a public-house outside which hackney coaches pulled up during the day. Hansom cabs were not yet known; Mrs. Rossetti said 'cabriolet' for cab. The omnibus was in use, but the Rossetti brothers walked every day to and from King's College School. There is an incident in 'Jenny', the poem about a young

17133

[33]

c

prostitute, most of which was written in 1858, referring to a memory of those walks down Regent Street on the way to school:

> And from the wise, unchildish elf,
> To schoolmate lesser than himself
> Pointing you out, what thing you are . . .

William, the younger brother, was the ' schoolmate lesser than himself '.[1]

The slow but serious failure of Gabriele Rossetti's health was a gloomy shadow over this industrious and cheerful household from about 1843; but illness was not unusual. Illness, indeed, played the prominent part which it seems normally to have played in family lives last century— perhaps because more information is available than there has been of former centuries. Neither of the girls in the Rossetti family enjoyed good health. Christina was for some years expected to go into a ' decline ' from consumption, but this proved to be less serious than the exophthalmic goitre from which she began to suffer in maturity. The swollen throat and protrusive eyes which are symptoms of this malady are clearly seen in the portrait done by her brother in 1877, reproduced to face page 90, as also in several others of his portraits. This fact is worth noting, as the suggestion has been made that the artist introduced a ' morbid ' appearance into the portrayal of his sister, which in fact her courageous and usually cheerful life contradicted. But a moment's consideration of the two likenesses, which he drew of mother and daughter, should show that he did not distort appearances, for there is no sign of such a condition in the face of his mother.

Maria's health also was not of the best; portraits of her, especially photographs, suggest some nervous malady. Nevertheless in the early years she fully sustained the family's exceptional promise of being intellectually remarkable. As a child she was in quickness and retention of

[1] See W. M. Rossetti's Notes to the ' Collected Works ' of his brother, 1911 edition.

[34]

information, though not in originality, the leader of the children, and although later she became a nun, and died in 1876, she broke into print at least three times: once with a religious allegory called *The Rivulets*; with her exposition and description of the 'Divine Comedy', entitled *A Shadow of Dante*, and in the more practical effort of producing a translation of some Italian exercises, with her own key, a task in which Christina endeavoured to help. The Italian exercises, like the governess's work, were due to the straitened means of the family after Rossetti senior ceased to earn money. First Mrs. Rossetti, who had taught Italian before her marriage, began to seek pupils again, and as she had trained Maria for a similar career, Maria was able to go out and stay in various families to teach the young ladies of the house refined subjects like Italian. Christina went out by day for a time, but lived at home.

Mrs. Rossetti had not only shared the housework with one servant, but she had herself given all her children the rudiments of education, and her desire that they should be an intellectual family included her daughters not less than her sons. She taught them all to read and write, and it was the custom for her to talk to them in English and for her husband to talk in Italian. The children did not see nearly so much of their father as they did of her. While he was still active he would usually be out in the daytime, and he spent most of his evenings surrounded by books and manuscripts. His personality, his eloquent recitals, snatches of song, and impromptu dissertations played a positive part in the mental growth of his children. A passage in Dante Gabriel's prose story, *St. Agnes of Intercession*, written in 1850, has an autobiographical air which has been recognized before, but it is worth quoting here:

Among my earliest recollections, none is stronger than that of my father standing before the fire when he came home in the London winter evenings, and singing to us in his sweet, generous tones: sometimes ancient English ditties—such songs as one might translate from the birds, and the brooks might set to music ; sometimes those with which foreign travel had familiarized his youth—among them the great tunes which have rung the world's changes since '89. I used to sit on the hearth-rug, listening to him, and look between his knees into the fire till it burned my face, while the sights swarming up in it seemed changed and changed with the music : till the music and the fire and my heart burned together, and I would take paper and pencil, and try in some childish way to fix the shapes that rose within me. For my hope, even then, was to be a painter.

An instance of the elder Rossetti's interests serving as a stimulus to his son's is afforded by the discovery of the famous portrait of Dante by Giotto. It was found under the plaster on the Bargello wall in 1839, and an early copy of it was sent to Gabriele Rossetti. This became a memory with his elder son who, in 1852, did the water-colour of Giotto on his scaffolding painting Dante's portrait.[1]

This must have been a rare example of an interesting art object in the home. The most prominent picture was a framed engraving of Queen Victoria in her opera box, a characteristic gift from Harriet Pierce, Mrs. Rossetti's aunt. There were also two small oils given to Mrs. Rossetti by a native painter of Vasto, Gabriele Smargiassi, about 1837, when he visited his old friend and fellow-townsman. One of these pictures represented the Blue Cavern at Capri, and the other a picture of sea-bordered Vasto. They do not seem to have made Italy an irresistible goal to Dante Gabriel, who never saw his father's native land. The dearth of pictures was also relieved by another Italian friend who gave Gabriele Rossetti ' The Marriage Feast of Tobias ' in oils, the donor mistakenly supposing it to have been by Paul Veronese. But this picture afforded Gabriele Rossetti a text for one of his dissertations. William Rossetti, who seems to have been the chief beneficiary on this occasion, says that soon after the picture came into the house, an Italian visitor was looking at it, ' and opined that the action of a certain page in the group

---

[1] No. 26 in H. C. Marillier's iconographical list. A pen drawing was done in 1849.

is wrongly represented: the page is pouring wine from a jar into a cup, and the Italian considered that, in the relative positions of the jar and the cup, the rillet of wine would never have reached the latter. This inaccuracy he rashly dubbed an " *anacronismo* " (anachronism). My father noticed the misuse of this term, and after the Italian had gone, mentioned it in my presence. I dare say I had never before heard the word *anacronismo*; from that moment, I knew what it does *not* mean, and also what it does '.[1] Incidentally, the future secretary and critic of the pre-Raphaelite Brotherhood heard an application of the pre-Raphaelite test of truth to nature. It suggests what has still to be explained more fully, that there was no originality in pre-Raphaelitism beyond the revolt from outworn conventions.

The scanty resources of the family exchequer were made to suffice for the boys' outside schooling. The local private school close to their home, and the King's College School in the Strand later, where their father lectured, seemed, however, to the boys a descent from the tone and the educational stimulus of their own home. Here there was more intellectual life and disinterested effort. They may have seen comparatively little of their father in early youth, but that energetic, plump, shortish figure, with the dignified brow and thinning hair and still resonant voice, the kindly humour and vehement egotism, had always the air of being an important man, especially before visitors. He projects out of the early years of his children. He seems more prominent than their mother; but that, as already suggested, is an illusive appearance. Prominence in this case counts for less than retirement. The matronly figure of the strong-willed and patient woman who mothered those children, in the end played by far the most important rôle in their lives, both deliberately and unconsciously. She, who was busied with them from morn till night, had from the children probably a deeper affection, certainly a

[1] *Some Reminiscences*, vol. i, chap. i.

feeling of greater dependence, than was evoked by the father, who, said his elder son long afterwards, 'liked riding the high horse'.

The solidarity of the Rossetti family, as one looks back at it, resembles closely that of the best type of Victorian middle class, but in range of interests and educational atmosphere its equivalent at that time would have been found only in the exceptionally cultured homes. Gabriele Rossetti's income, at its highest, did not permit of intellectual luxuries, any more than of material ones, and the intellectual was given preference over the material. In the matter of clothes none of them ever showed to advantage, and no doubt the two boys at school were often on the defensive, with all the boy's sensitiveness to outward appearances. William Rossetti recalled how he went to a birthday party of a school chum whose parents were well-to-do, and how his only jacket, an old blue serge, was worn so white at the elbows that he spent some time beforehand in patiently inking over the bad patches! There is also the account of a contemporary student at the Academy, when Dante Gabriel joined the Antique School there in July of 1846, of how, 'with a slightly rolling gait, Rossetti came forward among his fellows with a jerky step, tossed the falling hair back from his face, and, having both hands in his pockets, faced the student world with an *insouciant* air which savoured of thorough self-reliance. A bare throat, a falling, ill-kept collar, boots not over-familiar with brushes, black and well-worn habiliments, including not the ordinary jacket of the period, but a loose dress-coat which had once been new—these were the outward and visible signs of a mood which cared even less for appearances than the art-student of those days was accustomed to care . . .'. The signs much more probably indicated the anxious concealment of shame by a lad highly sensitive to anything like ridicule. Since he could not reach the modest standard expected of the art students, he fell back on his immense pride and an assumed pugnacity, and swaggered a little. The incident belongs to a later period, when childhood was just passed.

Travelling also was a hardly attainable luxury for the Rossetti children, and a ride in a public conveyance was a memorable ' treat '. They had glimpses of ' the country ', because grandfather Gaetano Polidori's family lived in a large cottage at Holmer Green, Little Missenden, in Buckinghamshire. Polidori gave up his work as a teacher of Italian and lived wholly at Holmer Green himself after 1835. His rooms in Wells Street, Oxford Street, which he had occupied before his retirement, were visited by the children, who were very fond of him; but they spent several holidays of three or four weeks at a time at the Holmer Green house, which later became known in the locality as Polydore House, Polydore being the Anglicized version of his surname, adopted later by Gaetano Polidori's son, Henry, a solicitor. Here in a pretty and sheltered country-side the children obtained their earliest impressions of rural sights and sounds. The pigs and pigsty at Poly-dore House, and their grandfather's carpentering shed were special attractions. Another joy, shared by the brothers, was to lie in wait by the edge of a pond in the grounds and to capture and release the frogs. But the boys went to Holmer Green only twice together; they would usually be sent with one of their sisters; Mrs. Rossetti usually accompanied the children. The journeys there were done by stage-coaches passing through Ux-bridge, Wycombe, and Amersham, for railways then were still an experimental idea. These country holidays ceased in 1839 when grandfather Polidori came to live at 15 (later changed to 30), Park Village East, Regent's Park, a house with a long back garden sloping down to the Regent's Canal. A shed in this garden contained Polidori's private printing press, on which he printed Dante Gabriel's first book, *Sir Hugh the Heron*, a metrical romance inspired by Scott, but of no startling promise. In maturity, having heard that a copy was in the British Museum, and fearing it would be unearthed, the poet made a note on *Sir Hugh the Heron*, rather severely describing it as 'a ridiculous first attempt of mine in verse ... which was printed when I was fourteen, but written, except the last page or two, at twelve. . . . When I was fourteen my grandfather (who amused himself by having a small private printing press) offered, if I would finish it, to print it. I accordingly added the last precious touches two years after writing the rest. I leave this important explanation as there is no knowing what fool may some day foist the absurd trash into print as a production of mine. It is curious and surprising to myself as evincing no promise at all—less than should have been even at twelve. When I wrote it the only English poet I had read was Sir Walter Scott, as is plain enough in it '.

It was inexact to describe this piece, which Polidori printed in 1843, as a ' first attempt ', for *The Slave*, dated in his fifth year, and a prose romance, never finished, called *Sorrentino*, written during school years, preceded it. But in writing to Swinburne in 1870 the poet describes a still later piece, written in 1845, as ' what I may call my first poem (after still more childish things) I believe, and enclose it you for a lark. Of course it is on nothing less than Napoleon at Waterloo!'[1] It is called ' The End Of It ', and has a biographical interest, showing that the youthful Dante Gabriel was not quite oblivious of the world's events. Here are two of the four stanzas which are printed in Mr. Wise's Catalogue:

> His brows met, and his teeth were set,
>   And his mouth seemed in pain,
> And madness closed and grappled with him
>   As they turned his bridle-rein.
> And albeit his eyes went everywhere,
>   Yet they saw not anything :
> And he drew the bit tightly, for he thought
>   That his horse was stumbling.

---

[1] Vol. iii, *Catalogue of the Ashley Library.*

There was a great shouting about him
    And the weight of a great din:
But what was the battle he had around
    To the battle he had within?
A pond in motion to the stress of the ocean,
    A lamp to a furnace-eye,
Or the wind's wild-weeping fits
    To the voice of Austerlitz
    When it shook upon the sky.

It seems appropriate to remark that by this time Shelley and Keats had been added to Scott as poets read, and when a little later Browning swam into his ken, all previous enthusiasms were temporarily put into the shade. But in any case Shakespeare and Byron had long been familiar, Shakespeare from a very early age. The boy's style shows an effort to wield a literary diction too loaded for so youthful a hand. There is the amusing and well-known letter written to his mother in 1842 from Chalfont St. Giles, where he was staying with his uncle Henry Polydore. It affords a glimpse of his reading at this time, as well as his writing, when he says: ' Yesterday I commenced reading *The Infidel's Doom*, by Dr. Birch, which work forms part and parcel of Uncle Henry's library. However, I have abandoned the task in despair. I then began *The Castle of Otranto*, which shared the same fate, and am now engaged on Defoe's *History of the Plague*. This morning we deposited Uncle Henry's books in a closet in Uncle Henry's bedroom, which, in common with all the other closets in this house, possess a lock but no key '.

He adds, with a slight accentuation of the florid sarcasm: ' I do not think that I shall go to church on Sunday, for in the first place I do not know where I can sit, and in the second place I find we are so stared at wherever we go that I do not much relish the idea of sitting for two hours the loadstone of attraction in the very centre of the aborigines, on whose minds curiosity seems to have taken a strong hold '.

Correspondence was frequent between all the members

of the family when parted, but Dante Gabriel especially kept a close contact in this way with his mother. We find him, aged twenty-five, after misunderstanding some remark in a letter of hers, writing to repel the notion that he is bored by writing to her. She answers promptly:

'Read my letter again, and you will see that I never said that you thought it a bore to write to me; but that my letters are so barren that they might well prove a bore to you to read. You have always had a fund of affection for me; and the remembrance of how, when quite little, you came forward in my defence if I was attacked, and tried to console me if I seemed unhappy, is one of the dearest reminiscences of my heart.'

Although his father wrote to him always in Italian and customarily spoke Italian with the children, in December 1844, during a visit for his health to the Maenzas (friends of his father's at Boulogne), he writes a letter in English to his father. He excuses himself on the ground that ' my Italian is so " stentato " [strained] that, although perhaps, when finished, it may be passably decent, still the labour of composing in a language in which I am so imperfect is an agony that I would willingly avoid '.

In the summer of 1842 he had left King's College School, which he entered in 1837. There he had acquired some knowledge of French and Latin, and enough German to enjoy some of the German romantic literature, from which his earliest translations were made in the next three years. Italian he was already tolerably at home with for reading, though it is a noteworthy fact that until he was about sixteen, despite the din, or perhaps because of the din of discussion of Dante in his father's house, he had read next to nothing of the poet whose *Vita Nuova* and *Divina Commedia* suddenly dawned upon him then and set him to work on his beautiful translations. It is possible that this attitude to Dante in boyhood expressed a natural opposition to the strong personality of his father, but a more reasonable explanation is that he was not prepared for his ' conversion ' before adolescence.

The father showed always the keenest ambition for his son's career as an artist, and his letters after this time frequently contain encouragements and exhortations. At one there is even a rebuke to the young artist for neglecting painting while writing poetry, since by painting he must expect to earn his living. It was to hasten this consumma- tion that in 1842 his father agreed upon the exchange of King's College School for regular art training. The son's desire in this matter received a reinforcement of practical considerations, because Gabriele Rossetti's health was beginning to fail, and the family could not but feel concern at the financial prospect in the event of his active career coming to an end. Among the elder Rossetti's friends had been the best known of the English translators of Dante, the Reverend Henry Francis Cary. His son, F. S. Cary, a minor painter, ran ' Sass's Academy ', a well-known drawing school in Bloomsbury Street, near the British Museum. Here Dante Gabriel attended the antique classes, but not any life classes. In July 1846 he was admitted as a student in the Antique School of the Royal Academy, but seems to have found the training not less dull and discouraging than at ' Sass's '. It was rather his intuitive prevision of his goal than deliberate industry which stimulated him to return after each lapse from industry. His difficulty in concentration of the systematic sort was no doubt accentuated by the concurrence of his progress in the art of poetry. So it is that the story, whether quite true or not, is quite significant, which is related of him at ' Sass's '. Cary asked him why he was absent the day before. Rossetti replied: ' I had a fit of idleness '. He then began to distribute a bundle of manuscript sonnets to his fellow students. His brother's view of this unsystematic energy seems to include all that it is possible to say of it:

· He once said to me—it may have been towards 1857 or later—' As soon as a thing is imposed on me as an obligation, my aptitude for doing it is gone; what I *ought* to do is what I *can't* do '.[1] This went close to the essence of his character, and was true of him through life. As the years rolled on, what he ought to do was very often what he chose and liked to do, and then the difficulty vanished; but in his student days it consisted in attending assiduously to matters for which, in themselves, he cared little or not at all, and a real obstruction was the result. As his gift for fine art was indisputably far superior to that of the great majority of his fellow students, and as his drawings from the antique, etc., were (I presume) in reasonable proportion to his gift, I know of no reason why he did not rapidly complete his course in the Antique School, and proceed to the Life and the Painting Schools—which he never did—except this same :—That the obligation which lay upon him was to fag over the antique and cognate first steps in art, and that, being obliged, he found the will to be lacking. A resolute sense of duty, firm faith in his instructors, and a disposition to do what was wanted in the same way as other people, might have furnished the will.[2]

Dissatisfaction and disappointment with his art training prepared Rossetti for his enthusiastic acclamation of work being done by Ford Madox Brown, a still struggling artist, but one with continental training and practical experience. Although the choice was haphazard, Rossetti could not have chosen an artist to work under more likely to help him than Brown. By a letter, written from Charlotte Street, in March 1848, to Brown, Rossetti introduced himself to the painter, as he had the previous November introduced himself to William Bell Scott, who was then the Master of the Government School of Design in Newcastle-on-Tyne. But whereas Scott's published poetry, especially *Rosabell* and *A Dream of Love*, had been the stimulus and the pretext for his enthusiastic opening letter, the occasion for the self-introduction to Brown was the latter's exhibited pictorial work. In both instances the letter which he wrote erred on the side of enthusiasm in admiration. Brown was some seven years his senior, and good-naturedly agreed to let the twenty-year-old Rossetti share his studio and learn what he could without any payment for tuition. On Brown's advice he attended a life school in the evenings. A letter to his Aunt Charlotte Polidori at this time tells her of his plans and

---

[1] A very similar observation was made on Coleridge by De Quincey.
[2] *Memoir*, ix.

acknowledges her offer to help him with the fees. His references to Brown are full of grateful respect. Soon he writes to Aunt Charlotte again (on 12th April 1848), saying that owing to ' a return of my old atrocious boils ' (an affliction he was often subjected to), he had not been out of doors for a week. ' It was therefore not till last night that I was enabled to join the Maddox Street Academy, according to the recommendation of Mr. Ford Brown. I find that the terms are half a guinea monthly—rather more than I had been led to believe. However, as you had made me so kind an offer, I thought that I should not be exceeding the bounds of moderation in joining, which I did. In order to pay for the first month I was obliged to inform Mamma of our correspondence and its object; so that it will now be as well to forward to her, instead of to me, the half-guinea in question, which she disbursed. For all this I will not repeat my thanks, because it would perhaps appear an affectation, but I hope you will believe me nevertheless not ungrateful. The academy is a capital one. The hours are from seven to ten in the evening, and the model sits four times a week.'

He concludes by telling his aunt that ' not long ago ' he sent some poems to Leigh Hunt, asking for his opinion, and that the answer was too flattering for him to quote any part of it. Rossetti's unsophisticated hero-worship of well-known men at this time is indicated by the further delighted remark to his aunt that Hunt had requested him ' to give him the pleasure of my acquaintance ', which calls for four marks of exclamation from the artistic neophite who had already written poetry of enduring beauty.

Answering Rossetti's enquiries about literature as a career, Leigh Hunt warned him not to expect to earn a living as well as immortality from poetry, and since he was a painter: ' if you paint as well as you write, you may be a rich man '. It seems that this exhortation to stick close to painting for a career was not out of place, for very soon Rossetti was bewailing the tasks which Brown set him.

[45]

His friendly instructor did not flatter him with any notion
that by leaving the Academy School he had escaped the
necessities of elementary technique, and he seems to have
put him at once to the painting of still-life objects, especially
bottles and pickle-jars. But Rossetti was no Chardin, and
he was all the time desirous of making original compositions
which should catch some of the ideas already seething
within him. While in Brown's studio he continued his
practice of doing character sketches and portraits, though
a portrait of his sister Christina in 1847, and one of his
father in this year were the only oils he had done, if one
excepts an unfinished 'Retro me Sathana', referred to later.
While at Cary's his sketches were remembered by a fellow-
student to have been mainly chivalric and satirical, and at
this time much of his reading, in poetry especially, would
have increased his impatience for plastic expression. In
this state of mind and development he attended the
Academy exhibition in the spring of 1848, to which both
Holman Hunt and Millais had contributed a picture.
Hunt's picture of the flight of Porphyro with Madeline,
taken from Keats's 'Eve of St. Agnes', caught his attention,
both by the distinctive style and no doubt in part because
it was a subject from Keats. He overwhelmed the shy
painter, who was only about a year his senior, with his
pleasure, and, says Hunt, 'in loud tongue made me feel
very confused by declaring that mine was the best picture
of the year'. Rossetti asked to be allowed to call on Hunt
at the latter's studio, which he did soon afterwards. When
he had aired his grievances about pickle-jar painting Hunt
sensibly advised him to combine the practice of still-life
painting with an original composition more attractive to
him, since some still-life objects would form a part of the
picture. Hunt suggested that one of the designs Rossetti
had contributed to a sketching society, which numbered
himself and Millais among its members, would be suitable
for the picture. In the event he did not chose either the
design of 'La Belle Dame Sans Merci' or of 'Gretchen in

Church' from *Faust*, which were, with 'The Girlhood of Mary Virgin' (the one chosen), the designs in question. He came to an agreement with Hunt to share the studio which the latter was about to occupy in Cleveland Street, Fitzroy Square. According to the record of F. G. Stephens, one of their associates and fellow students, the studio was a truly dismal room, but it was nevertheless the scene of Rossetti's first serious work as a painter. This, however, belongs rather to the phase associated with the pre-Raphaelite movement.

He had reached now the first rungs in the ladder of a successful career. It would be a serious error to suppose, however, that Rossetti was entirely a neophite, except in the management of pigment. The portraits he had already done of members of his family, and of the Polidori family, amply prove that he *could* draw, and had a sensitive feeling for faces, and also that he could be painstakingly faithful to nature, before pre-Raphaelitism was born. At this time one of the most skilful of draughtsmen in the new generation of artists was the youthful Millais. The members of the sketching society already mentioned, called the Cyclographic Society, made a practice of criticising the designs of other members as well as contributing their own to the collection sent round in a portfolio, and thus it is that Millais' criticism [1] of Rossetti's early 'Gretchen' design is available to reinforce this impression of the ability which was already apparent in his pictorial work. The first sentence, 'a very clever and original design, beautifully executed', and the last, 'chairs out of perspective' are both significant. The originality of Rossetti's designs never ceased to win the admiration of his fellow artists, but perspective was one of his greatest technical weaknesses, though it was a weakness due in part to conviction that perspective was comparatively unimportant. The Devil, Millais thought 'a mistake'; but for some time after Rossetti discovered Goethe's *Faust* he was very fond of the medieval Devil. In 1847 he had begun to paint his

[1] Quoted in *Memoir* by W. M. Rossetti, section 12.

[47]

first picture in oils, which was never completed, and after-wards destroyed. But the preserved pen and ink design of 1848, called 'Retro me Sathana', which Marillier says was the same as the oil, has an amusing devil, with horns and a long tail, but otherwise dressed up like a man; he is slinking behind a young girl who walks austerely in a chapel cloister beside a priest who holds up a crucifix. The attempt at the painting in 1847 received a dis-couragement from the prospective purchaser of the picture who, like Millais, thought the Devil was 'a mistake'. But the Devil, being found in *Faust*, suggests the import-ance of Rossetti's eager and continuous reading.

While Rossetti was still a boy one of the attractions of his grandfather's house at Park Village East had been the library, which contrasted favourably with the Dantesque studies of Gabriele Rossetti. An eighteenth-century French illustrated edition of Ariosto, the Waverley novels, Allan Cunningham's tales, and, especially, an assortment of romances of the Monk Lewis and Maturin type were greatly enjoyed. Both pictorially and poetically his in-clination to the mysterious and inexplicable, and a corre-sponding indifference to matter-of-fact information, re-mained an essential element in his creative impulse.

Rossetti's taste for the occult, whether in 'thrillers' or in more pretentious forms, is the subject of some curious remarks in one of the letters, unpublished in English, written from Reading Gaol by Oscar Wilde to Robert Ross. Wilde was writing in January 1896, and in the course of his lengthy letter referred to William Michael Rossetti's *Letters and Memoir* of his brother, Dante Gabriel, which book apparently he had been reading in prison. As a lecturer on the pre-Raphaelites he may have felt himself to be particularly interested in the truth about Dante Gabriel Rossetti. At any rate, he declares: 'Ros-setti's Letters are terrible transparent counterfeitings of his brother. In spite of that, I have seen in them with interest that my Great-uncle's *Melmoth* and my mother's

Sidonia the Sorceress were among the books which entranced him in his youth. As to the conspiracy, which later is said to have arisen against him, I believe that such a thing really occurred, and that the means thereto were afforded by Hake's Bank. . . .' [1]

A typical example of the kind of literature which aroused Rossetti's youthful imagination is the romance by T. Gordon Hake, *Vates, or the Philosophy of Madness*, illustrated with bizarre etchings by Thomas Landseer. This made a vivid impression on him when he was about sixteen. The book was afterwards entitled *Valdarno, or the Ordeal of Art Worship*. Rossetti did not meet Dr. Hake until 1869; in 1872 Hake became his physician. The Newgate Calendar was another youthful delight, but of all the weird or melodramatic literature in his readings only Dumas seems to have remained as a favourite recreation in later life, apart from authentic work like Poe's.

In more serious reading it is noteworthy that Keats, Coleridge, and Browning inspired some of his earliest designs, though the drawing for 'La Belle Dame Sans Merci' is enough to link his feeling for romantic poetry with his sense of the mysterious. This drawing, done in 1847, not only in atmosphere but in the forms of the white-faced lady and the bemused knight, is an unmistakable anticipation of the design of 'How They Met Themselves', his vivid pictorial presentation of the *doppelgänger* legend, which always attracted him from the moment he came across it first. He was destined, against all the superficial probabilities of his varied and broad education and ample social opportunities, to become a lonely seeker of lonely knowledge.

[1] This is not Wilde's original English, which is not published, but a translation from the German edition of the *De Profundis* with some of his letters. It is quoted as being little known and not without biographical interest, but there is no evidence to support allegations of William Rossetti being a dishonest biographer. The question of the 'conspiracy' can never be quite cleared up, but it is referred to in subsequent chapters.

CHAPTER III

LIZZIE SIDDAL

I plucked a honeysuckle where
The hedge on high is quick with thorn.
—*D. G. ROSSETTI.*

ROSSETTI's first contact with Elizabeth Eleanor Siddal, the daughter of a Sheffield cutler, was due to the young painter Walter Deverell, a friend of the P.R.B.'s, who found her in a milliner's shop near Leicester Square. Holman Hunt tells the beginning of the story in his reminiscences. The year is 1850. Rossetti and Hunt were dining in the latter's studio one evening when Deverell broke in unexpectedly and sat down with them.

He had not been seated many minutes, talking in a somewhat absent manner, when he bounded up, marching, or rather dancing to and fro about the room, and, stopping emphatically, he whispered, 'You fellows can't tell what a stupendously beautiful creature I have found! By Jove! she's like a queen, magnificently tall, with a lovely figure, a stately neck, and a face of the most delicate and finished modelling; the flow of surface from the temples over the cheek is exactly like the carving of a Pheidean goddess. Wait a minute! I haven't done; she has grey eyes, and her hair is like dazzling copper, and shimmers with lustre as she waves it down. And now, where do you think I lighted on this paragon of beauty? Why, in a milliner's back workroom when I went out with my mother shopping. Having nothing to amuse me, while the woman was tempting my mother with something, I peered over the blind of a glass door at the back of the shop, and there was this unexpected jewel. I got my mother to persuade the miraculous creature to sit for my Viola in "Twelfth Night", and to-day I have been trying to paint her. . . . To-morrow she's coming again; you two should come down and see her; she's really a wonder; for while her friends, of course, are quite humble, she behaves like a real lady, by clear commonsense, and without any affectation, knowing perfectly, too, how to keep people at a respectful distance.'

[1] Hunt, chap. viii.

[50]

Rossetti accepted the invitation and returned to Hunt the next day with the announcement that he had prevailed upon Miss Siddal to sit to him. Hunt, who wanted to make the young woman tending the priest in his picture of 'Christians escaping from Persecuting Druids' 'a fair Celt with red hair', asked Rossetti whether he thought that he (Hunt) could ask her to sit. Rossetti's advice was to write to her, which Hunt did, and so she became the model for a figure in this, one of the much abused P.R.B. pictures at the 1850 exhibition. Rossetti was then at work on his 'Ecce Ancilla Domini', for which his sister Christina and his brother William were the models. Hunt says that although Rossetti admired Miss Siddal from the time he first saw her, he 'did not for a full year or two profess any strong personal feeling for her'. Probably Hunt, if he remembered correctly, was misled by Rossetti's reserve. Ford Madox Brown wrote in his Diary in 1855:[1] 'I had a letter from Rossetti, Thursday, saying that Ruskin had bought all Miss Siddal's (" Guggum's ") drawings, and said they beat Rossetti's own. . . . She is a stunner and no mistake. Rossetti once told me that, when he first saw her, he felt his destiny was defined. Why does he not marry her?' This pregnant entry launches the reader at once into the problem of Rossetti's relations with Lizzie Siddal. It is probable that she was his model within a few months of their introduction, which had been appropriately effected by both of them sitting to Deverell for figures in the same picture, 'Twelfth Night, the Duke with Viola listening to the Court Minstrels'. She was Viola, he the Jester, which his brother described as 'a fair likeness, but rather grim'.[2] A small water-colour by Rossetti, 'Rossovestita', belonging to the year 1850, is probably painted from her, but the first of his really beautiful studies of her

[1] 10th March 1855: *Ruskin, Rossetti, Pre-Raphaelitism, Papers,* 1854-1862, edited by W. M. Rossetti, 1899. Subsequent quotations from Brown's Diary are in this book.

[2] *Memoir,* xvii.

face is the Beatrice in 'Beatrice at the Wedding-Feast Denying her Salutation to Dante', of 1851, and for some years after this she comes into all his Beatrice pictures. In 1855 Ruskin commissioned a replica of the water-colour, which Rossetti, being 'hard-up', had sold for about £10 to H. T. Wells. To copy it, Rossetti borrowed the picture, which is considered one of the finest specimens of his early work. Ruskin's dictatorial methods, which partly caused the alienation of the two men, is revealed in two of his letters of 1855 referring to the replica. Among Ruskin's remarks are: 'Please put a dab of chinese white into the hole in the cheek and paint it over. People will say that Beatrice has been giving the other bridesmaids a " predestinate scratched face "; also a white-faced brides-maid behind is very ugly to look at—like a skull or body in corruption'. Eventually the replica went to Ruskin's, and later Rossetti's, friend, Professor C. E. Norton, of Harvard.

After 1852 the face of Lizzie appears more frequently in Rossetti's designs, the next important water-colour how-ever being the 'Dante Drawing the Angel' done in 1853, another of the subjects taken from his translation of Dante's *Vita Nuova*. An earlier version of this, done in pen and ink, was given by the artist to Millais, who parted with it a little later. In both cases the passage illustrated was:

On that day which fulfilled the year since my lady had been made of the citizens of eternal life, remembering me of her as I sat alone, I betook myself to draw the resemblance of an angel upon certain tablets. And while I did thus, chancing to turn my head, I perceived that some were standing beside me to whom I should have given courteous welcome, and that they were observing what I did. Also I learned afterwards that they had been there a while before I perceived them. Perceiving whom, I arose for salutation, and said: 'Another was with me'.

It should be noted that the themes for which Rossetti found Lizzie Siddal a beautiful model were familiar ones to him, and that she served where previously his sister Christina served as the original.

Not the least surprising feature in the twelve-years'-long relationship of these two is the development of artistic genius in Eleanor Siddal, who was barely seventeen years old when she first met Rossetti. The environment of the brilliant though still rather ragged and Bohemian art world of the P.R.B.'s must have been a revolutionary change for the young milliner, who needed all her native intuition and fine dignity to cover her inability to follow the young men's clever (or nonsensical) talk and to share in their ideals. Except for her instinctive refinement of mind, she faced the situation precisely as any insufficiently cultured but proud working girl would have done, adopting an habitual taciturnity varied by somewhat flippant and cynical remarks. Everything goes to show that Rossetti's interest in her was returned. The millinery business was abandoned so that she could be not only his model, but his pupil, and so this astonishing creature in 1852 is already practising with the success of genius, not of trained talent, the art which absorbed Rossetti. She was an apt pupil. In those eager, ambitious years for Rossetti, when the P.R.B. had dissolved and left its chief members as notable individuals in the world of art, she accompanied him here and there: to his own family; to his friends Mr. and Mrs. Madox Brown then at Finchley; to the Ruskins at Denmark Hill; and a few years later, when married, to the homes of Morris and Burne-Jones. His nearest friends, such as the Browns, saw more of Lizzie than his own relatives indeed. Ruskin and Swinburne especially were devoted adorers of ' the Sid '. There are many glimpses of her in letters and jottings of this time.

Ruskin's letter to Rossetti on 2nd May 1854, which was probably his first after their first meeting early in the preceding month, refers to Miss Siddal as Rossetti's pupil: ' I hope to be back in London about the middle of August, and will immediately come to see your pupil's drawings '. It is clear that Rossetti had taken the earliest opportunity of interesting Ruskin in her work. The following are a few brief relevant extracts from Brown's Diary: [1]

6th Oct. 1854. Called on Dante Rossetti. Saw Miss Siddal, looking thinner and more deathlike and more beautiful and more ragged than ever; a real artist, a woman without parallel for many a long year. Gabriel as usual diffuse and inconsequent in his work. Drawing wonderful and lovely Guggums one after another, each one a fresh charm, each one stamped with immortality, and his picture never advancing. However, he is at the wall, and I am to get him a white calf and a cart to paint here; would he but study the *golden one* a little more. Poor Gabriello. . . .

12th. . . . Gabriel gone to town to see Miss Siddal. Getting on slowly with his calf.

10th March 1855. . . . I had a letter from Rossetti, Thursday, saying that Ruskin had bought all Miss Siddal's (Guggum's) drawings, and said they beat Rossetti's own. This is like Ruskin, the incarnation of exaggeration. However, he is right to admire them. She is a stunner and no mistake. Rossetti once told me that, when he first saw her, he felt his destiny was defined. Why does he not marry her?

17th. To Seddon's, to meet Millais, Rossetti and Collins. Rossetti in joyful state about Miss Siddal, who has got lots to do, and Mrs. Tennyson insists upon her having a share of the illustrations to Tennyson. Sooner than not, she writes to Moxon, 'she will pay for them herself'.[2]

13th April 1855. . . . A letter from Gabriel saying Ruskin . . . had made two propositions to Miss Siddal . . . one to buy all she does one by one, the other to give her £150 a year for all she does, and, if he sold them for more, the difference to be hers; if not, to keep them. D.G.R. in glee.

21st. Rossetti and Miss Sid came per 'bus to-night.

22nd. Rossetti and Miss Sid here all day, one of perfect repose. Talk till 2 a.m.

23rd. Do. and do. here still. . . .

6th August. To Rossetti . . . till at last they [the company] all went off together about 12, and I remained talking to Rossetti till 3 a.m. He showed me a drawer full of 'Guggums'; God knows how many, but not bad work, I should say, for the six years he has known her; it is like a monomania with him. Many of them are matchless in beauty, however, and one day will be worth large sums.

[1] *Ruskin, Rossetti, Pre-Raphaelitism.*
[2] Nothing came of the scheme. Tennyson's volume was illustrated by Millais, Rossetti, and others.

16th. Emma [Mrs. Brown] went into town with Miss Siddal before Rossetti was come in from his room at the Queen's Head, so that when he did come his rage knew no bounds at being done out of the society of Guggum, and vented itself in abuse of Emma, who 'was always trying to persuade Miss Sid that he was plaguing her', etc., etc., whereas of course Miss Sid liked it as much as he did, etc., etc. . . . I did not know whether to laugh most or to be angry, laughed at him and damned him, and at length thought it best to tell him where he could find them, as Betsy was to follow them as soon as she could dress Nolly [1] and join them in Kentish Town. This appeased him, and presently off he started. I took a shower-bath, not having had one since Miss Sid came, she having my room.

The life was too unrestful for Elizabeth Siddal, whose continually bad health became the chief anxiety of Rossetti's existence, while it gave the generous Ruskin his best excuse for repeated offers of financial help. As early as 1853 Rossetti writes to Brown that ' Liz ' is to do a picture for the R.A.; but this astonishing fertility of her mind had accompanied the development of phthisis, which was already in her constitution. Brown makes a significant entry in his Diary for 22nd October 1855. He has lent Rossetti £15. 'Guggum' has gone to France. 'She is gone, and I hope Gabriel will work all the better for it.' Miss Siddal was accompanied by Mrs. Kincaid, a relative, who seems to have been extravagant. They were to go from Paris to Nice. 'After she had been gone six weeks or so ', Brown writes, 'letter came to Gabriel saying she had spent all his money at Paris. Gabriel, who saw that none of the drawings on the easel could be completed before long, began a fresh one, 'Francesca di Rimini', in *three compartments*; worked day and night, finished it in a week, got thirty-five guineas for it from Ruskin, and started off to relieve them. Saw her off by rail for Nice, and came back in another week. This is how Gabriel can work on a pinch. I must say, however, that as yet my £15 are in abeyance, but I live in hope.'

Before the departure for the Continent that autumn, in

---

[1] Oliver Madox Brown, then an infant.

the preceding February of 1855, Rossetti wrote a Valentine in light vein for her:

> Yesterday was St. Valentine.
> Thought you at all, dear dove divine,
> Upon the beard in sorry trim
> And rueful countenance of him,
> That Orson who's your Valentine? . . .
>
> The bore was heard ere noon; the dun
> Was at the door by half-past one:
> At least 'tis thought so, but the clock —
> No Lizzy there to help its stroke—
> Struck work before the day begun. . . .
>
> Some time over the fire he sat,
> So lonely that he missed his cat;
> Then wildly rushed to dine on tick—
> Nine minutes swearing for his stick,
> And thirteen minutes for his hat. . . .
>
> Come back, dear Liz, and, looking wise
> In that armchair which suits your size,
> Through some fresh drawing scrape a hole,
> Your Valentine and Orson's soul
> Is sad for those two friendly eyes.

Lizzie was probably in the country or by the sea for a change of air at this time. At any rate, in the previous May she was so ill that she was packed off to Hastings, accompanied by Rossetti. He writes anxiously on 23rd May 1854 from 5 High Street, Hastings, to his friend Brown, and says: 'Lizzy, poor dear, continues on the whole much the same. I have been here rather more than a fortnight, and shall now be returning for a short time to London, leaving her here till I can come again. She is looking lovelier than ever, but is very weak. . . . She has spent two very pleasant days at Barbara Smith's farm, some miles from here, and just while I write a letter reaches me asking us to go down again to-day, but I do not suppose we shall, as it is wet. Everyone adores and reveres Lizzy. Barbara Smith,[1] Miss Howitt, and I made

[1] Afterwards Mrs. Bodichon, who would lend Rossetti 'Scalands', Robertsbridge, Sussex, in later years.

Photo W. F. Mansell

LIZZIE SIDDAL. A DRAWING BY ROSSETTI, *c*. 1855, OF HIS MODEL AND FIANCÉE

Photo W. F. Mansell

LIZZIE AFTER HER MARRIAGE IN 1860. A SKETCH BY ROSSETTI OF HER RECLINING ON A PILLOW

sketches of her dear head, with iris stuck in her dear hair, the other day, and we all wrote up our monograms on the panel of the window, in memorial of the very pleasant day we had spent at the farm '.

Those who share the pardonable curiosity about the autobiographical facts in a poem may be able to connect certain lines of ' The Portrait ' with this visit to Hastings of Rossetti and Lizzie Siddal, for they were engaged about this time. The sixth and seventh stanzas especially may be claimed to justify this detective piety:

> But when that hour my soul won strength
>   For words whose silence wastes and kills,
> Dull raindrops smote us, and at length
>   Thundered the heat within the hills.
> That eve I spoke those words again
> Beside the pelted window-pane;
>   And there she hearkened what I said,
>   With under-glances that surveyed
> The empty pastures blind with rain.
>
> Next day the memories of these things,
>   Like leaves through which a bird has flown,
> Still vibrated with Love's warm wings;
>   Till I must make them all my own
> And paint this picture. So, 'twixt ease
> Of talk and sweet long silences,
>   She stood among the plants in bloom
>   At windows of a summer room,
> To feign the shadow of the trees.

Unfortunately, it is necessary to this supposition to assume that the above stanzas were added long after the poem was first written in 1847.

Rossetti goes on to tell Brown how ' Guggum ' and he are to illustrate Allingham's anthology of border ballads, and ' she has just done her first block (from " Clerk Saunders ") and it is lovely. Her power of designing even increases greatly, and her fecundity of invention and facility are quite wonderful, much greater than mine '.

Ruskin's letters to Lizzie show that he was very anxious lest she should overwork herself. While pressing in the most tactful way his offers to finance a holiday for her (about April 1855) he says: ' I don't expect you to be able to work at all for about four months yet; that by that time I believe you may have gained strength enough to do a little water-colour drawing, and next year to begin the oil; and that if I hear of your being any more restive I shall be very seriously saddened and hurt '. He says that if the doctor recommends the south of France or Italy he wants to meet the expense, but ' if you were my own sister, I should plead hard for a little cottage in some sheltered Welsh valley. My own belief is that you want calm, sweet, but bracing air, rather than hot, relaxing air '. About the same time he is writing to Rossetti asking to be taken into his confidence concerning Rossetti's ' plans or wishes respecting Miss S which you are prevented from carrying out by want of a certain income, and if so what certain income would enable you to carry them out '. He follows the letter hastily with a longer one, to make sure there can be no misunderstanding. It is a very fine letter, going out of the way to meet the confidence of his correspondent, and to remove any embarrassment to Rossetti which might result from the idea that Rossetti's marriage to Eleanor Siddal should depend upon Ruskin's money. In a letter to her Ruskin had likened his assistance to the offer of a cup of water to a thirsty person, and here he tells Rossetti that it is just as natural ' I should try to be of use to you as that I should offer you a cup of tea if I saw you were thirsty, and there was plenty in the teapot, and I had got all I wanted '. So far as money was concerned this was the bare truth, but few men with money are so generous and wise as Ruskin was, or so tactful in offering it. Although he was undoubtedly in love with Eleanor Siddal, whom he called ' Ida ' (a name borrowed from Tennyson's ' Princess '), the mere offers of help with money *were* ' natural ' to him, and needed no such stimulus of deep feeling. Brown, it will be remembered, also had asked in his Diary ' why does he not marry her? ' and quite likely had asked Rossetti personally the same question. Rossetti's impecunious condition alone would hardly be a sufficient explanation of his delay in marrying Lizzie until the spring of 1860. But this is hardly an adequate reason for charging him, as some writers have done, with a callous disregard of Lizzie's welfare, and with hastening the ruin of her health by delaying the marriage. It might have been well for both of them if they had never married. Ruskin was right in constantly urging rest and quietness for Lizzie, but, as he says in a letter to her,[1] ' the difficulty is to keep you quiet and yet to give you means of passing the time with some degree of pleasure to yourself'. When at last these strange children married life was anything except restful for her. Ruskin went as far as anyone could go on her behalf by urging her to go to quiet and bracing places and to rest. He also did what he could to discourage her taste for gloomy and spectral subjects in painting, but her themes were by no means merely the sign of sympathy with the new mood of romantic archaism which possessed Rossetti in the 'fifties. They are, like her pathetic poems, the forced fruit of a fine spirit morbid at the core. Lizzie Siddal from the first that we know of her is clearly doomed to nervous instability and excessive irritation. To blame Rossetti because the incipient phthisis developed rapidly with the mature development of her eager mind and passionately repressed temperament is to go laboriously out of the obvious path of truth in judging a man who, by the kindest eyes that are also clear-sighted can never be seen in too favourable a light. But it is probable that delay in marriage was not the offence against love of which Rossetti was guilty, if he is to be indicted at all. With all their morbidity Lizzie's poems impress the mind not only as being almost uniformly painful, but as harping monotonously upon the theme of betrayed and disillusioned love. One of her poems was published in the *Memoir* by William Rossetti. This, ' A Year and A Day ', is an exception, not

[1] No. 35 in *Ruskin, Rossetti, Pre-Raphaelitism.*

because it is cheerful, but because there is in it the sad lassitude of a person dying too soon, rather than the bitterness of one betrayed. It begins:

> Slow days have passed that make a year,
> Slow hours that make a day,
> Since I could take my first dear love,
> And kiss him the old way:
> Yet the green leaves touch me on the cheek,
> Dear Christ, this month of May.

The third and fourth stanzas, however, hardly justify us in treating the poem as an exception to the rule of bitterness:

> The river ever running down
> Between its grassy bed,
> The voices of a thousand birds
> That clang above my head,
> Shall bring to me a sadder dream
> When this sad dream is dead.
>
> A silence falls upon my heart,
> And hushes all its pain.
> I stretch my hands in the long grass,
> And fall to sleep again,
> There to lie empty of all love,
> Like beaten corn of grain.

This was the poem described by Oscar Wilde as ' A 1 ', when he wrote to Robert Ross from prison about William Rossetti's *Memoir*.

Sometimes the poems become a prayer for death.

Among the other pieces which William Rossetti published, ' Early Death ' begins:

> Oh grieve not with thy bitter tears
> The life that passes fast:
> The gates of heaven will open wide,
> And take me in at last.

The one entitled ' He and She and Angels Three ', like ' Early Death ', has only three quatrains, the first of which runs:

> Ruthless hands have torn her
> From one that loved her well;
> Angels have upborne her,
> Christ her grief to tell.

The title is taken from a verse in the last stanza. When the soul of the dead girl's lover has been brought to her by ' three winged angels ',

> He and she and the angels three
> Before God's face shall stand :
> There they shall pray among themselves,
> And sing at His right hand.

The next piece, ' A Silent Wood ', opens:

> O silent wood, I enter thee
> With a heart so full of misery—
> For all the voices from the trees
> And the ferns that cling about my knees.

Two more quatrains follow and then a couplet of five-foot lines :

> Can God bring back the day when we two stood
> Beneath the clinging trees in that dark wood?

which might be compared with the fourth stanza of Rossetti's ' The Portrait '. ' Love and Hate ', throughout its five quatrains, is in the key of the first one :

> Ope not thy lips, thou foolish one,
> Nor turn to me thy face :
> The blasts of heaven shall strike me down
> Ere I will give thee grace.

Other lines,

> Lift up thy false brow from the dust

and

> And turn away thy false dark eyes

give the poem the poignant tone of a jealous woman's reproach. The next piece in this series, ' The Passing of Love ', concludes :

> Oh Heaven help my foolish heart
> Which heeded not the passing time
> That dragged my idol from its place
> And shattered all its shrine!

But the sixth and last, ' Lord, May I Come ? '—which contains thirty-two lines undivided into stanzas, though broken at intervals by refrains, has a rather different character. It ' is written in a very shaky and straggling way ', says William Rossetti; ' I surmise that it must have been done under the influence of laudanum . . . and probably not long before her death '. The poem opens:

> Life and night are falling from me,
> Death (and day) are opening on me.
> Wherever my footsteps come and go
> Life is a stony way of woe.
> Lord, have I long to go?
> Hollow hearts are ever near me,
> Soulless eyes have ceased to cheer me:
> Lord, may I come to Thee?

Two references to some dead person called forth a special note from William Rossetti, ' Loved eyes, long closed in death, watch o'er me ', and the second one in

> I am gazing upwards to the sun,
> Lord, Lord, remembering my lost one.

The note runs: ' I do not know of any " lost one " unless the reference is to the still-born infant [1861]. I learned, however, of late years from Mr. James Siddal [brother of Lizzie] that, shortly before her acquaintance with Dante Rossetti, she had been in lengthened and very exhausting attendance on the sick-bed of another much-loved brother, whose illness ended in death '.[1]

The pieces published in 1899[2] are in keeping with these. They are entitled ' True Love ', ' Dead Love ', ' Shepherd Turned Sailor ', ' Gone ', ' Speechless ', ' The Lust of the Eyes ', ' Worn Out '. A reading of these brief lyrics, crude though they generally are in mere technique, is as painful as reading a diary in which some nerve-tortured person has recorded unmitigated anguish. But there is resentment and bitterness every now and again. ' The Lust of the Eyes ', for instance, needs to be quoted in full for an appreciation of the strange mingling of irony and despair:

> I care not for my lady's soul,
> Though I worship before her smile:
> I care not whereby my lady's goal
> When her beauty shall lose its wile.

---

[1] *Some Reminiscences*, chap. xiv, by William Michael Rossetti.
[2] Section 79, *Ruskin, Rossetti, Pre-Raphaelitism.*

Low I sit down at my lady's feet,
  Gazing through her wild eyes,
Smiling to think how my love will fleet
  When their starlike beauty dies.

I care not if my lady pray
  To our Father which is in Heaven;
But for joy my heart's quick pulses play,
  For to me her love is given.

Then who shall close my lady's eyes,
  And who shall fold her hands?
Will any hearken if she cries
  Up to the unknown lands?

Now the sentimental view would be at once that Rossetti must have been brutally callous to produce such a state of mind as these monotonously sad poems reveal. The view could not be held for long however, granted either some understanding of morbid psychology, or even some acquaintance with the rest of the biographical literature which is available to any inquirer. Perhaps enough has been said about Lizzie's failing health. Her most productive years, from 1855 to about 1857, were marked by visits to doctors and health resorts one after the other. Besides the phthisis, she was found to have a curvature of the spine in 1854. She grew increasingly subject to attacks of neuralgia, and began on medical advice to get relief in laudanum. Ruskin became sufficiently in love with her to arouse, justifiably or not, Rossetti's jealousy. Some other painter in the Rossetti circle seems to have troubled her with unwelcome attention. So much did she resent his presence that there was a quarrel with Rossetti concerning a project which he and Burne-Jones and Morris were discussing in February 1857. This was for a sort of communal 'college' of various artists. The letter which Rossetti wrote to Madox Brown from Chatham Place on 26th February 1857 throws light on some of the difficulties of the relationship between Rossetti and his fiancée. It seems desirable to quote the letter at length:

Last night a misunderstanding occurred between Lizzy and me about what passed, when you were there, concerning the scheme of a college.

She seems under the impression that you came there in great surprise at hearing that I had not consulted her on the matter, and with the wish to speak to her yourself. Though I should be grateful to you for anything done in friendship to her, I cannot but imagine that, as my friend, you would have preferred first asking me what had passed between us, before speaking to her; especially as you could have been under no impression that I was acting in this without reference to her as well as myself; seeing that on the night when Morris, Jones, and I, came to you, and were discussing the scheme, I expressly said that I should be married by the time it came into operation, and require space accordingly in the building. When you first spoke on Tuesday evening of two married couples as beginning the scheme, I thought you meant Lizzy and me for the second; and, on finding that you did not, I refrained from saying anything, simply because Lizzy has sometimes lately shown so much displeasure on my mentioning our engagement (which I have hoped was attributable to illness) that I could not tell how far her mother was aware of it, or how Lizzy would take my mentioning it before her.

I *had* spoken of the scheme to her some days ago, but she seemed to take little interest in it, and I did not say much. She now says that she understood only a range of studios, and would strongly object to the idea of living where G[1] was, of which objection of hers I had no idea to any such extent. I have myself wished to keep him and her apart hitherto, as I do not think he has acted lately as a friend towards me in her regard, but that feeling would have left me when once we were married. However, my wishes as to this scheme would entirely depend on hers, supposing that it would really affect her happiness; in which case I should cease to care for it or to think of it. As it is, she seemed last night quite embittered and estranged from me on this account, whether for the moment or permanently I cannot yet tell, and it has made me most unhappy ever since, more so than anything else could make me. . . .

And a day or two later he thanks Brown for a friendly reply, and says he must not show it to Lizzie however, ' as her health will not bear any excitement. . . . She does not better in health, never eating anything to speak of, and I am most wretched about her. What to do I know not. . . . I cannot trouble her about it or feel any anger at her, only constant pain at her sufferings. Kind and patient she has been with me many and many times, more than I have deserved; and I trust this trouble is over '.

[1] 'G' is William Rossetti's alternative to giving the painter's name.

Ruskin's arrangement for making a regular payment to Lizzie for her work was ended at this time by her and Rossetti. It had been difficult to persuade her to accept Ruskin's sensible if unbusinesslike plan (her work had then no market value), and when she was unable to give Ruskin any pictures owing to her travels she and Rossetti agreed that she should not depend on Ruskin's generosity any longer. Ruskin made a good-humoured protest at their decision, but showed no resentment, and after their marriage wrote to Rossetti much as before.

E

CHAPTER IV

LIZZIE ROSSETTI

'I and this Love are one, and I am Death.'—D. G. ROSSETTI.

ROSSETTI himself was conscious of having hesitated too long over their marriage. Before 1856 or 1857 certainly his impecuniosity provided a fairly reasonable objection to such a step, but what with Ruskin's allowance to him and other commissions at improved prices, he was receiving towards the late 'fifties enough to dispose of the most serious monetary difficulties. When Brown, in 1855, asked in his Diary, ' Why does he not marry her ? ' he was hardly allowing for the difference between his own steady character, which could face marriage in almost as uncertain financial conditions as Rossetti's, and his friend's disorganized and impulsive temperament, which would have made marriage a hopeless business without a dependable surplus for extravagance. Moreover, Brown did not marry an invalid. Nevertheless, Rossetti's letter about the misunderstanding over the ' college ' of artists shows that in 1857 he and Lizzie were on the verge of the dangerous step, and also makes it seem very probable that further delay was due not less to some fear or resentment in her than to his own hesitation.

One of the important incidents in Rossetti's life at this time was the discovery of the beautiful Jane Burden at Oxford. If the story is quite true that the enthusiastic young men who were painting in the Oxford Union Hall held an agitated meeting about the strangely beautiful ' type ' they had seen in the theatre at Oxford, then it must have been Rossetti who ' moved ' that ' Topsy ' Morris, as the only eligible bachelor, must marry her so that such a

[66]

' stunner ' should remain in the family, as it were, available as a model. The curious thing about the whole business is Morris's seeming lack of enthusiasm over his marriage to Jane Burden. It is not possible to read J. W. Mackail's *Life* of Morris without getting the impression that Morris was as troubled about his marriage to Jane Burden as Rossetti a little later was to be about his own marriage to Lizzie Siddal, and the conclusion that I have reached from a study of the documentary material is that the impetuous and unconcentrated Rossetti had betrayed too deep an interest in the dark beauty whom he was to immortalize some years later in the pictures of his mature period. ' Beauty like hers is genius ' he declared, and one is forced to wonder if the phrase contained an unconscious comparison of Jane Burden with the ailing Lizzie, who had possessed genius itself. Jane Burden was only eighteen when Rossetti made her acquaintance and first drew her, in 1857, for his ' Study for Queen Guenevere '. She was Mrs. William Morris before he married Lizzie Siddal.

The Oxford incident was not the first distraction of the years of his engagement to Lizzie. The chief of his models, apart from her, had been Fanny Cornforth, afterwards Mrs. Schott, who became the principal original for the florid and sensual types in his pictures. The fair-haired, solidly built Fanny was to be his mistress for more years than any other woman, exercising a corresponding power over his desires. Before his marriage she was no doubt a cause of Lizzie's bitterness. Rossetti would probably have married sooner than he did but for such a disorganization of his emotional life as would result from engagement to a woman who would not be his entirely before marriage, and the simultaneous intimate contact with another woman capable of satisfying his senses and content to do so. Ruskin was well aware of these complications and found himself painfully situated between his admiration of Rossetti and his chivalrous fears for Lizzie, who, of course, would not have welcomed the interference of any third person. Nevertheless, the model for ' Fazio's Mistress ' (judiciously re-titled ' Aurelia '), for the woman in ' Found', was decisively, though we can be sure not ungenerously, banished when at last he rushed down to the sick Lizzie at Hastings in the spring of 1860, and after wearing anxiety suddenly married her during a recovery of her strength, taking her off to Paris there and then on their honeymoon. The impetuosity of the delayed action was entirely characteristic of him, but no one has a right to sit in judgment on Rossetti for the sufficient reason that Lizzie herself was by no means a passive agent and her temperament was decidedly morbid where his was merely complicated by confused desires. It was the poet and artist in him which drew the man into the complete union of marriage with Lizzie Siddal, and the very delay of the final step, in so far as it depended on his own decision, may reasonably be traced to an unresolved emotional conflict in him. A consciousness of his own fault in delaying the marriage is clearly shown by the letter written to his mother [1] from Hastings. In the weeks preceding the marriage his letters to Brown and to his brother William are painfully full of Lizzie's illness and his fears for her. After they get to Paris he writes, on 9th June, from the rue de Rivoli, asking William to insert in *The Times* the following notice: ' On the 23rd ult., at St. Clement's Church, Hastings, by the Rev. T. Nightingale, Dante Gabriel, eldest son of the late Gabriel Rossetti, of Vasto degli Abruzzi, Kingdom of Naples, to Elizabeth Eleanor, daughter of the late Charles Siddal, of Sheffield '.

Characteristically he adds: ' If the governor's birth-place is wrong at all, please alter '.

Rossetti would have been caught unprepared however

---

[1] Reproduced to face this page. The conclusion of the letter is:
' Grieved to hear her health is no better as yet.
' Love to all,
' Your affect: Son
' D. G. ROSSETTI.'

(Gabriel's marriage) Hastings
Wednesday
℞ May 23rd 1860

My dear Mother

Lizzie and I are
just back from
Church — We are
going to Folkestone
to-day, hoping
to get on to
Paris if possible
but you will be

ROSSETTI'S LETTER AFTER HIS MARRIAGE. 'GABRIEL'S MARRIAGE'
AND THE DATE ARE WRITTEN BY HIS MOTHER
(By courtesy of the owner, Mr. Thomas J. Wise. See Appendix C)

long his marriage had been delayed. As it was, he was thrown into a state of chaos by this honeymoon, dragged by the call of his profession and of commissioned work overdue, by grief for Lizzie's condition, and fear of the wandering desires in himself. To his brother he wrote from Hastings just before the marriage that they had the ordinary licence ready, ' and I still trust to God we may be enabled to use it. If not, I should have so much to grieve for, and what is worse, so much to reproach myself with, that I do not know how it might end for me '. To Brown, concerning a temporary relief from ' this dreadful attack' through which he had been nursing Lizzie, he wrote: ' this improvement is so sudden and unaccountable that one fears to put full trust in it, but can only hope and wait. At any rate, it makes me feel as if I had been dug out of a vault, so many times lately has it seemed to me that she could never lift her head again '. His letter concludes: ' I had wished to snatch a few days' work in London before our marriage, but this seems daily more impossible—indeed it hardly seems to me as if I should ever work again '.

One of the significant signs of his perturbation is the drawing ' How they Met Themselves ', which he did during their honeymoon. It was done from the memory of an earlier design of the same subject, but after making allowance for his interest in romantic and occult legends, that weird and powerful representation of the belief in the *doppelgänger* comes strangely during a honeymoon. A man and woman, walking as lovers through a dark wood, are confronted by their doubles, around which shines an unearthly halo of light. The man is startled and supports the woman, who is falling back in a faint before the vision of herself. The vision of a ' double ', according to the old legend, signifies the approaching death of the person whose ' double ' is seen.

Lizzie's health seemed to improve after the marriage, but was shattered again a year later when she gave birth to a stillborn child. A few months later Ruskin is writing to her about painting. In a letter from Brighton about September 1860 Lizzie writes to 'My Dear Gug' apologizing for worrying him about coming back. She has evidently been staying at Brighton with her sister for the benefit of her health, and says, 'I seem to have gained flesh within the last ten days, and seem also much better in some respects, although I am in constant pain and cannot sleep at nights for fear of another illness like the last'. But she thinks she may be better there with Lyddy (her sister) than alone in the lodgings they have taken at Hampstead. 'I really do not know what to advise about the little house in the lane. If you were to take it, you might still retain your rooms at Chatham Place, which I think would be the best thing to do until better times. However, I do not see how the £30 are to be paid just at this time, so I suppose that will settle the matter.' She adds that she would like her water-colours sent down, 'as I am quite destitute of all means of keeping myself alive. I have kept myself alive hitherto by going out to sea in the smallest boat I can find. What do you say to my not being sick in the roughest weather?' She would like to see the picture, 'Regina Cordium', which he has painted from her, but supposes it will be sent away to a purchaser. She concludes: 'I can do without money till next Thursday, after which time £3 a week would be quite enough for all our wants—including rent of course. Your affectionate Lizzie'.

About the same time Ruskin wrote a letter after calling at Chatham Place and finding no one in. He had looked over the collection of sketches which Brown referred to in his Diary as 'lovely Guggums', and wrote: 'I think Ida should be very happy to see how much more beautifully, perfectly, and tenderly you draw when you are drawing *her* than when you draw anybody else. She cures you of all your worst faults when you only look at her'.

There was no sign of any developing domesticity about

Lizzie, and probably No. 14 Chatham Place became, as a consequence of the journeying to Hampstead and elsewhere, more untidy than ever, while Rossetti's habits of working and feeding would have been as irregular as they had always been; they could not have grown more irregular. Rossetti, nevertheless, during 1860 and 1861 was very prolific in designs and new plans of work, and with Ruskin's financial assistance produced *The Early Italian Poets* at long last, inscribed: 'Whatever is mine in this book is inscribed to my wife. D.G.R., 1861 ', of which Ruskin writes after seeing the book, ' I like the inscription so much '. This period is marked by the death of Mrs. Browning[1] and what they hear of Browning bereaved. Woolner told William Rossetti of a lady who was walking with Browning about Paris, and how she reported ' that the poor fellow was often in tears '. Rossetti is much occupied with the early activities of the new firm, Morris, Marshall, Faulkner & Co., of which he was a contributing member. There is correspondence with Ruskin and with members of the Rossetti family about Christina's *Goblin Market and Other Poems*, her first book, which he illustrated in the summer of 1861. Rossetti finishes his long-delayed triptych for Llandaff Cathedral, and makes other designs for Morris at Red Lion Square. Morris is applying a new method of painting glass. Holman Hunt and Millais at this time are both becoming comparatively affluent in their profession. Rossetti, throughout the summer and autumn of 1861, is trying to finish pictures paid for by Plint, a purchaser who died before receiving them, and for whose estate the pictures are to be put on the market. The Hogarth Club's doings also engage Rossetti's attention, and he often refers to them in correspondence with Madox Brown.

On 31st October 1861 Rossetti writes to his mother

---

[1] William Rossetti's Diary for 22nd July 1861: 'Gabriel tells me (having heard it from Val Prinsep) that Mrs. Browning died through catching cold on the journey from Rome to Siena '.

from the house of J. A. Heaton, near Bingley, in Yorkshire. He had gone there to paint the portrait of Mrs. Heaton; the portrait became one of the pictures entitled ' Regina Cordium '. He tells his mother that he had left Lizzie staying with the Morrises. ' Now she writes me that she has left them in a hurry, making me very uneasy, as I know there was not a halfpenny of money at Chatham Place. If at all possible would you go there, and take her some few pounds, which I shall be able to repay you on my return immediately, and will punctually do so?' It was impossible to bring her here with me, both from her very delicate state and from the very reason that what money we had hardly sufficed for my own journey. On my return I shall have earned 50 guineas and shall certainly be back in a week from to-day.' Glimpses of this kind at the Rossettis' married life do not encourage any feeling that it could ever have endured even if it had not been violently and tragically terminated.

At the end of 1861 came the unexpected death of Alexander Gilchrist. Rossetti writes to Brown the news, and says that ' the Sunday evening before last I spent with him at his house [when two children and a servant were already attacked [1]], Ned Jones and Swinburne being there with me '. He adds a P.S. hoping that there is less danger than in some cases of the family being unprovided for. He had been associated with Gilchrist in the famous *Life* of Blake and was before long to be associated with Gilchrist's widow in the completion of the work.

A glimpse of married life is afforded by the long letter to Norton on 9th January 1862,[2] referring to his quarters at 14 Chatham Place. The passage explains, though not very convincingly, why he had not moved away from the river if this was not thought good for Lizzie's health. ' Our wish was to live at Hampstead, where for some time after our marriage we took lodgings, and looked for a permanent habitation, I meanwhile coming every day to

[1] By scarlatina.   [2] No. 154, *Ruskin, Rossetti, Pre-Raphaelitism.*

my work in the old quarters. But everything that seemed eligible at Hampstead persisted in slipping through our fingers; and the inconvenience and expense of divided dwelling and studio was so great that at last my wife resolved to settle here with me till we could suit ourselves in more suburban quarters. Accordingly, to get elbow-room, we took the second floor of No. 13 in addition to my second floor at 14, and opened a door of communication between the two suites of rooms. . . . Indeed, there is something so delightfully quaint and characteristic about our quarters here that nothing but the conviction that they cannot be the best for her health would ever induce me to move. However—this being so—I would move at once if I found a nice place elsewhere, and hope to do so before long. I write this in our " drawing-room ", entirely hung round with her water-colours of poetic subjects, which I wish you could see, as many of them would delight you. However, she is unhappily too confirmed an invalid to leave a hope now that she will ever be able to make the most of her genius. Indeed, the strength to work at all is only rarely accorded her.' One is entitled to say that the explanation hardly exonerates Rossetti from a charge of being too ready to make the best of the situation. Yet, although it was but too characteristic of him to hesitate over the move and to postpone the decisive step, there is no reason to doubt the sincerity of his intention to make the move ' before long '. But Lizzie was dead less than five weeks later, though not from the disease which might have been encouraged by a prolonged stay at Chatham Place. It seems necessary to treat this matter in some detail at this time of day so that Rossetti's complex and puzzling personality may not for ever excite extravagant vagaries of biographical comment.[1] After their marriage Lizzie had

---

[1] A good example of what I mean is Violet Hunt's way of writing about Rossetti and Lizzie Siddal. Violet Hunt does not scruple amid other wild perversions of the sane view to charge Rossetti with callously making Lizzie live over the 'miasmic swamps' of the river and so producing chronic developments of her consumption.

actually spent a smaller proportion of her life at Blackfriars than during the years from 1851, when she became her future husband's model and pupil. It has not been suggested that he should have given up his studio then to prevent her coming to the riverside; yet he is blamed as a husband for keeping her there, although they were married for less than two pitiful years, and she could not have spent half of that time at Chatham Place. And her death was from the laudanum which was her constant refuge from neuralgia. So far as the available documentary evidence shows, Lizzie's health seemed slightly improved during the first year of her marriage, until the birth of a stillborn child, which must have prepared the way for the serious relapses which followed her temporary recovery. There is another poem of hers not mentioned here yet, which is probably to be dated 1861,[1] called 'At Last', a strange mixture of her usual mood with suggestions of Tennyson's 'May Day' and Keats' 'La Belle Dame Sans Merci'. None of her poems sublimates emotion enough not to be autobiographical in the ordinary sense. The second stanza of 'At Last' runs:

> And, mother dear, take my young son
> (Since I was born of thee),
> And care for all his little ways,
> And nurse him on thy knee.

The concluding stanzas are:

> And, mother dear, break a willow wand,
> And if the sap be even,
> Then save it for my lover's sake,
> And he'll know my soul's in heaven.
>
> And, mother, when the big tears fall
> (And fall, God knows, they may),
> Tell him I died of my great love
> And my dying heart was gay.

---

[1] See W. M. Rossetti's note to it: *Ruskin, Rossetti, Pre-Raphaelitism*, No. 126.

And, mother dear, when the sun has set,
    And the pale church grass waves,
Then carry me through the dim twilight
    And hide me among the graves.

On the afternoon of 10th February 1862 Lizzie and
her husband joined Swinburne for dinner at the Sablonière
Restaurant in Leicester Square. A few days earlier she
had sat to him (for the last time) for the figure holding the
knight's helmet in ' St. George and the Princess Sabra '.
At that dinner she was animated, but enjoying only a
temporary relief from neuralgia, which had been causing
her so much distress that it was against Rossetti's advice
that she came out with him to the dinner party. When they
returned he went out again and advised her to go to bed.
Whatever the atmosphere in that doomed home was when
the harassed husband left the suffering wife to herself,
there is no reason for any attempt to allot blame by
biographers who must know far less of the facts than the
mutual friends of the Rossettis knew.

His brother William's Diary contained the following
entry for 11th February:

Death of poor Lizzie, Gabriel's wife. Coming home last night past
11 from the Working Men's College, he found her almost gone from
the effects of laudanum, and, spite of the efforts of four doctors, she
died towards 7½ this morning. I was called from Somerset House
about 12½ (by Mrs. Birrell, the housekeeper of the Chambers, 14
Chatham Place, who had been there during the entire duration of my
brother's stay). Brown, whom Gabriel had called on before 5 in the
morning, was there (his residence was then near Highgate Rise), and
told me the circumstances. Lizzie and Gabriel had dined at a Hotel
with Swinburne that afternoon. The poor thing looks wonderfully
calm now and beautiful.

    ' Ed avea in sè umiltà sì verace
    Che parea che dicesse, io sono in pace.' [1]

I could not but think of that all the time I looked at her, it is so
exactly like.

---

[1] From the *Vita Nuova*, in D. G. Rossetti's translation :

    ' And with her was such very humbleness
    That she appeared to say, I am at peace.'

[75]

The remaining facts, as distinguished from implications which may be read into them, concerning Lizzie's part in her husband's life, are well known and need not occupy much space here. Unobserved by his friends, the grief-distracted poet slipped into his wife's coffin at the last minute the manuscripts of the poems he had been collecting for a volume to follow *The Early Italian Poets*. When they heard of the sacrifice, the commonsense Brown condemned it, William Rossetti remarked that the feeling it showed did his brother credit. That feeling was no doubt a mixture of bereaved love and of remorse. In such an inharmonious marriage, so beset by the trivial difficulties of life which may assume momentous importance with highly strung people, there must have been incidents enough to make so affectionate and imaginative a man remorseful after that tragic end. For we have to face the probability that Lizzie Rossetti took that overdose of laudanum in an hysterical moment with the knowledge that it was fatal. The mere suspicion of such a thing would have been cause enough for Rossetti's distress, apart from the bare loss of the ' lovely Guggums '. The depth of his feeling is most beautifully expressed in one of his finest pictures, the ' Beata Beatrix ', painted in 1863. The student of Rossetti will find in that picture a profound tenderness and an exquisitely controlled ardour of grief; but that picture is less a man's memorial to a frail and lovely creature who needed his protection, than the aspiring prayer of a childlike and yet beautiful soul to an ideal removed to desperate distances by the death of a loved person. It was, like the placing of the manuscripts in the coffin, a childlike confession, the expression of a desire to atone for shortcomings. The great genius employed does not change the spiritual character of ' Beata Beatrix ', which was the culmination of Rossetti's peculiar idealism.

Lizzie was an accidental influence, as Dante's *New Life* had been, in the unfolding of Rossetti's innate tendencies. He followed a normal course after Lizzie's death by seeking social pleasures and in art passing through the phase which has been called that of 'women and flowers'. The call of the Sirens was the inevitable call of Death after the failure of Love. And again Rossetti was normal in accompanying his sensual phase with the excitement of the quest for dark knowledge. His interest and experiments in spiritualism were roused and stimulated by the undying sense of loss. His perturbation in 1869 at his own decision to allow the exhumation of his wife, so that the buried manuscripts might be recovered, came from the revived strength of the old love and the fear of the unknown which his dangerous dabbling in spiritualism had strengthened. There is no evidence that Rossetti shared any superstitious feelings about the sacredness of graves. He would have felt more sharply the condemnation of his friends, who, as a matter of fact, encouraged him to recover his poems. Rossetti had half convinced himself that the dead wife, who now had assumed in his imagination a mothering love towards him, would have been foremost in urging him to this courageously selfish act. His feelings were, however, complicated by a far more difficult problem in his conscience. He had fallen seriously in love again. The recovery of the buried poems—and really not much more than 'Jenny' and 'A Last Confession' would have suffered seriously if the exhumation had not taken place—was only the first phase of the revival which produced the great poetic creation of 1869-1871. Among the poems produced in these years were all the passionate love sonnets in *The House of Life*. The reader of chapter xi may be disposed to agree that the exquisitely refined and passionate confession which is in the love poetry of this period made the poet a naked target for heedless arrows of criticism, whether honest or dishonest. Writers who befouled his words and thoughts were treading on the man's very heart with clumsy and filthy boots. Had he not written 'Vain Virtues' in 1869? Just as he was reconciling the opposed impulses in himself, hampered by the progressive psychic disintegration caused through insomnia, chloral and alcohol, he was assailed in his most vulnerable self-feelings by ferocious and biased judgments upon his work.

William Rossetti [1] has given a full account of his brother's state of health at the time of Buchanan's article in the *Contemporary Review*, and it is only necessary to remind the reader that Rossetti showed comparatively little immediate strain as a result of the first publication in October 1871. His feelings can be seen in the vivacious correspondence with his publisher Ellis at this time, and they are reflected in the limerick which he wrote:

> As a critic, the Poet Buchanan
> Thinks Pseudo much safer than Anon;
> Into Maitland he shrunk,
> But the smell of the skunk
> Guides the shuddering nose to Buchanan

coupled with his paper on 'The Stealthy School of Criticism'. But the malicious article was expanded into a pamphlet published in the spring of 1872, so that there never was any ground for Buchanan's defence, of having written in a hurry. The *Poems* had been published eighteen months when the article first appeared, and caught Rossetti still in full creative tide. But a less cause for agitation might have sufficed to begin a period of renewed fears and self-criticism. When the attack was renewed, with still more evidence of unscrupulous vindictiveness, six months later, the poet's self-confidence began to crumble, with disastrous consequences. His latent superstition, strengthened by a vivid imagination, was roused again to discover signs of 'a widespread conspiracy for crushing his fair fame as an artist and a man, and for hounding him out of honest society'.[2] The chloral drugging alone, accompanied by a use of alcohol which is always most dangerous to

---

[1] *Memoir*, xxxiii.

[2] *Memoir*. His brother's choice of words is interesting, for Rossetti's fears always took the external appearance of concern about people's opinions. The world seemed to be taking sides against his own desires.

people of Rossetti's imaginative and emotional type, offers a quite adequate scientific explanation of his development of a persecution mania. It only needed the continuity of the attacks, the cumulative effect of suggestion, to drive his mind, recently agitated by the new crisis in his erotic life, to the pathetic stage in which he attempted to kill himself by the same means which had caused Lizzie's death. The chronological extremes of his crisis are marked by two sonnets in *The House of Life*—No. 85, 'Vain Virtues', in 1869, and No. 61, 'The Song-Throe', in 1880. He had learnt but too well,

> By thine own tears thy song must tears beget,
> O singer! Magic mirror thou has none
> Except thy manifest heart. . . .

The finest of his lyrics in the last years of life, such as 'Insomnia' and 'Spheral Change', harp on the theme which he brings into his letter to Mrs. Gilchrist, written on 2nd March 1862, three weeks after his wife's death. 'I thank you sincerely in my turn for the words of sorrow and sympathy which, coming from you, seem more terribly real than any I have received. . . . I have now to be thankful for obligations connected with my work which were a source of anxiety before; for without them it seems to me that I could never work again. But I already begin to find the inactive moments the most unbearable, and must hope for the power, as I feel most surely the necessity, of working steadily without delay. Of my dear wife I do not dare to speak now, nor to attempt any vain conjecture whether it may ever be possible for me, or I be found worthy, to meet her again.' He adds that he is staying at his mother's, and is looking out for a new home which will house perhaps all the family as well as himself. The return to his mother was instinctive. Finally he says: 'I have just read your letter again, and again feel forcibly the bond of misery which exists between us, and the unhappy right we have of saying to each other what we both know to be fruitless. Pray believe that I am not the less grateful to

[79]

you, at least for the heartfelt warmth with which it is said '. Such a letter should dispel any light of melodrama which may be thrown luridly over Rossetti's remorseful grief for the death of his wife. The abnormal element in the situation came almost entirely from the deeply ailing wife and the nature of her death. Remorse can be a better indication of sensibility than a measure of guilt.

Seven years later Rossetti writes to C. E. Norton: ' I have long wished to make a proposal to you. It would be a great satisfaction to me to possess the drawing you have by my late wife, of " Clerk Saunders ", to add to those of hers which are now mine, and which every year teaches me to value more and more as works of genius, even apart from other personal interest to me. None would ever have been parted with, of course, had we not then hoped that these little things were but preludes to much greater ones—a hope which was never to be realized '.

CHAPTER V

CHRISTINA ROSSETTI

' To poverty as to Death none opens the door with gladness.'
                                                    —*DANTE.*

ROSSETTI's younger sister was born on 5th December 1830. If there is any truth at all in the popular belief that one's temperament is somehow indicated by the month and season of one's birth, it receives no confirmation when Christina is compared with Dante Gabriel. He was born on 12th April, which was the old style May Day, upon which fact he exchanged some half serious speculations with Hall Caine in 1881. In his verse spring is praised more than any other season. The same is true of Christina's verse, however, and the reason also is the same: the poet's interest in death and desire for the fulfilment through re-birth of unsatisfied longings. If the work of Dante Gabriel and Christina is examined from this point of view, a remarkable and possibly rather surprising similarity of temperament between them is to be recognized. So much could be gathered from only a part of the biographical facts. As children they were the two troublesome ones of the family, passionate, petulant, volatile, and later on unable to subdue the movements of their minds to ordered study. Maria, the eldest child, and William, shared all the learning between them: the elder brother and Christina shared nearly all the genius, for such we must call the power of transmuting the experiences of the unrestful personality into a steadily shining beauty. She also resembled her elder brother in appearance. Besides the account of her in early childhood already quoted,[1] we

[1] See page 33.

have Watts-Dunton's description, which is half recollection, half hearsay:

She had Gabriel's eyes, in which hazel and blue-grey were marvellously blent, one hue shifting into the other, answering to the movements of the thought—eyes like the mother's. And her brown hair,
though less warm in colour than his during his boyhood, was still like
it. When a young girl, at the time she sat for the Virgin in the picture
now in the National Gallery, she was, as both her mother and Gabriel
have told me, really lovely, with an extraordinary expression of pensive
sweetness. She used to have in the little back parlour a portrait of
herself at eighteen by Gabriel, which gives all these qualities.[1]

The expression of her eyes indeed inspired her brother,
and accounted largely for his reputation for painting
women's faces with such a delicate profundity. Holman
Hunt asked her to sit for him so that he could catch the
expression he wanted in the face of the Christ in his
picture ' The Light of the World '. The picture Watts-
Dunton refers to is, of course, the ' Ecce Ancilla Domini ',
in which, however, the Virgin is not properly a portrait of
the painter's sister, as it was partly repainted.

In the more superficial sense Christina's life was very
different from Dante Gabriel's; hers does seem curiously
self-effacing and discreet by contrast with that of the
wilful poet-painter. In the early years, however, before the
self-training in restraint had begun, she showed a self-
assertion and an outward radiance of personality as clearly
as her brother, but the conflict of unreconciled impulses
which made him wayward and self-indulgent as well as
unhappy, drove her into herself with a concentration
which was prevented from becoming tragic by taking the
prepared way of religion. As already explained, the family
was divided, just as that of the Polidoris had been, in
religious matters. The males followed an unorthodox
father, the females a pious mother. This family division
is probably more common in Latin races than in the north,
and derives some of its traditional force from older ideals
of womanly conduct. Dante Gabriel himself preferred

[1] Quoted in *Christina Rossetti*, by Mackenzie Bell, p. 18.

women to be orthodox in piety, and was always sympathetic
to Christina's devotional writings. He did not share
Swinburne's views at all in that direction. Mrs. Rossetti,
besides being the most intellectual of the Polidori girls,
was less narrow than her sisters Marguerite and Charlotte,
but nevertheless she was strictly orthodox in her own way,
and her daughters closely followed her progress from
evangelistic tendencies towards the 'High' English
Church. Her mother had been Protestant, her father an
easy-going Roman Catholic, like Gabriele Rossetti. When
Maria, her eldest daughter, became a nun in an Anglican
order, Maria's peace of mind in Christina's eyes was the
fruit of saintliness. If it was, there had been some change
in Maria, for she seems to have been inclined to jealousy
and criticism of others, and no doubt during the children's
early years was their austere little mistress. Christina
would have been put in her place very early. But then
came the verse-writing, and it was not long before she was
recognized in that mentally alert family as unusually gifted.
When Christina was put back one way she always reappeared in some other way, but this became increasingly
the introspective way, and with the development of
emotional power came a readiness to submit to external
authority and a growing shyness of the outside world. So
it is that the confused emotions in her led to the rejection
of the physical satisfaction of an erotic nature. In her
brother the consequence of emotional disharmony was,
after earliest manhood, a disastrous tendency towards the
separation of eroticism and the spiritual side of love. In
much of his poetry and painting he strove to bridge over
this divorce. Although family tradition had passed on to
him and his brother the unorthodoxy of their father, with
him this remained a comparatively superficial element of
his mind, for he was influenced irrationally by his mother's
attitude. Her moral idealism was too strong an influence,
combined with the capacity for religious emotion in his
nature, to permit him the pleasures of love without the

remorse of sin. He acted for some years like a butterfly of love, but he could not feel the unreflective happiness of irresponsibility. In the case of Christina, whose temperament was not less ardent and sensuous, the immense power of moral sanctions embodied in the Christian faith was reinforced by contemporary conventions respecting the relations of the sexes. Such conventions were comparatively harmless to the average young lady with average depth of feeling and an uncomplicated attitude towards marriage; so long as she appeared always to accept passively a man's love, and walked sedately before the marriage ceremony had been performed, she was as reasonably secure from persecution as one can expect to be in this uncharitable world. But how far from this rather mythical average young lady was Christina! Her first book of *Verses*, printed before she was seventeen, included a few of her best poems; among others, ' Vanity of Vanities '. No wonder if the budding young girl that wrote so finely of

> Pleasure that bringeth sorrow at the last

should have written another equally characteristic sonnet later, on ' The World ', declaring:

> By day she stands a lie: by night she stands,
>   In all the naked horror of the truth,
> With pushing horns and clawed and clutching hands.
> Is this a friend indeed; that I should sell
>   My soul to her, give her my life and youth,
> Till my feet, cloven too, take hold on hell.

It is the mood which is responsible for much of her poetry classed as ' devotional ', and this mood is one largely of fear, the fear which in her daily life found such touching and often noble expression, so that in her conduct she seems often to us to have the characteristics of a saint. Yet William Rossetti was right in counting her ' wire-drawn scrupulosity' as a weakness.[1] Remembering again the contemporary conventions of ocnduct for pious young

---

[1] See his Introduction to the *Collected Poems of* 1904.

ladies, something might be attributed to such influence when we find that she refused always to go into a theatre after the age of eighteen. But later in life, being very fond of playing chess, she gave it up lest such self-indulgence should become a sin too hard to conquer. With her sister Maria, at the time of entering a convent, these disciplinary exercises would have been a normal form of spiritual training. In Christina they indicated a straining will to be what she knew she was not.

From her eighteenth to her twentieth year Christina was, in the phrase of a journalist, 'Queen of the Pre-Raphaelites'. James Collinson, the dullest member of the P.R.B., was engaged to her. But for Dante Gabriel he would not have been elected when the Brotherhood was formed in the autumn of 1848. It seems as if he would not have wished to become a P.R.B. but for the beautiful and clever young sister of the painter whose ' Girlhood of Mary Virgin ' had pictured her as she was then. Rossetti good-naturedly assisted Collinson's purpose of meeting his sister and even spoke kindly of him to her. But he had already attracted the favourable remarks of the females of the Rossetti household by his regularity and pious demeanour at the church services which they attended. Before he proposed to Christina he had been converted to Roman Catholicism. When she heard of this she made the difference of their churches an insuperable obstacle to the engagement. William Rossetti's explanations of this matter would be merely puzzling without an assumption that she had a scarcely conscious fear of marriage which found expression in seizing an excuse with a religious colour. The vacillating Collinson presently recanted and rejoined the English Church; he proposed again and was accepted. This might seem to dispose of the necessity for any other explanation than that she feared the possible dissension between her and a Roman Catholic husband concerning the religious training of any children they might have; for such is the best that William offered to explain her refusal of Collinson. The miserable Collinson now changed his mind again and reverted to Roman Catholicism. ' He had ', says William Rossetti, ' ... struck a staggering blow at Christina Rossetti's peace of mind on the very threshold of womanly life, and a blow from which she did not fully recover for years. He died in 1881.' For again she rejected him, cancelling their engagement. William attributes this to her force of will. Some time later, when walking in the street with her younger brother near Regent's Park, she unexpectedly caught sight of Collinson coming their way, and fainted from the shock, an incident by which the tumult of her inner life at this time may be gauged.

Christina's second love affair was more enduring though less violent. The man was Charles Bagot Cayley, a scholarly, timid, untidy, absent-minded individual, with a sweet and unworldly disposition. He must have met Christina first at her father's house between 1847 and 1854, when he was a pupil in Italian of Gabriele Rossetti. He later translated Dante's *Divine Comedy* in the original metre; the translation was admired by William as being closer to the Italian than the Miltonic version of Cary, but Ruskin would have none of it. Cayley's religious opinions were indefinite, so much so that William Rossetti could not say what they were beyond the fact that he ' was brought up in the Church of England '. He and Christina saw very little of each other till about 1860, the year in which Dante Gabriel married Lizzie Siddal. He, like Collinson, was as different in temperament and ability as possible from her admired brother. Christina soon loved him ' deeply and permanently ', and when he died in 1883 she could not have cherished his memory and his literary remains more ardently had she been his wife all those intervening years instead of the poet of the starving heart. For she rejected him as a husband. When her brother William thoughtfully urged her to marry him and offered to share home with them if monetary difficulties stood in the way, she explained that her decision was based on considerations that were to her more important and higher than money. William says, ' she must have probed his faith, and found it either strictly wrong or woefully defective '. She must indeed, if apart from this she could have married him without an emotional conflict too terrible to face. Yet ' she loved the scholarly recluse to the last day of his life, 5 December 1883, and, to the last day of her own, his memory '. No reader of all the biographical material available will doubt the truth of this last statement, setting aside the possibly controversial evidence of some of her most moving poems, such as that beautiful sonnet, ' Remember me when I am gone away '. But Christina could not have feared dissensions with the gentle Cayley over their children's religious training.

The rejection of earthly love left her path clear though terribly difficult: it was a path of stern duty and self-repression, for which she found a compensation in religious aspiration and poetry. Her dutiful devotion to her mother, and after Mrs. Rossetti's death in 1886, to her aged aunts, became an ingrained habit, but it began as an expression of self-distrust. In spite of her faith, her mind, like her poetry, was often despondent and full of bitterness. Some of her poems she destroyed because they offended against her religious convictions; others she would not publish. Even so, with the poems published posthumously and some published during her lifetime, the very human side of her is not unrepresented. ' Maude Clare', 'Light Love', ' Sister Maude ', ' Noble Sisters ', and ' Cousin Kate ', although sometimes inspired by the dramatic old ballads or by novels, are examples of sincere feeling in poetry which is far from the Christian mood of the truly devotional poet, though not at all alien to the mood of many of the pieces classed as ' devotional '. So in her daily life we have, happily, some glimpses of a woman who was never inhuman in her austerity but humorous and capable of ordinary reactions to other people. There seems to have been a little friction at first between her and both of her brothers' fiancées, Lizzie Siddal and Lucy Madox Brown (who became Mrs. William Rossetti). The incidents which gave rise to it were probably trifling enough, but sufficient to supply her with food for reflection and self-abasement. In the case of Lizzie Siddal the temporary coolness started between Christina and Dante Gabriel, who thought that his sister seemed inadequately impressed by ' the Sid ' in those enthusiastic early fifties. What was to him merely a spontaneous expression would have caused long reverberations of self-criticism in Christina. There is a decidedly human, not to say humorous, side to the situation which may be reconstructed from the recorded facts. One of Rossetti's reproaches was expressed in this way: ' Well, Christina, your heart may be like a singing bird, but you dress like a pew-opener '. But ' the Sid ' found it a simple matter of using experience to preserve the external signs of her queenliness. Brown, who was more constantly in touch with the young affianced couple than any other friend of Rossetti, entered in his diary in 1855, ' saw Miss Siddal, beautifully dressed for about £3, altogether looking like a queen '.[1] As Christina seems to have been incapable of dressing like that, she decided to try her hand at the art in which Lizzie had been making such astonishing progress under Rossetti's guidance. It is amusing to find the brother writing to Christina, in 1852, when she was staying at Frome with her mother: ' Maria has just shown me a letter of yours by which I find that you have been perpetrating portraits of some kind. If you answer this note will you enclose a specimen, as I should like to see some of your handiwork? You must take care however not to rival the Sid, but keep within respectful limits. Since you went away, I have had sent me, among my things from Highgate, a lock of hair shorn from the beloved head of that dear, and radiant as the tresses of Aurora, a sight of which may perhaps dazzle you on your

---

[1] *Ruskin, Rossetti, Pre-Raphaelitism.*

return. . . .'[1] But pictorial art proved to be also beyond reach, and her brown hair certainly was never ' radiant as the tresses of Aurora '. Those interested in Christina's beautiful mentality may be tempted to link together the portrait which Elizabeth Siddal painted of herself[2] and the dream of faces noted down by Christina soon after.[3] The portrait belongs to 1853. William Rossetti dated the dream roughly as about 1855. Christina wrote:

Night, but clear with grey light. Part of church in the background with the clock-side towards the spectator. In the churchyard many sheep with good innocent expressions; one especially heavenly. Amid them with full face a Satan-like goat lying, with a kingly look and horns. Three white longish-haired dogs in front, confused with the sheep though somewhat smaller than they: one with a flattering face, a second with head almost entirely turned away, but what one sees of the face sensual and abominable. My dream, C. G. R.

Many years later (about 1880) she added: ' This *real* dream left me with an impression it was my duty to paint the above subject as a picture—contingent duty perhaps. Of course I never became competent '.

Three years after Lizzie's death, when she is preparing her second volume of published poetry, *The Prince's Progress*, which appeared in 1866,[4] Christina writes to her brother from Hastings to thank him for the loan of Lizzie's poems. She wonders if it would be possible to let some of them come out in a volume of her own, for the sake of getting them published. A few days later she writes: ' how full of beauty they are, but how painful—how they bring poor Lizzie herself before one, with her voice, face and manner! ' She expresses a preference for the piece called ' Dead Love ', ' piquant as it is with cool bitter sarcasm ', while ' Gone ' reminds her ' of Tom Hood at his highest ', which was high praise indeed, for she and her

---

[1] *Family Letters*, August 1852.
[2] Reproduced in the *Memoir*, p. 175.
[3] *Ruskin, Rossetti, Pre-Raphaelitism*, p. 13.
[4] Not counting the privately printed *Verses* of 1847, the first volume was *Goblin Market and Other Poems* of 1862.

brother were great admirers of Hood. This constant communication between brother and sister persisted to the end of his life, and was no doubt facilitated by the fact that she always lived with their mother, with whom he was an unfailing correspondent. He no longer needed to use Christina as a model as he had done for many of his earlier pictures until Lizzie came upon the scene and took her place as the Madonna-Beatrice-Princess type. She is, however, recognizable in a few pictures of the 1850's. She is the central female figure who is hiding her face in momentary shame in ' Hesterna Rosa ', the picture of two gamblers dicing and their mistresses, the motive for which came from Elena's song in Sir Henry Taylor's *Philip van Artevelde*:

> Quoth tongue of neither maid nor wife
> To heart of neither wife nor maid,
> ' Lead we not here a jolly life
> Betwixt the shine and shade ? '

> Quoth heart of neither maid nor wife
> To tongue of neither wife nor maid,
> ' Thou wag'st but I am sore with strife,
> And feel like flowers that fade '.[1]

She is also recognizable in the ' weeping queens ' who watch King Arthur in Avalon, the illustration for the 1857 Tennyson volume. The face on the extreme left and the profile on the extreme right seem both to be done from Christina. Several fine portraits of her were done during her maturity, and show the patient strength as well as the ardent aspiration of the dreamer. That of 1866, a three-quarter profile, with chin poised on her hands, is a deservedly well-known one, and so is that of 1877, including her mother. Here the consequences to her appearance of Christina's ophthalmic goitre may be clearly seen in the prominent eyes. This disease, which has very distressing effects on the nervous organization, overtook her first in 1871, and troubled her off and on during the rest of her life. William Rossetti stated that her least unhealthy years

[1] H. C. Marillier remarks that this pen-and-ink, though dated and altered in 1853, was probably drawn in 1850.

THE ARTIST'S MOTHER AND SISTER (CHRISTINA)
CRAYON DRAWING, 1877
In The National Portrait Gallery

were about 1861 and again about 1867-1870, not a very cheering record in a life lasting from 1830 to 1895. She had the slightest material resources during most of her life, seldom earned £10 in a year until after the publication of *Goblin Market* in 1862, and then averaged about £40 a year. From 1867 she had a small private income, which towards the end of her life was augmented, but she always lacked the means for her elder brother's extravagances in middle life. This is not to imply, however, that while he wasted his income, which must have averaged over £2000 a year after the middle sixties, his mother and sister were stinted of comforts. His huge house in Cheyne Walk cost him slightly less in rent for the greater part of the time he was a tenant, than their house in Torrington Square, from which they were often absent at the seaside or in the country, with or without the company of the Polidori aunts. Apart from these trips Christina did not travel much, and went abroad only twice, but the consequence of seeing Italy roused the southern memories of her blood. She sang of her father's country as her brother never did. It became opposed in her mind to ' that bleak North ' where she had her ' day's work ' to do. To hear no more ' the half-familiar speech ' of the country half her own, she could say ' Amen ' to that:

> But when our swallows fly back to the South,
>   To the sweet South, to the sweet South,
> The tears may come again into my eyes
>   On the old wise,
> And the sweet name to my mouth.

If an attempt is made here to survey her work so that it may be compared with her brother's, we have to come back to that ' wire-drawn scrupulosity '. This affected even her reading. Although she enjoyed Italian literature, she would not read an author like Boccaccio. Tasso she enjoyed immensely, but would not read him straight through lest she should come across ' improper ' passages. These trifles are significant of the general watchfulness of her conscience, which so shaped her life that she became the poet of spiritual re-birth. The weary hunger and aspiring hope of the dreamer deprived of earthly satisfactions of love by no means account for all of her work, but they are the dominant motives of her inspiration. The tremendous emotional power in her poetry comes from a conflict as ravaging as any experienced by Dante Gabriel. The constant turning towards death as towards a haven of perfect rest is due to a mood essentially religious, since it is the first stage on the path of the illumination to which she never securely attained. When confronted by the beauty which she made out of tedious tears and weary years, it is irrelevant and ungrateful to mutter ' pessimism ' and ' morbidity '. There is no need to deny the pessimism or the ' morbidity ': what has that to do with the virtue of poems like ' Dream-Love ', ' Dream Land ', ' Echo ', ' When I am dead, my dearest ', ' Remember '? They are perfectly beautiful expressions of the universal human heart, and as such they need no philosophical or moral justification. She is the poet of the silent land and the poet of the passion that is lived only in the echo of a dream. As a dreamer in poetry she more than rivals her brother: she is the finer of the two, for frequent though the imagery of dream is in his work, it is hardly ever so free from mingled concepts not belonging to the dream. Yet here alone, from the time when, as a young girl, she wrote ' Dream Land ' (which appeared in *The Germ*) she proved her poetic kinship with the poet of ' Love's Nocturne ', ' The Staff and Scrip ', ' Sleepless Dreams ', and other pieces noted elsewhere.[1]

Christina Rossetti is also the poet of the false dawn of love and of remorse for the unfulfilment of love on earth. ' An Apple Gathering ',

> I plucked pink blossoms from mine apple-tree
> And wore them all that evening in my hair:
> Then in due season when I went to see
> I found no apples there. . . .

---

[1] In chapter xiv.

Lilian and Lilias smiled in trudging by,
    Their heaped-up basket teased me like a jeer;
Sweet-voiced they sang beneath the sunset sky,
    Their mother's home was near.

Plump Gertrude passed me with her basket full,
    A stronger hand than hers helped it along;
A voice talked with her through the shadows cool
    More sweet to me than song. . . .

voices a mood which is familiar to the poet. So 'Mirage',

The hope I dreamed of was a dream,
    Was but a dream; and now I wake,
Exceeding comfortless, and worn, and old,
    For a dream's sake. . . .

and the still franker 'Another Spring':

If I might see another Spring
    I'd not plant summer flowers and wait:
I'd have my crocuses at once,
    My leafless pink mezereons,
        My chill-veined snowdrops, choicer yet
        My white or azure violet,
Leaf-nested primrose; anything
    To blow at once, not late.

If I might see another Spring
    I'd listen to the daylight birds
That build their nests and pair and sing,
    Nor wait for mateless nightingale;
        I'd listen to the lusty herds,
        The ewes with lambs as white as snow,
I'd find out music in the hail
    And all the winds that blow.

If I might see another Spring—
    Oh stinging comment on my past
That all my past results in 'if'—
    If I might see another Spring
I'd laugh to-day, to-day is brief;
I would not wait for anything:
    I'd use to-day that cannot last,
    Be glad to-day and sing.

Would not the poet of the 'House of Life', supposing
him a woman and denied all the physical side of love, have
written poems like these as well as the dream songs?

DANTE GABRIEL ROSSETTI

Christina's range is not completed here, for she is super-
latively the poet of guilty passion. The tremendous
' Convent Threshold ' collects with a sort of desperate
force all the fierce agony of the self-starved heart. Few
poets attain to such an ' apocalypse of soul ' even though
they may write about it, as Mrs. Browning did. Among
English women poets only Emily Brontë and Edith
Sitwell have done anything comparable to ' The Convent
Threshold '. The secret of Christina's unrest is voiced in
' A Pause of Thought ':

> I looked for that which is not, nor can be,
> And hope deferred made my heart sick in truth :
> But years must pass before a hope of youth
> Is resigned utterly.

It ends with:

> Alas, thou foolish one! alike unfit
> For healthy joy and salutary pain :
> Thou knowest the chase useless, and again
> Turnest to follow it.

The strain of pain continually broke through the ardent
faith inspiring such a poem as ' Advent ', which the
atheistical Swinburne surprisingly admired so much that
he considered it her finest. It is not her best poem, though
very fine, as also was ' Passing Away ', another specially
admired by Swinburne. When Hall Caine expressed a
preference for ' The World ' and ' Dead before Death '
among her sonnets his correspondent, Dante Gabriel,
answered that he did not quite agree, and thought ' Dead
before Death ' ' a little sensational *for her* ', and his doubt
was justified, when there remained ' Remember Me ' to
put in its place. Rossetti, however, said ' I think " After
Death " one of her noblest, and the one " After Communion "'. He added: ' In my own view, the greatest of
all her poems is that on France after the siege—" To-day
for Me "', a verdict as surprising, coming from Rossetti, as
that on ' Advent ' coming from Swinburne. But we do not
need to settle such a question, and indeed several of Chris-

tina's finest poems have not been so much as mentioned
here. The important fact in a study of Rossetti is that his
sister's art shows quite as clearly as his the vicissitudes of
the spirit, the stress of a powerful emotional conflict never
properly resolved. And there occurs also the same diminish-
ing of inspirational force as the poet leaves youth behind,
so that nearly all the inferior work she did, marked by
repetition of her earlier poems, and by skill operating
without sufficient impulse, belongs to the later part of her
life. Her best prose, too, like his, among which must be
counted the story of ' The Lost Titian ', is generally early
work, and, again like his, has often a strong autobiographical flavour. These are facts which need to be
reckoned with before attributing to Rossetti's moral faults,
or his remorse for life misspent, a lessening of his powers
as an artist. So far every critic discussing the fluctuations
of Rossetti's genius has ignored the instructive comparison
with his great sister, whose life certainly offers no such
field for the introduction of moral condemnation. Not
only did Christina's soul pass through valleys of gloom
like his, but her art gradually lost the divine validity of its
youth, recapturing the rapture of vision with more and
more difficulty. The evidence of divided aims and confused desires in her poetry is supported by the biographical
material up to the end. Her very death was no more
serene than her brother's. She took to her death-bed,
says her brother William, ' in a calm and resigned mood,
but, as the time advanced, with troublous agitation, both
of the spirit and of the bodily frame. Not that she was
ever abashed by pain, or craven-hearted—far indeed from
that; but the terrors of her religion compassed her about,
to the overclouding of its radiances '. Dear, beautiful,
tortured soul! Who that knows her poetry deeply does
not adore Christina Rossetti, and understand more than
words can express except in poetry like hers?

CHAPTER VI
FRIENDS

' So now the whole Round Table is dissolved.'—TENNYSON.

BY THE time he was twenty-one Rossetti had not only established himself among the great English poets, he had also made a serious beginning of one of the greatest painting careers in the history of British art. In 1848 he had painted 'The Girlhood of Mary Virgin', and helped to establish the pre-Raphaelite movement. Exhibited in the spring of 1849, the picture was recognized as the work of a promising new artist. He, with Holman Hunt and Millais, formed a group which could not be ignored even though it could be violently assailed. The Pre-Raphaelite Brotherhood was a social-artistic centre of remarkable interest for a young man just coming of age. Through one member or another of that group he was brought into touch with Tennyson, Coventry Patmore, and Ruskin. He had by his own initiative made a friend and adviser of Ford Madox Brown in painting, of William Bell Scott, brother of David Scott, a painter of weird pictures whose works later on interested Rossetti, as did the *Memoir* prepared by W. B. Scott. The latter was Master of the New-castle Government School of Design when Rossetti opened a correspondence in 1847; but the immediate cause of Rossetti's advances was the desire to send some verse for criticism by a fellow scribe. Rossetti had seen poems—he mentioned especially ' Rosabell ' and ' A Dream of Love '—by Scott in a periodical; after which he obtained a copy of the long blank poem, ' The Year of the World ', which, he wrote, ' I fell upon like a vulture '!

Scott was thirty-six years old, and the boldness of his ideas in poetry were a genuine stimulus to Rossetti. ' Rosabell ', the story of a country girl who became a rich man's cast-off mistress, contained a theme popular in the Victorian age. Rossetti seized on the idea of the shamed girl being met by her former bucolic lover, to whom she had been engaged in marriage before the bad rich man had lured her to London; this formed the subject of the picture called ' Found ', which, in spite of Scott's own exhortations years later, was never completed for Leathart, the buyer whom he had found for Rossetti's picture. Scott was not a little annoyed about this, feeling that the picture was a great illustration of ' Rosabell '. It never was that however, for the situation depicted by Rossetti is not described in the poem, though something like it is implied. ' Rosabell ' had already been used as the title of a poem by Walter Scott, and at Rossetti's suggestion Scott altered it to ' Mary Anne '. In his *Autobiographical Notes* Scott expressed his annoyance at Rossetti appropriating ' The Stream's Secret ' for a poem when he, Scott, had already used it, but he made no mention of the fact that he himself had used a title of a poem already published in book form by another poet. William Bell Scott was a forcible character, and several other causes of friction between him and Rossetti make their long friendship rather surprising. The reader ought to beware of Scott's scarcely repressed desire to score points off his old friend in the *Autobiographical Notes*.[1]

Rossetti in those eager, youthful years also addressed Browning a letter full of his exuberant admiration after recognizing the author of the anonymous ' Pauline ', which he read in the British Museum during the days he spent there rummaging in old English literature, looking for ' stunning words for poetry '. Browning was never a close personal friend, not being in London often, but Rossetti remained his admiring reader. His admiration

[1] *E.g.* in connexion with Rossetti's efforts to have the *Poems* of 1870 reviewed by competent friends, see page 133.

for Tennyson's work did not endure quite so well, neither did his admiration of the youthful Millais.

New acquaintances were constantly made through older ones. The sculptor Alexander Munro, an Inverness man (Rossetti seems to have got on well with Scots), was a close friend, and Munro introduced him to Major Calder Campbell, a bachelor aged fifty, retired from the Indian Army, who used his time in writing sketches and verse for periodicals. That the Rossetti brothers were glad to spend an evening every week for about two years around 1847 at Campbell's lodgings off the Tottenham Court Road, in west-central London, argues their unspoilt eagerness for literary friendships. On one occasion, to please Dante Gabriel, who had discovered for himself that astonishing volume, the *Studies in Sensation and Event*, Campbell arranged for him to meet Ebenezer Jones. Jones, says William Rossetti, 'was a well-grown, thin, pale man, still young, with decayed teeth and a general air of shaky health, which brought him to his grave before many years had passed'.[1] The brothers never met Ebenezer Jones again, but Rossetti remained interested in his strange, lurid poetry. His remarks in *Notes and Queries* in 1870 are supposed to have led directly to the republication of the forgotten *Studies*.

Rossetti's critical initiative was indeed as extraordinary as the personal adventurousness of his approach to poets and painters. He bought a manuscript notebook of Blake's from a British Museum attendant (after borrowing the necessary ten shillings from his more provident brother) at a time when hardly anybody thought about Blake, and thereafter became so constant an advocate of that great genius that Watts-Dunton, writing at the end of the century, attributed to Rossetti's preaching the widespread recognition of Blake. With a fervour which showed a similar spiritual affinity he preached the merits of Chatterton in later life, thus following up Keats's recognition, and

[1] *Memoir*, xi.

forced critics to take serious notice of Chatterton's actual work as well as his mere blighted promise. The contents of Mr. Walter de la Mare's anthology entitled *Come Hither* suggest that Chatterton has found an equally appropriate champion in this epoch. Several writers whose acquaintance with Chatterton's work may be suspected of severe limitations, have repeated each other's comments, borrowed from William Rossetti, that Dante Gabriel showed an exaggerated, not to say eccentric, opinion of the value of the 'marvellous youth's' poetry. But there was less eccentricity than extraordinarily acute perception—stimulated always by temperamental predilection—in Rossetti's anticipations of critical respect for neglected work. It is hardly necessary to repeat the story of how he came across FitzGerald's *Omar Khayyam* in a penny book-box—the first edition having been remaindered—and sang its praises until the mighty 'boom' which overtook it was in its birth-throes of eclectic appreciation. A more curious instance of his literary enthusiasm was that for Charles Wells, whose *Joseph and His Brethren* he continued to belaud for many years, imposing his judgment on his most influential and brilliant friends. Watts-Dunton recalled when he and Dr. Gordon Hake were guests of Rossetti at Kelmscott Manor House after 1870, and how he then first heard about this lyrical drama. The retention of the dialogue in Watts-Dunton's account is unusually interesting.

Rossetti and I went strolling one day beside the banks of the Upper Thames, when he said, 'You are a Shakespearean student, *n'est-ce-pas?*' [Dr. Hueffer had been showing him an essay upon the lost *Hamlet* by me.]

'You may call me so if you like', I said; 'I know enough of Shakespeare and his contemporaries to be amazed at his infinite superiority to all the others.'

'Are you aware that we have discovered', said Rossetti, 'an unknown poem more Shakespearean than anything else out of Shakespeare?—You smile.'

'Men of genius', I said, 'should sometimes be mistrusted in their poetical finds. There are not many lumps of quartz which the auriferous light shed from the poet's own eye cannot transmute into very respectable nuggets.'

'You are sarcastic!' he said.

'The fact is', I said, 'I have got a good deal wearied with the iteration and reiteration of this word "Shakespearean". Through all this century, or at least since Coleridge wrote about Shakespeare, critics have been writing and talking of him as though they had

> "Eaten on the insane root,
> That takes the reason prisoner".

'You must', said he, 'have been in touch with Dion Boucicault and the cockney Shakespeares who have lately, I believe, been comparing their own dramatic efforts with the much poorer stuff of the Bard of Avon. . . .'

'No. I know nothing of the cockney Shakespeares. . . . All I mean is that Shakespearean critics will insist upon formulating new canons of criticism expressly for one author.'

'There is something in that, I must say', he replied.

'They treat characters of all other imaginative writers as being imaginary: Shakespeare's characters they treat as being real. This is not fair either to the dramatist Nature or to the human dramatist. . . .'

When the two friends returned to the old manor house and entered Rossetti's tapestried studio the subject was resumed. Watts-Dunton suggested that the very name of Wells's play was enough to kill it.

'Why?' asked Rossetti.

'Because the only female interest it suggests is that of Potiphar's wife, a very unsavoury female. What surprises me is that Wells managed to get a publisher for a play on such a subject. I have always understood that the first thing a publisher asks an author about his manuscript is not, "What is in it?" but, "What are you going to call it?"

'That is true', said he, with one of his loud guffaws. 'In literature as in life, "What are you going to call a thing?" is the first question; that is especially so when the publisher is bargaining on the slopes of Parnassus. But as to the unsavouriness of Potiphar's wife; in every drama, you know, there must be a villain or a villainess to do battle with the hero or good person, and, as Wells has not tampered with the Scripture narrative, but has given us a portrait of a lecherous woman, perfectly unique—perfectly astounding for vigour—you will find that she makes a pretty successful villainess.'[1]

---

[1] *Rossetti and Charles Wells: a Reminiscence of Kelmscott Manor*, by Theodore Watts-Dunton. This followed Swinburne's Introduction to a reprint of *Joseph and His Brethren*, in 1908 in The World's Classics. The play had been previously reprinted in 1876, with Swinburne's Introduction. It is clear that Rossetti was responsible for this.

Mary Magdalene at the door of Simon the Pharisee.

Ford Madox Brown
from his friend
D G Rossetti

ONE OF ROSSETTI'S AUTOGRAPHED PHOTOGRAPHS, PRESENTED TO
FORD MADOX BROWN. THE HEAD OF CHRIST IS SAID TO HAVE BEEN
DRAWN FROM THE YOUTHFUL BURNE-JONES. [*See Appendix B*]

Watts-Dunton says that after reading the poem he concluded that Wells deserved most of Rossetti's praise, and on a subsequent visit told Rossetti of the Persian story of Zulaikha—in Jamis' ' Yusuf and Zulaikha '. ' That wonderful creature FitzGerald translated one of the poems of Jamis, his masterpiece, I believe, "Salaman and Absal". Garnett was talking to me about it the last time I saw him ', Rossetti said.

We have in Watts-Dunton's recollection a unique glimpse of Rossetti in the act of his literary proselitizing, and considering his personal influence and the type of men who were his friends, it is not so surprising that his judgments took so much effect. Wells's *Stories After Nature* also had Rossetti's partisanship from his early years, and perhaps because of the title (those young men were never severely logical) that also of the Pre-Raphaelite group. Rossetti even accorded Wells the flattery of some degree of imitation in the prose of ' Hand and Soul ' and ' St. Agnes of Intercession ', but the elusive resemblances are submerged in the brilliant originality and imaginative power of these stories, which were written in 1849 and 1850 respectively and appeared in *The Germ*.

The founding of *The Germ* was a pleasant extension of the range of personal interests offered by the P.R.B., and it brought into the fold several writers, including Christina Rossetti, Coventry Patmore, and Madox Brown, in addition to the P.R.B. contributors themselves. Rossetti's enthusiasm may be measured by the fact that he wrote ' Hand and Soul ' especially as a contribution to number One of the brief-lived periodical, finishing it almost at a sitting by working all day and night. This was his brother's recollection. He himself wrote to Hall Caine, about 1881, saying that, except for ' an opening page or two ', it was written ' all in one night in December 1849, beginning I suppose about 2 a.m. and ending about 7. In such a case landscape and sky all unsurmised open gradually in the mind—a sort of spiritual Turner, among whose hills one ranges and in whose waters one strikes out at unknown liberty. But I have found this only in nightlong work, which I have seldom attempted, for it leaves one entirely broken; and this state was mine when I described the like of it at the close of the story, how long ago!'[1]

If indeed he 'seldom attempted' such impetuous creative production, it is certain he attempted it too often for his subsequent health. Holman Hunt remembered his amazing concentration in painting, once he had been seized by the inspirational force which was expressing itself. The apparent lack of artistic discipline in his earlier years was no doubt largely accountable to this impetuosity of his newly fledged genius. Every fresh conception and mood, working itself out either in a poem or a picture, battled with every other interest, claiming for the time being the whole force of his mind, with the consequence that a task involving prolonged care and deliberate craftsmanship would, if unfinished, be set aside and almost forgotten while the new idea predominated. This characteristic of his method of work on ' The Girlhood of Mary Virgin ' so impressed Holman Hunt that the latter doubted if ' Gabriel ' would ever become a proficient painter. If he could be suddenly absorbed by a new design it is easy to conceive how much more readily a new poem would seize upon his attention, though perhaps for a briefer period. But these aberrations were complete. ' When he had fairly got entangled in a new design he would refuse the attraction of home, meals, out-of-door engagements, or bed, and sit through the night, sleeping where he sat for an hour at the time, recommencing his work when he woke. He ate whatever was at hand when hunger suggested. . . .'[2] Hunt has also given us a picture of the young poet-painter under the spell of an inspiration: ' When he had once sat down, and was engaged in the effort to chase his errant thoughts into an orderly road, and the spectral fancies had

[1] See page 103.
[2] Pre-Raphaelitism, by Holman Hunt, chap. vii.

[102]

all to be kept in his mind's eye, his tongue was hushed, he remained fixed and inattentive to all that went on about him, he rocked himself to and fro, and at times he moaned lowly, or hummed for a brief minute, as though telling off some idea. All this while he peered intently before him, looking hungry and eager, and passing by in his regard any who came before him, as if not seen at all. Then he would often get up and walk out of the room without saying a word. Years afterwards, when he became stout, and people, not without some reason, found a resemblance in him to the bust of Shakespeare at Stratford-on-Avon, and, later still, when he had outgrown this resemblance, it seemed to me that it was in his early days only that the soul within had been truly seen in his face. In these days his inner life was untainted to an exemplary degree, and he worthily rejoiced in the poetic atmosphere of sacred and spiritual dreams. . . .'[1]

Another friend, the painter-critic Frederick George Stephens, also described Rossetti's absorption in his work and said that the work accomplished in a day, the painter using every minute of the light, was often 'astounding'. A similar observation was made by Madox Brown. This eagerness was the cause of his irregular feeding, and the acquirement of a gift (of doubtful advantage) for consuming a prodigious, a fabulous amount of food for breakfast. It is said that Rossetti's preference for a large plate of ham with a circle of fried eggs all round the rim, which astonished Dr. Hake and other friends in his later life, was a cause of Meredith's hasty abandonment of his subtenancy at Rossetti's large house in Chelsea in 1864.

During the early fifties he was still a slender, hungry, gaunt, somewhat untidy figure, his conversational brilliance and wide gazing eyes superficially hinting at the fierce-blooded spirituality of the young man. In 1850 he had first met his future wife, Elizabeth Eleanor Siddal, and two or three years later was engaged to be married to

[1] *Ibid.*, chap. vi.

her, though the agreement between them was kept secret for some time in deference to her wish, which may have arisen from the difficult social change for her involved in Rossetti's friendship. Up to this time there is every reason to think that Rossetti's powerful sexual nature had been completely sublimated or repressed. His enthusiastic companionship of Lizzie Siddal was no doubt a contributing cause of the dissolution of the Pre-Raphaelite Brotherhood. *The Germ* had died, under the changed title of *Art and Poetry* after the issue of the third and fourth numbers had been financed by a friendly and trustful printer, and meetings of the Brotherhood had practically ceased in 1851. In 1853 Millais was elected to the Academy, and thereupon Rossetti wrote to his sister, 'So now the whole Round Table is dissolved'. Christina, in the true Rossetti spirit, wrote an epitaph:

The P.R.B.

The P.R.B. is in its decadence:
    For Woolner in Australia cooks his chops,
    And Hunt is yearning for the land of Cheops;
      D. G. Rossetti shuns the vulgar optic;
    While William M. Rossetti merely lops
      His B's in English disesteemed as Coptic;
    Calm Stephens in the twilight smokes his pipe,
      But long the dawning of his public day;
      And he at last the champion great Millais,
Attaining Academic opulence,
    Winds up his signature with A.R.A.
So rivers merge in the perpetual sea;
    So luscious fruit must fall when over-ripe;
And so the consummated P.R.B.

A purely comic poem on the kindred theme of 'The Death of *The Germ*, otherwise known as *Art and Poetry*' was perpetrated by John Tupper, a contributor, and a son of the head of the printing firm which financed the last two numbers. It is to be hoped that his father was able to see the comic side for as many years as he had to await Rossetti's ability to square up the printing account. The

final stanza shows that Rossetti had made Browning a
subject of debate at the P.R.B. meetings:

> A time *Sordello* shall be read,
> And arguments be clean abolished,
> And sculpture punched upon the head,
> And mathematics quite demolished;
> And *Art and Poetry* instead
> Come out without a word of prose in,
> And all who paint as Sloshua [1] did
> Have all their sloshy fingers frozen.

A pleasant incident was a meeting of ' The Round
Table' in 1853 to draw pictures of each other to send to
Woolner, who had departed to the Australian gold-diggings.
Rossetti had already written him a sonnet, concluding

> Ah, still for thee and me,
> Winter or summer, Woolner, here or there,
> One grief, one joy, one loss, one victory.

After the return of Woolner to England, the friendship
of the two men came to an end when a mutual acquaintance interrupted Rossetti's praise of Woolner to tell him
that Woolner spoke very differently about *him*. Upon
receiving confirmation of this, Rossetti avoided his old
friend. Woolner was a pugnacious Suffolk man whose
critical asperity had been perhaps sharpened by Rossetti's
growing distinction and widening circle of brilliant friends.
Moreover he had disavowed, most forcibly of all the
P.R.B.'s, ' antiquarianism ' in art, and could have found
little else, in his eyes, in Rossetti's work up to the sixties.

This ' antiquarian ' strain, which is treated in a later
chapter as ' romantic archaism ', becomes associated with
the second group of young men of which Rossetti was
the inspirational centre. Let us call it the Oxford group.
Ruskin's prolonged interest in this, as in the P.R.B., was
largely through Rossetti. Between the formation of the
two Ruskin had become an important buyer and supporter
of Rossetti's paintings, mostly water-colours; these were
of a character to enthrall the young men at Oxford, who

[1] *I.e.*, Sir Joshua Reynolds.

[105]

were about to hail Rossetti as their chief. An unexpected activity of Rossetti during the fifties, teaching art in the Working Men's College, was a consequence of Ruskin's enthusiasm and Rossetti's friendly acquiescence. One of the difficulties of personal intercourse which taxed Rossetti's diplomatic gift, was the hostility of the independent Madox Brown to Ruskin, who showed a contemptuous indifference to Brown's work which must have been as provoking as it was unjust. Ruskin, most generous of men, was full of crotchets and capable of surprisingly unfair judgments. But this we cannot pursue, except to observe that only a tactful and really good-natured man could have preserved a friendship with Ruskin so long as Rossetti did without adopting the rôle of an unquestioning pupil. That Rossetti also preserved the friendship of Madox Brown is a testimony to Brown's sensible loyalty as well as his affection for Rossetti. The eventual drifting apart of Rossetti and Ruskin is thus explained by E. T. Cook, Ruskin's biographer: ' There was enough of the *idem velle et idem nolle* between Ruskin and Rossetti to make a friendship possible; enough, too, of difference to add piquancy to it: but not enough readiness to give and take on equal terms to lend it permanence. Ruskin hoped to be obeyed; Rossetti was accustomed to dominate '.[1]

Several men recorded the tremendous personal influence of Rossetti during the fifties and sixties. The contact of his personality seems to have been almost hypnotic. Even the intellectually positive, not to say opinionative, Ruskin is said to have told a friend that Rossetti's presence robbed him of all initiative in thinking, so that his mind could only follow Rossetti's. If this was so, Ruskin seems to have found his compensation in the letters he wrote to Rossetti about paintings. Except for the understood facetiousness of banter between them, Ruskin's attitude is often that of a father speaking to a fractious child. The dominance of Rossetti in any company was certainly often

[1] *Life of Ruskin*, vol. i, chap. 24.

noted, and as one writer has it, ' to be his friend was in a sense to be his disciple '.[1] But this dominance was not a snatched privilege, nor was it the result of overbearing, bullying conversational manners. Coventry Patmore, who was not lacking in individuality, declared that Rossetti ' had the sweet and easy courtesy peculiar to his nation ' (meaning the Italian). This charm of manner was noticed by new friends in the latest years of Rossetti's life.

Hall Caine has given a vivid picture of Rossetti, recumbent on the sofa, legs higher than head, talking in his characteristic mixture of banter and thoughtfulness.[2] In an article in the *Times* for 11th May 1928 (the eve of the centenary of Rossetti's birth), Sir Johnston Forbes-Robertson, who was the model for the head of Love in ' Dante's Dream ' (the large 1871 oil) wrote: ' Let me try to describe him as I, a boy of 16, remember him at the age of 42. His face was pale, the colour of old ivory as it were, but it glowed under excitement. His forehead was high-domed and broad, the brown eyes deep-sunk, lambent, and sad, with the skin about them of a much darker tone than the rest of the face. His beard was black and slightly forked, and his hair was thick, black, and curly. The lips were rather full and red, seen slightly through his moustache, which was not heavy. The face was very handsome, deeply striking, with its calm nobility and impressiveness—one of those rare faces, in short, that once seen are never forgotten. His voice was rich and deep, soft to ear as velvet to the touch. His frame was robust, thick-set, and muscular. He stood, I should say, a little under 5ft. 10 in., but his whole appearance expressed his powerful personality '. Concerning ' Dante's Dream ' Sir Johnston wrote: ' The model for the Beatrice was Mrs. Morris, and one of the two figures—the one on the left holding up the drapery over Beatrice—was painted from the beautiful Miss Spartali, afterwards Mrs. Stillman. I often used to meet

[1] Joseph Knight.
[2] *Recollections of Dante Gabriel Rossetti.*

[107]

her at Madox Brown's receptions in Fitzroy Square. With her long, graceful figure and wistful expression she was exquisite, and of course quite the living type of the Rossetti beauty, as was Mrs. William Morris, though a much older woman. When the picture was nearly finished Rossetti asked my father if I might sit to him for the head of Love, and this I did, much to my 'pride and delight. I remember well that the space left for the head was scumbled over with Venetian red, on to which he painted the profile. I had to pose over a cushion on a sofa, and at the first sitting he said, " My dear Johnston, I am sorry I have not a beautiful creature for you to kiss ". I was 16 at the time and I remember to this day my blushing confusion. I sat three times for about an hour and a half, being delightfully entertained all the time by his lively and interesting talk: he treated me as a grown man, which naturally was very flattering.'

The home of the Prinseps, Little Holland House, in West London, where G. F. Watts had a studio and was the god of a group of aspiring young painters for some years, was often visited by Rossetti and other Pre-Raphaelites. At Little Holland House took place most of the discussions preceding the persuasion of various painters to go down to Oxford and help in the work on the Union Hall. This impulsive scheme,[1] mooted between Benjamin Woodward, the architect, and Rossetti and Morris, has been described in all its phases. Rossetti was being shown the new Union Hall and noticed the blank wall spaces between the windows above the bookshelves in the gallery (the Hall afterwards became the Library). Woodward cordially agreed to his plan to paint over the empty spaces. Morris offered to help. Alexander Munro, the sculptor, was enlisted to do a relief in stone from Rossetti's design, for the tympanum of the doorway. Morris started work

[1] Owing to careless ignorance all the painting—some of it marvellously beautiful, according to Patmore, Ruskin, and others—was done on an unprepared brick surface and peeled off in a few years.

first, finished his bay, and then began on the ceiling, with results which astonished his friends, for here he at last discovered his flair for decoration. Morris's great friend at Oxford, Burne-Jones, came in quickly. He wrote of this: 'When Rossetti and Morris came back they were full of a scheme, and I was to put everything aside and help it. Woodward had just built a new debating-room for the University, and there were large bays above the gallery that ran round the room, hungry to be filled with pictures— Gabriel equally hungry to fill them, and the pictures were to be from the *Morte d'Arthur*, so willed our master '.[1]

Burne-Jones had to put aside the picture of 'The Blessed Damozel' which he was painting; and during the long vacation of 1857 Rossetti proceeded to enlist others. 'Mr. Prinsep clearly recalls the day that Gabriel came out to Little Holland House, and by the power of his personality made him promise to "join him and some other fellows in decorating the Union at Oxford".' The young artist, Prinsep, was flattered, but recollected: ' I had not studied with Watts without being well aware of my own deficiencies in drawing—so I told Rossetti that I did not feel strong enough to undertake such work. "Non-sense", answered Rossetti confidently, "there's a man I know who has never painted anything—his name is Morris—he has undertaken one of the panels and he will do something very good you may depend—so you had better come! " Rossetti was so friendly and confident that I consented and joined the band at Oxford '.

Long afterwards Burne-Jones recalled how Rossetti took him to Little Holland House for the first time and prepared him for the visit and for a sight of Watts, who lived there then: ' One day Gabriel took me out in a cab—it was a day he was rich and so we went in a hansom, and we drove and drove until I thought we should arrive at the setting sun— and he said, " You must know these people, Ned; they are remarkable people: you will see a painter there, he paints

[1] *Memorials of Edward Burne-Jones*, by G. B.-J., vol. i, p. 159.

a queer sort of pictures about God and Creation " '.[1]
Prinsep's recollection of the same visit was: ' This time
Rossetti was accompanied by a younger man, who he
declared was the greatest painter of the age—a shy, fair
young man, with mild grey-blue eyes and straight light
hair which was apt to straggle over his well-developed
forehead . . . he did not impress me much; but then, as I
said, he was almost painfully shy and my mind was filled
with Rossetti. It was Burne-Jones, or, as Rossetti and all
of us called him, " Ned Jones " '.[2]

Prinsep went down to Oxford according to his agreement, and dined the first evening with Rossetti. The band
of artists were doing themselves proud at an hotel, the
foolish committee who had consented to the painting of the
Union having professed inability to pay the artists for their
work but agreed to pay their expenses! ' I was, of course,
proud to accept the invitation ', says Prinsep, ' so at the
hour mentioned I was punctually at the house. There I
found Rossetti in a plum-coloured frock-coat, and a short
square man with spectacles and a vast mop of dark hair.
I was cordially received. " Top ", cried Rossetti, " let me
introduce Val Prinsep ". " Glad, I'm sure ", answered
the man in spectacles, nodding his head, and then he
resumed his reading of a large quarto. This was William
Morris. Soon after, the door opened, and before it was
half opened in glided Burne-Jones. " Ned ", said Rossetti,
who had been absently humming to himself, " I think you
know Prinsep." The shy figure darted forward, the shy
face lit up, and I was received with the kindly effusion
which was natural to him. When dinner was over,
Rossetti, humming to himself as was his wont, rose from
the table and proceeded to curl himself up on the sofa.
" Top ", he said, " read us one of your grinds." " No,
Gabriel ", answered Morris, " you have heard them all."
" Never mind ", said Rossetti, " here's Prinsep who has
never heard them, and besides, they are devilish good."

[1] *Ibid.*   [2] *Ibid.*

"Very well, old chap", growled Morris, and having got his book he began to read in a sing-song chant some of the poems afterwards published in his first volume. All the time he was jiggling about nervously with his watch-chain. I was then a very young man, and my experience of life was therefore limited, but the effect produced on my mind was so strong that to this day, forty years after, I can still recall the scene: Rossetti on the sofa with large melancholy eyes fixed on Morris, the poet at the table reading and ever fidgetting with his watch-chain, and Burne-Jones working at a pen-and-ink drawing.'

According to Prinsep, while they were at work on the walls of the Union Hall, the window panes were whitened, to tone the light, and the glass was soon covered with sketches, chiefly of wombats. ' "Do you know the wombat at the Zoo?" asked Rossetti: "a delightful creature—the most comical little beast." He was drawn by Edward in endless different positions and situations, and Rossetti's admiration led him years afterwards to buy a live one and try to make it happy at Cheyne Walk.' [1]

Soon after, Burne-Jones and his wife were invited to meet Rossetti and his wife. The assignation was at the wombat-house in the Zoological Gardens. William and Christina Rossetti had first 'discovered' the wombat and passed on their pleasure to Dante Gabriel.

In Mr. J. W. Mackail's *Life of William Morris*,[2] amid an interesting account of this merry and brilliant work going on at the Union, a passage is quoted from the diary of Cormell Price, Burne-Jones's old friend, who was one of this new Round Table. The following dates refer to 1857:

Oct. 17. Breakfasted with Top at Johnson's in George Street. Rossetti, Hughes, Prinsep, Ted, and Coventry Patmore there. To the Union to see the frescoes.

---

[1] *Ibid.*, p. 163.
[2] *Life of William Morris*, by J. W. Mackail, vol. i, chap. lv. Other vivid glimpses of the same time can be found in *A Painter of Dreams: Spencer Roddam Stanhope.*

Oct. 24. Spent afternoon in daubing in black lines on the Union roof for Topsy. Whist in the evening as usual [at Rossetti's].

Oct. 30. Evening at George Street. Rossetti, Ted, Topsy, Hughes, Swan, Faulkner, Bowen of Balliol, Bennet of University, Munro, Hill, Prinsep and Stanhope there. Topsy read his grind on Launcelot and Guenevere—very grand.

Oct. 31. Stippled and blacklined at Union. Evening at George Street. Rossetti and I versus Top and Faulkner at whist. Madox Brown turned up. Rossetti said that Topsy had the greatest capacity for producing and annexing dirt of any man he ever met with.

Nov. 1. To Hill's, where Topsy, Ted, Swan, Hatch, Swinburne of Balliol (introduced I think by Hatch) and Faulkner.

Swinburne had come up to Balliol in January 1856, and this meeting was probably the beginning of Swinburne's friendship with the group. Again the bond of union was Malory, and Swinburne, besides having written a long poem on Iseult of Brittany, was one of the most fervid admirers of Morris's early poetry. Rossetti had been contributing some of the poems which had appeared in *The Germ* and also 'The Burden of Nineveh' to *The Oxford and Cambridge Magazine.* Swinburne and Morris both dedicated their first volumes of verse to Rossetti, and began to write poems to his pictures. The impression that the group of young men made on an intelligent and refined girl is described by Lady Burne-Jones: ' I felt in the presence of a new religion. Their love of beauty did not seem to me unbalanced, but as if it included the whole world and raised the point from which they regarded everything. Human beauty especially was in a way sacred to them, I thought '.[1] Her feeling, and that of a woman friend who shared her memories of their youth, was ' that the men were as good as they were gifted '.

An entry in Cormell Price's diary for 14th November 1857, after receiving the news from Burne-Jones, bodes the ending of the great days at Oxford: ' Rossetti unhappily called away through Miss Siddal's illness at Matlock '.

Thus there was a tremendous personal influence to reinforce the fruitful admiration for his work felt by

[1] *Memorials of Edward Burne-Jones,* vol. i.

Burne-Jones, William Morris, and Swinburne, who came into contact with Rossetti from 1856 onwards. Swinburne wrote in 1866 (9th October) to William Rossetti in a letter yet unpublished:[1] ' It is nice to have something to love and believe in as I do in Italy. It was only Gabriel and his followers in art (l'art pour l'art) who for a time frightened me from speaking out; for ever since I was fifteen I have been equally and unalterably mad—tête montée—as my mother says—about this article of faith '. A close associate of the Oxford group, himself an Oxford poet, Canon Richard Watson Dixon, wrote just after Rossetti's death: ' My recollection of him is that of greatness. His work was great; the man was greater. His conversation had a wonderful ease, precision, and felicity of expression. He produced thoughts perfectly enunciated with a deliberate happiness that was indescribable, though it was always simple conversation, never haranguing or declamation '. The ' main features of his character ', Dixon believed, ' were fearlessness, kindliness, a decision that sometimes made him seem arbitrary, and condensation or concentration. He was wonderfully self-reliant '. Philip Bourke Marston wished Rossetti had been some splendid exiled king that they might have served him with their lives. More restrained and balanced, but all the more convincing, are the glimpses of Rossetti's personal ascendancy over Burne-Jones and other Oxford men afforded us by the beautiful *Memorials of Edward Burne-Jones.*

[1] Quoted in Mr. Wise's Catalogue.

CHAPTER VII

THE WORLD

*' If you will behold your own self and the outer world, and
what is taking place thereon, you will find that you, with
regard to your external being, are that external world.'*—

BOEHME.

THE MOST important consequence of the Oxford
association for Rossetti was probably not the subsequent working association at Red Lion Square in
London, with Morris's firm of decorators, but the meeting
with Jane Burden. Lizzie Siddal had departed on one of
her holidays for the recovery of her ailing health when
Rossetti went to Oxford. Towards the end of that memorable Long Vacation of 1857 Rossetti had gone with Burne-
Jones after their day's work at the Union Hall to the
theatre. They noticed two girls sitting just behind them,
the daughters of Robert Burden, an Oxford tradesman.
' The elder attracted their attention at once by her remarkable beauty, of a type not common in England, and
specially admired by Rossetti. They made her acquaintance; and after some little negotiation she was persuaded
to sit to him and his friends, and continued to do so while
the work at the Union was going on.' Morris, it is said
at the instigation of his friends who regarded him as the
most eligible bachelor, proposed to Jane Burden, and
became engaged. After this, says his biographer, ' the
instability which he found, or thought he found, in his
own character became for a time acute '.[1] Morris's time
was thereafter occupied with excursions to London and
Red Lion Square, to his mother's new house at Leyton,

[1] Mackail.

to various friends' houses, a tour of northern France, buying old manuscripts and armour and ironwork and enamel, and finally with plans for his own ' small Palace of Art '. This was the Red House at Abbey Wood, just out of London, in Kent, to which he took Jane Burden soon after as his bride.

The firm of Morris, Marshall, Faulkner & Co. was formed in 1861. The most important partners, from the public's point of view, were at first Madox Brown and Rossetti. Burne-Jones was hardly known then. Faulkner had resigned a mathematical tutorship and a Fellowship at Oxford, to join the firm. He did church decoration. ' As for Rossetti,' says Mr. Mackail, ' he contributed a few designs for both glass and tiles, but if asked why he had become a partner in a manufacturing firm, he might have, with some truth, given the reply, *Quia nominor leo*: he was looked up to by the younger men as their master mind, and they would hardly have thought of starting any new scheme without him.' Peter Paul Marshall, a surveyor and sanitary engineer, was a friend of Madox Brown's. In the firm's prospectus the intention was announced of reviving the decorative arts in England and of enabling all people of taste to obtain what then was unobtainable in the way of beautiful objects of furniture and decoration. In that prospectus, which is very forthright, Mr. Mackail thought ' it is not difficult to trace the slashing hand and imperious accent of Rossetti, now as always contemptuous of all difficulties and not over-scrupulous in accuracy of statement (*i.e.*, concerning the quality of the artists who worked for the firm). The most generous of men towards brother artists, he at once put all young men in whom he saw the elements of genius on an equal footing with himself, and claimed for them the full status and privilege which he and Madox Brown had earned by long years of work '. But though Rossetti's initiative was the most powerful, it was Morris's industry and versatility which made the firm succeed. Until the dissolution of the firm in 1874 the paid-up capital was never more than £140. William de Morgan was one of the outside designers employed by them, and so was Simeon Solomon. Mrs. Morris and her sister Miss Burden helped in embroidery, and Mrs. Burne-Jones also did some work. In the first year of the firm's operations, Faulkner writes to Cormell Price from Red Lion Square saying how busy he has been, and that ' Rossetti, with remarkable confidence, gave me a wood-block to engrave, which I with marvellous boldness, not to say impudence, undertook to do, and by jingo I have done it, and it is published, and flattering friends say it is not so bad for a beginning '. This was Rossetti's illustration as frontispiece for Christina's *Goblin Market and other Poems*.

Space will permit only one more glimpse of the group at Red Lion Square, the firm's headquarters. Morris and Burne-Jones had first taken rooms there, and with Rossetti had set about decorating them. A few of Rossetti's most attractive paintings were done on the furniture. The maid-of-all-work, known as Red Lion Mary, was a perpetual joy to the young men, who appreciated her willing helpfulness through all disasters. There is an attractive picture of her pathetic willingness to do anything she could. Burne-Jones said to her one day, ' Why were you made so short? I could do all I require while you are fetching Miss Joliffe [a model] if only you were taller '. Upon this she asked if she ' would be of any use if she stood on a stool! ' ' When Gabriel heard of this he was so touched by it that he said, " Mary shall go into a picture ", and so she did, as one of the ladies accompanying Beatrice in the " Meeting of Dante and Beatrice in Florence ". He also made a careful pencil drawing of her head and gave it to her upon her marriage '.[1]

The unfortunate dispute about money which arose when the firm was dissolved in 1875 snapped the last link of attachment between Rossetti and Morris. In the summer

[1] *Memorials of Edward Burne-Jones*, vol. i.

of 1875 Rossetti had given up his half-tenancy of the manor house at Kelmscott, which he had occupied jointly with the Morrises from 1872. When the Morris firm had developed, new premises were taken at Hammersmith, and Morris left the Red House at Upton. Morris took his wife and children to the old manor house in July 1871, before visiting Iceland, to which he had been attracted by its literature. The break-up of the original Morris firm was due to Morris's desire to stabilize his finances. By the original rules all the members were really entitled to an equal share of the value of the business, but practically all the money contributed, and most of the labour, had been Morris's. Three of the partners, Burne-Jones, Faulkner, and Webb, abandoned all claims to any legal share. Madox Brown and his friend Marshall, and Rossetti carried on negotiations until March 1875, through Brown's solicitor, and Watts-Dunton for Rossetti. They received compensatory payment out of the firm's funds. There was some reason in this, since Brown and Rossetti had certainly been useful to the firm, especially in the early days when none of the others' work had any market or publicity value, but Rossetti seems to have been actuated by abstract principle with possibly an admixture of loyalty to Brown, who proved stubborn in disregarding anything but his logical and legal rights. Rossetti at any rate intended not to use his share for himself, and set it aside for the eventual benefit of a member of the Morris family, though ' ere his death circumstances had induced him to trench upon it not a little '.[1] This financial instability and confusion was typical of Rossetti's whole life. In the early lean years he was constantly borrowing small sums from his brother and his aunt Charlotte. Madox Brown also was a banker in much request. Sometimes his borrowings were merely to give to some charitable cause, for he parted with money more easily than he acquired it, though after the 1850's he

---

[1] *Memoir*, xxxvii, by William Rossetti. The dissolution of the firm is described in more detail in Mackail's *Life of William Morris*.

was able to earn a big income from painting. As late as
April 1870 his brother William lent him £20 when he
was returning to Scalands, the farmhouse at Robertsbridge,
in Sussex, which Mrs. Bodichon had lent him. He needed
the £20 to meet current bills at 16 Cheyne Walk, Chelsea,
before he could depart. The bills included £12 15s. for
fire insurance, representing an insured sum of £5,100.
There are several instances of his efforts to raise money for
old friends' surviving relatives. He continued remitting
money to relatives of his dead wife. He enjoyed ordering
things for his mother and Christina, a sealskin coat for
' the Teak ' (short for the Antique, his favourite name for
his mother), or a case of champagne (' from my own wine
merchant ') for Christina! The large house at Chelsea
which he rented after the death of his wife enabled him to
indulge his social inclinations more fully than the rooms
at Chatham Place, Blackfriars, where most of his working
career had been located up to then. A heavy expenditure
was made possible by his skill in handling the dealers and
the big Victorian merchants who patronized the arts. If
he borrowed from his friends, there is ample evidence that
he was constantly assisting them to sell their work. He
must often have been very careless of the money which he
extracted from buyers with admirable skill. Probably
Mrs. Schott during the sixties was very well paid for the
sittings for ' Lilith ' and a few other pictures. There is no
telling what sums may have been handed over to women
with his characteristic lavishness. He showed a similar
desire for pleasantness at any price in his relations with
one or two men, like the Anglo-Portuguese Howell, who
amused him as well as proved useful in business ways.
Howell almost certainly was responsible for some of the
forgeries of his work which got about.

Writing to Brown from Chelsea in July 1867 he said:
' I'm sorry to say I shall have to use your cheque on
Monday. I am at present still waiting for Agnew's visit.
If with good result, I can easily lend the sum again. How

you manage to have a banking-account I don't know. I never can '. At this time his income was at least £2,000 a year, which was equal to more than twice as much now. In the same letter he refers, as so often in his correspondence, to a prospective purchaser of his or his friends' pictures. In the same month he is writing again to Brown, who has gone to Calais, to say that 'yesterday Mr. Matthews the Brewer came to see the design [*i.e.*, of Perseus and Medusa] and commissioned the picture for 1500 guineas. It is a very straightforward work and will not involve delay or great labour; so this is a capital thing for me '. On 5th August he has to explain that he can send Brown only £15 of the £25 Brown asked for, and that ' the other 10 shall come very soon '. On 15th August, in response to another appeal, he writes: ' Dreffle bad, ain't it? All would be well as to the £10, were it not that I had on Monday to send that very sum to Lizzie's brother Harry, who has the small-pox '. He supposes he must ' draw on Leyland on my own account, and can then do the needful. I wished to avoid doing this further till all his daubs were daubed; but other matters than yours will force me to it, I fear. As for the wretch Gambart, his damned £200 (minus 5s. which he stopped for something like cab-hire) are had and spent now——and now he wants more done to the drawings and has left two of them with me. Let him write, and won't he get it!——this at least will be a tit-bit. I'm on the right side of the hedge this time. . . .'

As for the Matthews commission of ' Aspecta Medusa ', which William Rossetti and H. C. Marillier[1] have shown was one of those subjects which he brooded over for years, it was a cause of a typical piece of careful negotiation. C. P. Matthews, of the brewery firm of Ind, Coope & Co., had commissioned Rossetti, at the price of 1500 guineas to paint in oils a picture from his pencil design of ' Aspecta

[1] William Rossetti's *Rossetti Papers*, pp. 281, 290. Marillier's *Rossetti*, p. 110.

Medusa '. Matthews then unexpectedly wrote asking the artist not to include the severed head of Medusa, which was an important element of the design, in the finished oil picture. Rossetti was evidently too indignant to reply at once, but weeks later, apparently in response to a further letter, he writes: ' your letter has given me matter for reflection, which has been the cause of my delay in answering '. No doubt the ' matter for consideration ' was the prospective 1500 guineas, which ought not to be scared away by too much candour. The artist starving for gold to meet his self-indulgent extravagances is at a disadvantage with the rich barbarian, who will care much less about losing Rossetti's picture than Rossetti will care about losing 1500 guineas. But Rossetti has not an ordinary mind. His nerve has been already tested with many a desirable purchaser. He will not show the weakness of his position. At first he tries to combine friendliness with the implacable purpose of Art. ' It would greatly decrease my pleasure in the picture I am engaged on for you ', he says, ' if I thought there was an unavoidable feature in its treatment to which you could never become reconciled.' Is that not a masterly sentence? It means, if the brewer wants the artist's best work, he had better let the artist have his own way. ' I am engaged on for you ' is a timely reminder at the very start, which is afterwards repeated with relevant details, that the picture is not only commissioned but that the artist has been working on it. The other key-words in that sentence are ' unavoidable ' and ' never '—the Gorgon's head is unavoidable: the only question troubling the artist is whether his client is going to become reconciled to it. A lucid defence of the feature objected to follows, and besides, ' the subject is one I have fixed on for years and much desired to carry out, and of which the treatment is as clear in my mind as if it were already done. No other object for a large work is so tempting to me at this moment, and the time which has elapsed since I last saw you has enabled me to mature all my ideas respecting its execution, and take various important steps towards it '. His client's persistence can only result in the abandonment, not the alteration, of this picture, though there will still remain some other picture to be done, of course. ' Thus nothing but the most decided impression against it in your mind would enable me to bear with substituting another subject for this, in the picture I am to paint for you.' This is not at all conciliatory, but good words cost nothing, so: ' And this at the same time I saw with the strongest wish that a commission so liberally given should be carried out to your entire satisfaction, quite as much as to my own. . . .'

Nearly three months later, on 3rd January 1868, he is replying to another letter and agreeing that ' our best course will be to abandon the Medusa subject for which you originally commissioned me, and to substitute another. As to the time and trouble already devoted by me to the work in preparation and studies, and your proposal to compensate me for this, I need only say that, as I shall of course continue the Medusa picture sooner or later on my own account, either on the life-scale or a smaller one, the studies made will serve me, and will also themselves be saleable. This matter therefore need not be pursued farther '.

But this matter was pursued farther, when the disappointed artist found that the fish would not nibble at another bait. He offers to do another picture, that of ' Dante's Dream ', which is ' among the subjects I most wish to carry out in my lifetime ', but unfortunately ' this being a composition of five figures, could not be painted for the same price as the Medusa ', which had only two figures. He will paint it for 2000 guineas. ' Though this proposal involves an extension of commission, it would be in fact of no pecuniary advantage to me, but the reverse; except in the one all-important particular, that I should thus be both complying with your wish for a change of design, and at the same time substituting for one subject after my own heart another in which I should take equal delight. Otherwise, the figures being more than twice the number of those in the first subject, I should be taking on myself an amount of labour much more than proportionate to the increase of price. I already explained to you, when we were discussing the Medusa subject, that the size of figures in a picture, whether that of life or less, made no difference in the labour of the work, supposing them to be still on a good scale.' But four days later he writes:

DEAR MR. MATTHEWS,

I cannot disguise from you that your last letter causes me great disappointment, which I feel sure you will not consider unreasonable on considering the course of events. After much careful preparation, during some months, for a work on which I built the greatest hopes, and the nature of which was so fixed that change seemed out of the question, I nevertheless felt it necessary to admit the force of an unconquerable objection coming thus late from you, since, if the work failed to please you at last, it could not but leave a painful regret with me. However, the substitution which you now suggest of small and comparatively casual works to the amount of the commission, instead of the one serious work, would destroy all the pleasure, and (in the higher sense) all the advantage, which I had promised myself from executing your order in its original form. In saying this, I speak without reserve, as you have rightly done, regarding an agreement which your wishes make it necessary we should modify, but in which my own interests are also greatly at stake.

When I proposed the Dante subject in my last letter, I thought that probably—considering what you had said as to compensation for my trouble till now with the work which (though I felt a difficulty in charging for it) has been in many ways very considerable, and most of all as regards the discouragement of the present change—you would not object to an extension of commission. This in fact involved no advantage to me, except that of painting a second subject I greatly desire to paint in lieu of the first, rather than having to seek something as a mere substitute: otherwise, as I said, the new plan was less advantageous to me than the old one.

He says that perhaps his correspondent fears an indefinite delay in the execution of the proposed new picture, since so much time went by without him seeing any of the preparatory work on the ' Medusa ', but ' with the substituted subject, I would now fix a precise longest date for the delivery of the work, if that seemed desirable to you '. He then offers to paint the ' Dante's Dream ' picture on a reduced scale as to size ' (which of course should still be not unimportantly small), and, so far as possible with justice to the work, reducing the labour throughout, as would enable me to execute it for 1500 guineas '. This will still be his best work and he hopes that his offer will be accepted, for among the difficulties he has borne owing to the change is 'the degree of discredit for an artist, which attaches to the subject of a commission being altered. During the time I have been getting the " Medusa " in hand, my work and the fact of its being commissioned have of course become known to various frequenters of my studio, and have been reported pretty widely; and the unavoidable consequence that, when I resume the work, I shall have to offer it to some one who will probably know it was originally ordered in another quarter, is not the least inconvenient feature of my position '.

The next letter, 9th January—two days after the above —opens: ' Dear Sir ' and begs his correspondent to ' acquit ' him of all intention to ' tie you down hand and foot ' to any plans. Whether he could or could not afford to paint pictures on speculation, he has too much self-respect as an artist to have dealings without mutual confidence. So ' I must now decline at once to paint you any picture at all '. Later, another letter, without opening or signature, says that Michael F. Halliday, the semi-professional painter who had first introduced Matthews to him, has had a talk with him, and as a result he will be ' as happy as ever ' to see or to hear from Mr. Matthews. ' As regards pictures (should you wish to renew that subject), I would carry out either of the proposals made by me, or else the original one.'

Rossetti's time in the sixties was divided between painting, among others, some of his greatest works and the variety of social interests which gave him pleasure

He amused himself by collecting, with great success, blue china and old furniture. His studio assistant, Treffry Dunn,[1] wrote some illuminating recollections of this phase. The story of the blue Nankin dish especially is much in tune with Rossetti's lighter side during the sixties.

Fine examples of Nankin and other china outshone most of the rare and curious things in the large house at 16 Cheyne Walk. Between Whistler and Rossetti especially there was the rivalry of collectors. Whistler's pieces of Chinese porcelain, on which slim figures of slant-eyed ladies were painted, came to be known as his 'long Elizas', an idiomatic version of the technical Dutch term, 'Lange leises' (tall damsels). The Anglo-Portuguese Howell, a remarkably versatile man, followed close on Whistler's and Rossetti's heels, and occasionally seems to have got there first in the pursuit of rarities. At a time when Rossetti and Howell may be said to have run neck-and-neck the latter discovered a beautiful blue Nankin dish in a second-hand furniture shop in Hammersmith. He invited Rossetti, Whistler, Morris, Burne-Jones, George Cruikshank, the rich Greek merchants, the Ionides brothers, John William Inchbold, and others of a select circle, to a grand dinner at his house, promising to show them something worth seeing. When the guests had progressed far enough through the feast to be appreciative, Howell brought in the dish wrapped up in a silk kerchief. A gasp of admiration came from the company when he placed it on the table. Rossetti's enthusiasm was equal to anyone's. He took the dish up and turned it all ways, and declared it flawless. Howell at last tenderly removed the dish and enshrined it in a cabinet. H. T. Dunn continues the story as follows:

It was now getting on well towards midnight, and most of the party began to think of getting home—Howell's Fulham villa was not a very easy place to get at, and after twelve o'clock it was only by chance a cab could be found. Whilst the ladies of the party were upstairs wrapping themselves up for their journey, and the men were downstairs occupied with their hats and overcoats, Rossetti was hanging about the hall in a thoughtful kind of way. He had on the Inverness cape which he generally wore at night, and I saw him go into the room where the dish was deposited, to have, as I thought, a last look at the treasure, but—shall I tell it?—he hastily dislodged that dish by stealth, concealed it beneath the cape of his cloak and carefully wrapped its ample folds around it, that none could perceive what he carried under his arm. Having done so, he took leave of Howell and his wife in the most charmingly innocent manner possible. . . . On our arrival at his door, having dismissed the cabman, he let himself in, and pulling out the dish from under his cape had a good look at it by the gaslight in the hall, chuckling the while with glee, for in his mind's eye he saw the long face Howell would pull on discovering his loss. . . . Then, finding his way to the back hall, he proceeded to carefully hide it in the recesses of the massive oak wardrobe that stood there, and the more effectually to conceal it, swathed it round and round with models' dresses and other artistic draperies for the custody of which the wardrobe was employed. Having done all this to his satisfaction, Rossetti took his candle and went to bed. Next morning, when he made his appearance at the breakfast table, we had our usual chat respecting the day's work, and whatever else required to be discussed. In the course of our conversation, Rossetti said, suddenly:

'Dunn, I shall give a return party to that of Howell's last night. This is Tuesday: I'll ask him for Friday, and tell him he must come as I have picked up a piece of "Blue" that will rival his.'

The dining-table at Cheyne Walk would accommodate twenty people, and it was well filled for the dinner. But Howell called in the afternoon, and found Rossetti and Dunn in the studio. A long conversation which touched upon everything except the missing dish ensued, and then Howell found a pretext for going out of the room. He had guessed at Rossetti's little game. While Rossetti was painting he crept to the old wardrobe, felt about among the robes, found his dish, extracted it and conveyed it softly outside to his waiting cab. Thence he took from his man, who was waiting for him, another dish of the same size and shape. Howell placed this in the wardrobe instead of the other, and returned to Rossetti for further conversation before departing. The dinner that night was a great success.

At last Howell managed to divert the talk to the subject of Blue China, and the dish of his that had excited so much admiration on the night of his party, whereupon Rossetti declared that he had something just as fine. Howell challenged him to produce it, so off went Rossetti to the wardrobe most confidently: he fished out the dish and brought it away swathed in drapery, just as he supposed he had left it. In a few minutes he returned to the dining-room with the package, and began to carefully remove the wrappings. As the dish became uncovered, a curious, puzzled expression came over his face, and when it was entirely exposed to view, he stood still in blank astonishment. For a few moments he was silent; then his pent-up feelings burst out in a wild cry:

'Confound it! See what the spirits have done!'

Everyone rose to look at the dish. A dish it was, certainly, but what a dish! Instead of the beautiful piece of Nankin that was expected, there was only an old Delft thing, cracked, chipped, and discoloured through the numerous bakings it had undergone. The whole party, with the exception of Howell, who looked as grave as a judge, burst into a roar of laughter. Rossetti soon recovered himself and laughed as heartily as any of his guests at Howell's ingenious revenge.

More serious than the pursuit of china was Rossetti's dabbling in spiritualism; for the claims that were being made at that time for various experiments found a ready response from the superstitious side of Rossetti. He shared his interest with others. Christina writes to him on 23rd December 1864, from Hastings, to express her interest in his account of a séance which he and his brother William attended.[1] 'To me', she wrote, 'the whole subject is awful and mysterious; though, in spite of my hopeless inability to conceive a clue to the source of the sundry manifestations, I still hope simple imposture may be the missing key: I hope it, at least, so far as the hope is not uncharitable. At any rate, I hope without any qualification that you and William escape bumping bangs to the maiming of your outer men.' In this year the Davenport brothers electrified London with a series of professedly spiritualistic séances in which they performed many clever juggling tricks. After attending sittings at other people's houses, and talking of spiritualism to all kinds of people, he started to arrange for little experiments at table-turning, spirit-rapping, and the like at his own house. Some of his friends would assemble with him round a table late at night. 'As each of the experimenters was suspicious of his neighbour's honesty when the table became rampant, the results were mostly unsatisfactory', says Dunn. To which one might add that as Whistler was one of the friends who

[1] *Rossetti Papers.*

attended, the suspicions of the others may not have been always unjustified. But Dunn adds that ' some remarkable messages were received from the spirits, which could not be accounted for '. But in so far as Rossetti's interest in spiritualism was associated with memories of his dead wife, it became something involving his serious feelings. If such superstitious observances as avoiding ' thirteen at table ' were noticed by him, it is not surprising that the poignant memories of his wife, and other ever-present painful associations, made him, as his brother said, ' prone to think that some secret might yet be wrested from the grave '. This tendency would have been accentuated when his insomnia and bad health increased towards 1870.

Although most of his friends, including his brother, smoked, Rossetti's sociable inclinations never induced him, or Swinburne, to this form of mild poison, which would have been much less injurious than chloral, could he have made it a substitute for the drug. Music was another blind spot in Rossetti, even as a relaxation. Dunn, who was an inmate of his house from 1863 till 1877 or after, says that he never heard a note of music there, although there was a queer collection of old and curious musical instruments, including lutes, mandolines, dulcimers, a spinet, and some strange Chinese instruments. They, like the odds and ends of jewellery and old furniture which Rossetti picked up in curiosity shops during his rambles, served as objects to paint from. Music was heard, however, at 16 Cheyne Walk, because the next door neighbours were much given to it. Theo. Marzials, a minor poet admired by Rossetti, was a good singer, and as he was often at the next door house, his baritone voice would come floating on the airs of summer evenings into the front windows of No. 16. Whether it was the music, or noises which Dr. Johnson would have called less bearable than music, a few years later Rossetti had the wall of his studio against the next door house pulled down and filled up with a deep layer of sand to deaden sound. Leyland, the Liver-

pool merchant, and a friendly picture buyer, took Rossetti
to the Royal Opera House to hear *Fidelio*. His assistant,
Dunn, was curious to hear the next morning what Rossetti
would say about it. ' The only notion he had of it was that
of a man who was taken out of prison, where he had been
for a couple of days without food, and who, when a loaf of
bread was given to him, instead of eating it like any
starving man would do, burst out into a long solo over it
lasting for ten minutes—which he thought was obviously
absurd!' Rossetti gave his impression also of a perform-
ance of Handel's *Messiah* at a Crystal Palace festival. It
seemed to him that everybody got up and shouted at him
as loudly as possible. But there are those who would
sympathize with him on this point!

Rossetti's health had been surprisingly good for some
years after the death of his wife, in spite of hard work and
irregular living, but his mind was ready to be unduly
darkened when one ailment and another began to afflict
him. The interest in spiritualism was not merely an idle
curiosity; it indicated the persistence of the sense of
bereavement following the death of his wife, and also the
inability of Mrs. Schott, or any other mistress, to make him
happy. The return to poetry after 1868 coincided with
the first outward signs of nervous strain, in insomnia.
Insomnia sets the mind in a vicious circle in which its
pursuit of rest and strength exacerbates its illness. Rossetti's
lively imagination strengthened every sign of ill-health.
He complained that his eyes were affected though his liver
was probably as important a cause of the ' films ' which he
said obscured his vision as any optical defect. The fact
that his father's eyesight had failed would have been
sufficient to set his fears on the alert. Then he was
recommended by his American friend Stillman to try
chloral for insomnia. It was a new drug, and it was said—
very mistakenly—to be harmless in its effects. Rossetti
was one of those people whose impulses, in every pursuit
of pleasure or alleviation of pain, will dominate the reason

[128]

until they are expended, and he was just the type of man
to sacrifice future health to momentary relief, as he sacri-
ficed future peace continually, to say nothing of his income,
to win a woman or to quieten her jealousy. If he showed
little sense in his relations with women, he showed less in
his care of himself. Treffry Dunn's impression of the
bedroom Rossetti slept in was confirmed later by Hall
Caine. Rossetti had the primitive liking for being closed
round, and shut in. All his life he used the same bed, the
one which his mother gave him after Gabriele Rossetti's
death. All the Rossetti children were born in it. Writing
of the room in which it stood, Dunn said:

I thought it a most unhealthy place to sleep in. Thick curtains,
heavy with crewel work in 17th century designs of fruit and flowers
(which he had bought out of an old furnishing shop somewhere
in the slums of Lambeth), hung closely drawn round an antiquated
four-post bedstead. A massive panelled oak mantelpiece reached from
the floor to the ceiling, fitted up with numerous shelves and cupboard-
like recesses, all filled with a medley of brass repoussé dishes, blue china
vases filled with peacock feathers, oddly-fashioned early English and
foreign candlesticks, Chinese monstrosities in bronze, and various other
curiosities, the whole surmounted by an ebony and ivory crucifix. The
only modern thing I could see anywhere in the room was a Bryant and
May's match box! On the other side of the bed was an old Italian
inlaid chest of drawers, which supported a large Venetian mirror in a
deeply-carved oak frame. Two or three very uninviting chairs, that
were said to have belonged to Chang the Giant—and their dimensions
seemed to warrant that statement, as they took up a considerable
amount of space—and an old-fashioned sofa, with three little panels let
into the back, whereon Rossetti had painted the figures of Amor,
Amans, and Amata, complete the furniture of the room. With its rich,
dark green velvet seats and luxurious pillows, this sofa looked very
pretty and formed the only comfortable piece of furniture visible. The
deeply recessed windows, which ought to have been thrown open as
much as possible to the fresh air and cheerful garden outlook, were
shrouded with curtains of heavy and sumptuously-patterned Genoese
velvet. On this fine summer's day, light was almost excluded from the
room. The gloom of the place made one feel quite depressed and sad.
Even the little avenue of lime-trees outside the windows helped to
reduce the light, and threw a sickly green over everything in the apart-
ment. It was no wonder poor Rossetti suffered so much from insomnia!
A few pictures, not of a very cheerful description, hung on the

walls where there was space. One, I remember, was particularly gruesome. It represented a woman all forlorn in an oar-and-rudderless boat, with its sail flapping in the wind about her, alone on a wide expanse of water. In the distance was a city in flames, over which the artist had inscribed *The City of Destruction*, in the sky were numerous winged dragons and sea monsters, all intent upon upsetting the boat.

William Bell Scott introduced Rossetti to his friend Miss Alice Boyd, and in 1868 and 1869 his despondency about his eyesight was temporarily relieved by visits to Penkill, her beautiful Ayrshire castle. Swinburne and Morris were now well known as poets, and he began to think again of the other art in which he had already done so much fine work. Scott, in his *Autobiographical Notes*, gives the impression that Rossetti's turning to poetry was due to his and Miss Boyd's suggestions, but this is not confirmed by William Rossetti, neither do the facts about Rossetti's state of mind lead to such a conclusion. He had been writing verse for his chief pictures in the previous few years, and the lines for ' Aspecta Medusa ', a design which was more poetic than the majority of the pictures he had done since the fifties, indicate the deep stirring of his imagination. During the second visit to Penkill he began writing in his best vein ' The Stream's Secret ' and other verse, and continued to do so on his return to London. The question of publishing the volume of poems which had been abandoned after his wife's death was now foremost, and at last, his decision strengthened by the persuasions of his friends, he agreed to the exhumation of the manuscripts buried with her in the North London cemetery. No one seems to know how the matter was made public property, since it was intended to keep the affair private, but it is hardly unfair to remark that Charles Howell was not the most reliable of mortals to be given charge of the actual operations, useful as the service was to the harassed Rossetti, who at this juncture revealed all his innate capacity for conflicting emotions and self-distrust. Insomnia and chloral, to which the increasing use of whisky (to take away the taste of the chloral) had been added, were bad preparations for so momentous a decision and deed. The recovery of the manuscripts was a good thing for us; the question of its moral justification could never be finally settled by anybody but the man who had to make the decision about it. All sorts of contradictory opinions have been expressed by different writers, according to personal feelings or to their sense of biographical propriety. The only indisputable fact is that Rossetti believed sufficiently that he was justified. He has been charged with violating the sacredness of the dead for literary ambition among other things. His severest critics have been women, including Mary Duclaux[1] and Eleonora Duse. The latter said to Mr. Arthur Symons:[2]

> Rossetti is like a perverse young man who has been nicely brought up: he does not give himself up to it, he is only half himself. Look at Watts's portrait, the fine, mad eyes, and then the weak and heavy chin. The eyes desire some feverish thing, but the mouth and chin hesitate in pursuit. All Rossetti is in that story of the MS. buried in his wife's coffin. He could do it, he could repent of it; but he should have gone and taken it back himself: he sent his friends!

This is, of course, precisely opposite to the point of view of Madame Darmesteter (Duclaux), who condemns the act as sacrilegious and a negation of himself. I think Rossetti was indeed divided about it, and that the sonnet ' Vain Virtues ' derived some of its force from the feeling of guilt associated with the reversal of his former sacrifice. But Duse's judgment is much too simple, though penetrating. The emotional complexity in Rossetti cannot be dismissed as mere weakness. It is a part of the greatness of his genius, and sprang from emotional causes too deep to be controlled by him. The recovery of the poems was also connected with the most passionate love affair of Rossetti's life, if his poetry, which is always extremely personal, is to be taken as an indication. Whatever the significance of ' Vain Virtues ', Rossetti certainly benefited spiritually by that decisive act, and entered upon a new

[1] *Grands Ecrivains d'outre-Manche.*   [2] *Studies in Seven Arts.*

period of creative expression. That is a far more potent defence than any casuistical controversy between people who never experienced his sufferings can bring forward. If the whole of Rossetti's creative energy had gone into poetry, instead of being half used up in painting, he would be recognized beyond dispute as a figure who, like Shakespeare, cannot be measured by superficial moral judgments which are necessarily without a full understanding of his inmost self. The most that we can do is to be guided by aesthetic feeling for and psychological apprehension of his work, aided by a careful examination of the superficial biographical facts.

Another bone of contention was cast into biography by William Bell Scott's exaggerated and irritated account of Rossetti's plans for getting the volume of his *Poems* reviewed by friends. Many a writer has done likewise, including the sarcastic Scott himself, as William Rossetti pointed out. There was good reason for the poet's care to have some of his most brilliant friends review his book as soon as possible. He expected the attack which was ultimately led by Buchanan,[1] though when the latter's article appeared in the *Contemporary Review* for October 1871, eighteen months after the publication of the volume, Rossetti did not know the identity of the 'Thomas Maitland' who signed it. This information was conveyed to him by the publisher, F. S. Ellis,[2] between whom and Buchanan there was no love lost. Buchanan had been involved in some shady transactions connected with horse-racing, of which he was a devotee. Ellis had once threatened him with disclosures which might have landed him in gaol.[3] Buchanan was already up against the Rossetti brothers and Swinburne. William Rossetti in a pamphlet review

---

[1] See chapter xi.

[2] Vide *The Letters of Dante Gabriel Rossetti to his Publisher, F. S. Ellis*, edited by Oswald Doughty, 1928.

[3] I owe this information to my friend Dr. Theodore Rake, an enthusiastic bibliophile who was a close friend of William Rossetti.

of Swinburne had described Buchanan as a ' poor and pretentious poetaster ' in response to some anonymous comic verses on Swinburne by Buchanan. However true William's description may have been, it was not conducive to good feelings.

In his letters to his publisher concerning the preparation of the *Poems*, Rossetti shows all his customary attention to details in practical and business affairs. Ellis was a fine example of a cultured and friendly publisher, patient and generous with Rossetti. Many a poet to-day with a bigger public than Rossetti's, who was practically unknown as a poet before the publication of the 1870 volume, would be glad to be paid in advance, as he was, at the rate of twenty-five per cent. on each edition before publication. Other matters besides the volume of *Poems* come into Rossetti's letters to Ellis. It is interesting to find him asking Ellis to procure him a complete edition of Edgar Allan Poe and—so that he can make a present of it to Mrs. Morris—a complete set of Scott's novels; or giving news of the progress of ' Dante's Dream '.

Readers of chapter 33 of William Rossetti's *Memoir*, and of William Bell Scott's *Autobiographical Notes* referring to Rossetti, will be able to judge for themselves whether the introductory remarks of Mr. Doughty to the letters to Ellis are just in charging William Rossetti with making an attempt at denial of his brother's scheme to get his book reviewed by Morris, Swinburne, and other competent men who were also friends. This question can be dropped here. In Mr. Wise's Catalogue is evidence additional to that published by Rossetti's brother of Rossetti's fear of being overpraised by so enthusiastic a champion as Swinburne. Rossetti wrote on 23rd February 1870:

DEAR SWINBURNE,

I rejoice to find I am really to have your invaluable support at starting, and do not care what happens now. Only do, do, my dear best of fellows, remember that I am your friend not only to the purpose of praising what I do to the utmost (which I know how surely you will fulfil), but also to the purpose of being on your guard against praising me beyond my deserts, which is pretty sure to be your first impulse, I know well. Remember that my verses are not yet my Remains or Manes, and do not sacrifice to them those poets—least of all the living ones—whom I respect and love, and with whom I would be but too proud to rank on such footing as the lesser quantity of my work could give me, if only its quality might be found worthy of being classed with theirs. The four I mean above all are Tennyson, Browning, yourself, and Morris. . . .

In the PS. he says ' I hope to send you before many days revised sets of sheets. And do pitch into me when I need it '.

At this time we are very apt to pay too much attention to Buchanan's attack on 'The Fleshly School of Poetry', as if it was an isolated instance of antagonism. Several famous men, including Dickens, joined the chorus. Moreover, the animosities aroused twenty years earlier by the Pre-Raphaelites had not been exhausted and they reinforced the stream of renewed prejudice and conservative alarm. A sidelight on the situation is afforded by the letter which Parker, the editor of *Fraser's Magazine*, wrote to Sir John Skelton in 1860. Skelton had sent in a sympathetic review of Morris's ' Defence of Guinevere '. ' For myself', said this editor, ' I am sick of Rossetti and his whole school. I think them essentially unmanly, effeminate, mystical, affected, and obscure.' Rossetti during the sixties, often wrote to Skelton urging him to review Morris or Swinburne. He did not approve of all Swinburne's wildnesses, and occasionally remonstrated with him, but he was concerned at the neglect of his friend's work. In 1865 he writes to Skelton, ' Do write something concerning Swinburne. You will find his Atalanta a most noble thing, never surpassed to my thinking '. In 1866, after Moxon, the publisher, had withdrawn *Poems and Ballads* in a fright at the storm the book had aroused (and really Swinburne's perversities asked for much of what they got), Rossetti writes again: ' Swinburne's book has been withdrawn by Moxon, quite unjustifiably from a business point of view. It will immediately be re-issued (unaltered, I regret to say) by another publisher. The attack in the press has been stupid, for the most part, and though with some good grounds, shamefully one-sided '.[1]

One of the sad consequences of Rossetti's morbid state of mind after his attempt to kill himself in 1872 by an overdose of laudanum was the growth of suspicions of his best friends. The idea of a widespread conspiracy against him had got a firm hold of his imagination after the appearance of Buchanan's second and amplified attack in pamphlet form, in the spring of that year, and the tale of those summer months in his brother's *Memoir* make pathetic reading. But with characteristic resilience Rossetti was again at work in the autumn of 1872, though now all the submerged tendencies in his mind to shun and fear the world had become active. He suddenly broke off all relations with his old friend Swinburne in 1872, and never spoke to him again. In Mr. Wise's Catalogue a letter from Rossetti to Swinburne is quoted which suggests, as a superficial cause of the break, Rossetti's bitter resentment of some criticism from Swinburne of certain poems, on purely technical grounds. In the state of mind which chloral and alcohol poisoning, and the increasingly cloistered life he led had produced in Rossetti, any pretext was enough for severing all but the deepest relations. The Morrises had stayed at his house in Cheyne Walk in 1868 and 1869, when he was painting from Mrs. Morris, whose ill-health and consequent inability always to sit are subjects of several letters, notably those to his friend Norton. In 1871, as already observed, he had agreed with Morris to share Kelmscott Manor House. After the attempt to kill himself he was but a gloomy tenant at times, though nothing is more delightful in his correspondence than the accounts he writes to his mother, brother, and sister of the pets at Kelmscott and of his games with the little Morris

[1] *The Table Talk of Shirley.*

girls. It was a relief to Morris however when, after a scene with some anglers whom he fancied had made insulting remarks about him, Rossetti finally left Kelmscott and began a life of greater seclusion than formerly at the Cheyne Walk house. When Hall Caine, a young and enthusiastic admirer, met him there, he was a ruin of the former kingly genius and personality, though still able to fascinate as well as cast a dreadful depression over his visitor. The stout and rather podgy figure (so much like that of his father) which had been redeemed up to 1872 by its vigour, was now flabby and sunken. His evil genius, Fanny Schott, still hovered over his life, encouraging his failings and damping the fitful fire of his still unextinguished creative spirit. He worked, at poetry, up to the last, and when he died in April 1882, aged fifty-four, prematurely old, as one can imagine Shakespeare to have been, a great man passed away, who had impressed many, notwithstanding the wealth of his work, as one who somehow had been greater than anything he accomplished.

One generalization of some importance ought to find a place here. In both the famous and fruitful groups of painters and poets which assembled around Rossetti's personality and genius, there was a pervading good fellowship, often boisterous, always humorous. In the mingling of these characteristics with a dynamic impulse to create beauty these movements, which are unified by the single figure of Rossetti, stood for something unknown in England on the same scale since the Elizabethan era. With the Oxford group especially, a sort of jolly coarseness in their everyday relations emphasizes the Elizabethan simile; it was the raw and boyish side of personalities which were absorbed essentially in work of an unconventional and bitterly assailed beauty. There was a deep temperamental gulf between the movements inspired by Rossetti and the decadent tendencies of the Wilde period which followed and exploited them. The only decadent tendency in the Oxford group was a temporary inclination

for refined preciosity in poetry, chiefly expressed by
Swinburne and Morris. It should be remembered that the
poet of ' The Blessed Damozel ' developed quickly into a
high-spirited, full-blooded, laughter-loving man in his
personal contacts with others, whatever deeper strain of
destiny lay waiting for fulfilment in his soul.

PART TWO
MAINLY CRITICAL

CHAPTER VIII
THE P.R.B. PHASE

' The world being inferior to the soul; by reason whereof, there is agreeable to the spirit of man a more ample greatness, a more exact goodness, and a more absolute variety than can be found in the nature of things.'—FRANCIS BACON.

HOLMAN HUNT, in recalling those student-days of the revolutionary forties, refers particularly to Bell's *Anatomy of Expression*, which was his guide in 1847, and from which the following passages are taken to show the critical point of view which preceded that of the 'Pre-Raphaelites':

Two of our greatest painters, Raphael and Domenichino, have painted demoniacal boys. In the convent of Grotto Ferraba, in the neighbourhood of Rome, Domenichino has represented St. Nilus in the act of relieving a lad possessed. The Saint, an old man, is on his knees in prayer; the lad is raised and held up by an aged man, the mother with a child is waiting the consummation of the miracle. Convulsions have seized the lad; he is rigidly bent back, the lower limbs spasmodically extended so that only his toes rest on the ground; the eyes are distorted; the pupils turned up under the eyelids. This would be the position of Opisthonos, were not the hands spread abroad, the palms and fingers open, and the jaw fallen. Had the representation been perfectly true to nature, the jaws would have been clenched and the teeth grinding. But then the miracle could not have been represented, for one, under the direction of the Saint, has the finger of his left hand in the boy's mouth, and the other holds a vessel of oil with which the tongue is to be touched, and the grandeur of the old man makes this one of the most admired paintings in Italy. . . .

In the same painter's great picture of 'The Transfiguration' in the Vatican there is a lad possessed, and in convulsions. I hope I am not insensible to the beauties of that picture, nor presumptuous in saying that the figure is not natural. A physician would conclude that this youth was feigning. He is, I presume, convulsed; he is stiffened with contractions and his eyes are turned in their sockets. But no child was

[141]

ever so affected. In real convulsions the extensor muscles yield to the more powerful contractions of the flexor muscles; whereas, in the picture, the lad extends his arms, and the fingers of the left hand are stretched unnaturally backwards. Nor do the lower extremities correspond with truth; he stands firm; the eyes are not natural; they should have been turned more inwards, as looking into the head, and partially buried under the forehead. The mouth, too, is open, which is quite at variance with the general condition, and without the apology which Domenichino had. The muscles of the arms are exaggerated to a degree which Michael Angelo never attempted; and still it is the extensors and supinators, and not the flexors, which are thus prominent

So these outspoken students concluded, Hunt having Sir Charles Bell to fall back upon for partial support, that the admired ' Transfiguration ' was a signal step in the decadence of Italian art. ' When we had advanced this opinion to other students, they as a *reductio ad absurdum* had said, " Then you are Pre-Raphaelite ". Referring to this as we worked side by side, Millais and I laughingly agreed that the designation must be accepted.'[1]

But although they stood out ultimately as reactionaries against excessive Raphaelism, that is, Raphaelitism, their first target, since they were Academy students, was no doubt the Academy tradition derived from Sir Joshua Reynolds, to whom Millais always referred as ' Sloshua ', this suggesting the current idiom, ' sloshy ', which they applied to comfortable vagueness in workmanship. The protest of the young students was aimed chiefly against the disregard and ignorance of ' nature ' encouraged in the followers of Reynolds by the acceptance of his methods. They objected ultimately to the slurring over of the work on those parts of the picture not in the centre of interest (though Millais's earliest paintings of any value were done in this manner), and in preferring also to paint in bright and clear colours they used the same argument, that these were more ' natural ' than the conventionally dark and heavy tones which imitated the appearance of ' old masters ', and which came of the bituminous painting made fashionable by Reynolds. They revolted also against

[1] *Pre-Raphaelitism*, by Holman Hunt, vol. 1, chap. 5.

'THE GIRLHOOD OF MARY VIRGIN', 1848. THE ARTIST'S
18-YEAR-OLD SISTER, CHRISTINA, SAT FOR THE VIRGIN, AND
HIS MOTHER FOR ST. ANNA. [*See Appendix A*]

the glaringly impossible flowers and trees, and the prevalence of Roman togas and unnecessary stone pillars and unlikely folds of curtain. They did not deny Reynolds's feeling for human sentiments and character, but they saw his disregard of other aspects of 'nature' serving as an excuse for dullness and incompetence. Examining the current artistic tradition in the light of works by 'old masters', they thus came to trace the oppressive conventions which were suffocating originality to the worship of Raphael. Art exhibitions in England, said Ruskin three years later in his polemical pamphlet, *Preraphaelitism*, were collections of ' " cattle-pieces ", and " sea-pieces ", and " fruit-pieces ", and " family-pieces ", the eternal brown cows in ditches, and white sails in squalls, and sliced lemons in saucers, and foolish faces in simpers '.

The revolt against Raphaelitism was given a direction when, at a meeting of the friends at Millais's studio, they examined the engravings by Lasinio from the Campo Santo frescoes in Pisa. These fresco paintings by mediaeval masters like Andrea Orcagna, Giotto, and Gozzoli served as a text. Anyone who has examined Lasinio's engravings and compared them with either the remaining originals or with good photographs must feel tempted to agree with Ruskin in describing them as ' execrable '. The engravings mostly reproduce Benozzo Gozzoli's and Orcagna's pictures, but their effect is to emphasize the crudities and to obliterate almost every delicacy of touch and devoutness of sentiment. But they were sufficient to give intense pleasure to art students enraged by the outworn conventions of Raphaelitism. In these designs may be felt individuality and earnest sincerity and even the mediaeval sense of humour, which in the hell scenes is gruesome and sadistic. But there are some angel groups representing Paradise, and such a thing as the beautiful concert of souls in the right-hand bottom corner of Orcagna's ' Triumph of Death ' which suggest what element of the ' early Christian ' art especially appealed to Rossetti. It was an element which might without extravagance of fancy be traced in Dante's paradisal visions. Between 1845 and 1848 Rossetti had been translating Dante; the first version of 'Dante at Verona' was written, and other poems already written were 'The Blessed Damozel', 'For an Annunciation, Early German', and 'Ave'. After Hunt and Millais had already become conscious 'pre-Raphaelites'—the term having been applied to them at first banteringly by fellow-students—Rossetti was still prone to talk of 'early Christian' instead of 'Pre-Raphaelite', and 'Gothic' instead of 'nature'.

At the beginning of 1848 Holman Hunt was twenty, Rossetti nineteen, and Millais only eighteen, but there never were three youths so radically various except in ardent idealism as artists. The wonder is not that the Brotherhood which they formed dissolved so soon, but that it endured for three or four years. Rossetti's irresistible enthusiasm was here the driving force which made the group so much of a reality as it actually was, and inspired it, hypnotized it, into the belief that the members would work for the same objects. But the first thing which the impetuous Rossetti did, after persuading them to be called a brotherhood rather than a society was to bring Thomas Woolner, the sculptor, into the group. Woolner was an experienced man of twenty-two and impressed and entertained them by his knowledge of pipes and tobacco and his personal anecdotes about celebrities. But there was not much artistic reason for his membership. James Collinson, a minor painter, and Rossetti's brother William were next brought in, while Hunt seems to have been responsible for the introduction of Frederick George Stephens, who later exchanged painting for criticism. Woolner went to the Australian gold-diggings three years later, in despair of earning a living by art. Eventually he was very successful and became an academician after his return from Sydney, where he had obtained work as a sculptor when he tired of digging for elusive gold. Collinson was a

pious young man who had been noted by the women of
the Rossetti household as a scrupulous worshipper at the
church they attended. He in fact secured Rossetti's
mediation in presenting himself to Christina Rossetti,
then seventeen, as her suitor. He resigned his membership
soon afterwards, ostensibly because he had become a
Roman Catholic, but probably because the engagement
with Christina which had been made was broken off by
her. In any case his work was not important. Of the seven
members of the Pre-Raphaelite Brotherhood only three
are important as painters, and Ford Madox Brown,
Rossetti's lifelong friend and his first artistic mentor,
although never a member of the Brotherhood, is as good a
' Pre-Raphaelite ' in his middle period as any of them,
except Hunt.

Unlike the members of the P.R.B., Brown had travelled
and studied on the Continent. He was the first to advise
Rossetti not to under-estimate the primitives of Italy, and
throughout the years 1848 and 1849 his influence upon
Rossetti's painting is much more obvious than that of
Hunt or Millais, or of the ideas which the P.R.B.'s professed to expound. Perhaps because he mixed up the
Overbeckian German sugariness (a part of the ' Gothic
Revival ') with the true ' early Christian ' art of the Italian
Primitives, Rossetti had shown an inclination to pooh-pooh
the new taste for these. Once directed aright—whether by
Lasinio or by Brown—Rossetti soon showed that he had
something in common with the early Italian painters which
his friends had not. His knowledge of and feeling with the
mediaeval Dante was alone enough to place him in a
mental atmosphere which Hunt and Millais could not
have shared at the moment when they formed their
Brotherhood, for none of the P.R.B.'s, except Stephens,
knew the Italian Primitives' work. The practice of the
Pre-Raphaelites was much more unanimous in the use of
colour than either in choice of themes or ' truth to nature '.
In Hunt's studio Rossetti, working on his ' Girlhood of

[145]   K

Mary Virgin ', practised painting on a white background with the clear and bright tones which are a feature of pre-Raphaelite pictures. Although Ford Madox Brown either was not asked to join or else declined membership of the Brotherhood, the younger men were probably influenced by his use of colour. This bright clarity of colour could already have been seen in Brown's exhibited works. Brown himself for a time was influenced by the German phase of the Gothic revival as it was revealed in painting by Cornelius and Overbeck, and this fact may have brought him nearer to Rossetti than to the others. It may also have given the impression—which Hunt, the chief of the pre-Raphaelites contradicted—that they were pursuing a kind of archaism. Nevertheless certain differences of aim even at the beginning were inevitable, and some hint of such may be gathered from the attitudes of Hunt and Rossetti towards the ' Chaucer Reading his Poems at the Court of Edward III '[1] by Madox Brown. Hunt was taken by the enthusiastic Rossetti on a visit to Brown's studio. The situation was a little delicate at the time, as Rossetti had left Brown rather suddenly and was now working in Hunt's studio. A certain reserve in Brown's manner, noticed by Hunt, soon gave place to cordiality, which showed at any rate that Brown did not feel deeply offended by Rossetti's change of tutors, and the young painters began their examination of the ' Chaucer '. Hunt seems to have objected chiefly to elements in the design which were derived from the decadence of baroque art. This had poured over Europe from Italy and Spain, and had recently taken a lease of renewed life in the ' Gothic Revival '. The ' back to nature ' tendency of the nine-teenth century, encouraged in painting by Ruskin and the Pre-Raphaelites, was already weakening the taste for the baroque element in Brown's pictures. In the ' Chaucer ' Hunt thought that what Brown described as ' architec-

[1] In which Rossetti is painted as Chaucer, and supplies a good likeness to both.

[146]

tonic construction ' reminded one of a builder's elevation, with its raised centre and panel-like wings. Thus it seemed akin to the work of the German subject painters, who carried into their pictures the groups in tiers contoured like cut-out cardboard which they had found in old mural painting. But Rossetti merely broke out into a tirade against the choice of poets in the side-groups of the design. ' He declared that Shelley and Keats should have been whole-length full figures instead of Pope and Burns, and the introduction of Kirke White's name, he said, was ridiculous.' [1] It would be true that Rossetti hardly knew enough about styles of painting to look at Brown's work with the slightly doctrinaire attitude of Hunt, but he would have felt intuitively the genuinely original element in it as well as the inadequate imaginative life. It is not unreasonable indeed to trace in ' Hand and Soul ' an autobiographical strain when Chiaro dell' Erma, the enthusiastic student, at last enters the studio of Giunta. ' But the forms he saw there were lifeless and incomplete; and a sudden exultation possessed him as he said within himself, " I am the master of this man ".' ' Hand and Soul ' was written in 1849.

The assemblies of the P.R.B.'s at one another's houses were occasions for stimulating excursions into other spheres than painting. At one of these meetings Woolner or Rossetti read out Coventry Patmore's poem, ' The Woodman's Daughter.' Woolner expressed the wish to know Patmore in person. Rossetti, with characteristic unhesitancy, told him to address a letter to Patmore, which Woolner did. The consequence was that eventually Woolner was able to introduce Patmore to the others, and Patmore was a valuable link with the most select circles of literature. He introduced them to Tennyson in 1849, and in 1851 Ruskin first became acquainted personally with their much abused work through the mediumship of Patmore. It is not inappropriate to mention also that in

[1] *Pre-Raphaelitism*, chap. v.

1845 Ruskin, during his enthusiastic Italian pilgrimage, had already found the Campo Santo of Pisa 'a veritable Palestine', and had cajoled the Abbé to let him put up a scaffold from which he could make outline studies from Gozzoli's frescoes, some of which were in those engravings by Lasinio which had roused the P.R.B. to enthusiasm. Such facts possess more than a casual relation to one another. No doubt all these men felt in their individual ways a stirring of ideas which came from a common source. The fallacy that must be avoided is to attribute to Pre-Raphaelitism much more than the power of catching attention possessed by a small group of young men who all shout out together. The shout was in their addition of the letters 'P.R.B.' to their signature of pictures. Until the secret of those initials was made public (owing to Rossetti incautiously telling his young friend Alexander Munro), their exhibited pictures were criticized, rather favourably, on their merits. The campaign of bitter abuse of them and their works was the reply of outraged convention and established interests to that pugnacious and concerted shout. Their first exhibition as P.R.B.'s in the spring of 1849 passed un-noted as such. Hunt with his 'Rienzi' and Millais with 'Lorenzo and Isabella' exhibited at the Academy, but Rossetti, without warning the other two (according to Holman Hunt's account) changed his mind at the last minute and instead of sending to the Academy, sent his 'Girlhood of Mary Virgin' to the Free Exhibition where his friend Brown was again exhibiting. This not only gave him an extra week to work on the canvas, but it caused his picture to be seen first, as the Free Exhibition opened before that of the Academy. The *Athenaeum* critic thought that 'for its invention and for many parts of its design, it would be creditable to any exhibition'. The 'Girlhood' was sold to the Marchioness of Bath, at Rossetti's own price of £80, which must have been a very timely relief to the family's exchequer. His Aunt Charlotte had been a governess in the home of Lady Bath, which

possibly helped to bring him his first success. Millais's
' Lorenzo ' was sold for £100. It changed hands several
times at increased prices, and in 1883 it was bought by
Liverpool Corporation for £1,120. Hunt, in his reminiscences, related the pathetic story of how his ' Rienzi '
remained unsold, and of the landlord's ultimatum having
been delivered that he must settle up or leave, when a
purchaser for it unexpectedly turned up and gave him a
£100 but, as events showed, did not want or value the
picture. The slender financial resources of the Pre-
Raphaelite brethren is indicated by William Rossetti's
statement that when he became the *Spectator's* art critic
at a salary of £50 a year in November 1850, this added to
his salary of £110 a year as a civil servant made him
' almost a capitalist among the P.R.B.'s. Millais perhaps
alone made more than this in the course of a year; most of
the others much less, or hardly anything '.

But Munro, having passed on the secret of ' P.R.B.'
to a brother Scot, Angus Reach, who wrote gossip for the
Illustrated London News, the young artists were about to
experience a blizzard of depreciation. When they exhibited
in 1850 the art critics made haste to atone for any former
appreciation. Rossetti's ' Ecce Ancilla Domini ', now in
the Tate Gallery, was shown in the ' Free Exhibition ' of
the National Institution, having been rejected by the
Academy. Millais, with his ' Carpenter's Shop ' and Hunt
with the ' Christians pursued by Druids ' were in the
Academy exhibition again. Instead of the praise accorded
to him the previous year for his ' Girlhood of Mary ' by
the *Athenaeum*,[1] Rossetti was told by the same journal that
his ' Ecce Ancilla Domini ' was a ' puerility ', ' an un-
intelligent imitation of the mere technicalities of old
painters '; it was ' a work evidently thrust by the artist
into the eye of the spectator more with the presumption
of a teacher than in the modesty of a hopeful and true
aspiration after excellence '. In fact (and here the cloven

[1] Quoted in *Appendix B*, pp. 324-325.

hoof showed itself), ' these crotchet-mongers ', ' professing
to look only to Nature in its truth and simplicity, are the
slavish imitators of artistic inefficiency '. The effect of this
kind of reviewing was rather serious for the impecunious
Rossetti, whose father's continually failing health had
placed the family in financial straits.[1] ' Ecce Ancilla
Domini ' did not find a purchaser until the useful and
shrewd buyer Francis McCracken, a Belfast business man,
steered by Holman Hunt's friendly suggestion, had
agreed to take it. But the long and disappointing delay,
convinced the painter that such themes were ' not for
the market ', and a companion picture of the ' Death of the
Virgin ', which he had intended to do after the ' Ecce
Ancilla Domini ', was abandoned. Dantesque themes
henceforth were the nearest approach to religious pictures
done by Rossetti. He also seems to have become appre-
hensive of charges of ' popery ' from the section of the
excited public of those days who would have been represented by Ruskin in his truculent Protestant mood. As a
precaution against such a confusion of his theme and his
attitude to ecclesiastical affairs, he changed the Latin title
of the picture into ' The Annunciation '. A reference in a
letter to the picture as ' the blessed white eyesore ', should
not be interpreted as anything more than a reflection of
disappointment at not disposing of it. He took pains to
improve it before despatching it to McCracken, and being
unable to ' get over the weakness of making a thing as
good as I can manage ', he was again looking it over with

[1] *Cf.* William Rossetti : ' In 1851 there was our father incapacitated ;
our mother and Christina fagging over an unremunerative attempt at a
day-school ; Maria giving lessons in Italian, etc., at two or three houses ;
myself with a small salary in the Excise-office, and another smaller sti-
pend from the *Spectator*. I can recollect that Dante Rossetti went round
once to some suburban station to see what a telegraph was like. The
sight, and the moderate amount of information given to him, afforded
him no satisfaction ; but, feeling the family's difficulties, he did not refuse to entertain the project. For one reason or another, and luckily for
all parties concerned—including maybe the railway passengers—it very
rapidly came to nothing '.—*Memoir*, xvi.

brush poised, in 1874, when at Kelmscott. But he decided (not without a touch of unconscious pathos): ' It is best left alone, except just for a touch or two. Indeed, my impression on seeing it was that I couldn't do quite so well now! '

The ' criticism ' of Hunt's and Millais's pictures at the Academy this year was far more vituperative than that which had assailed Rossetti's picture, but while the hunt was in full swing Ruskin's letters to *The Times* on 13th and 30th May 1851 came in defence of the P.R.B.'s, and counter-attacked very vigorously against the established interests in British art. This interruption came bolt-like out of the unclouded academic sky. This timely championship undoubtedly saved the professional career of several of the rash young men. It is not so clear that Ruskin's defence produced similarly definite effects in the aesthetic field. He defended the Pre-Raphaelites valiantly, but he did not inspire or influence them in any obvious way, beyond helping them to work. Indeed one doubts if their work would have appealed especially to him had he not seen them being hounded by the Philistines. His defence at this distance of time seems more ingenious than convincing. We find in reading his biographer[1] that he had not met any of the P.R.B.'s by the spring of 1851, and that, recalling this period in a letter written in 1882, he said that Dyce, the Royal Academician, ' dragged me, literally, up to the Millais picture of " The Carpenter's Shop ", which I had passed disdainfully, and forced me to look for its merits '. Certainly it is noteworthy that the pamphlet (an amplified version of his letters to *The Times*) published in the autumn of 1851, pays more discerning attention to Turner, whose fame he had already established, than to the youthful works of the Pre-Raphaelite revolutionaries. His chief argument to counter the hostile attacks against them was essentially a deliberate confusion of the Pre-Raphaelite style with Turner's. The critic

[1] *Life of Ruskin*, by E. T. Cook, I, xiv.

who existed inside Ruskin the crusader may have had
doubts concerning their work which he did not feel about
Turner's; but their pictures were undoubtedly above the
average of the work which was then regularly shown at the
Academy exhibitions, and he was stimulated by their
unjust treatment to make the most of any points of sympathetic contact. Their obvious sincerity and seriousness
enabled him to build his idealistic scaffolding around their
works. Even so, the exploitation of Turner's quality was
not a sign of strength in his position while defending them.
Turner was a mystic in pigment who pursued the one
beauty, and he was devoted to particular impressions of
general truths, not to particular impressions of particular
facts. The declared principle of the Pre-Raphaelites, of
' truth to nature ', seems to have been applied by some of
them, though not very effectually, in aiming at the false
realism of accuracy in detail which gives to secondary facts
an unjust prominence in a composition. Moreover, in
some of even their best pictures one feels that the skill and
care about detail outreach the painter's imaginative scope.
Millais's ' Lorenzo and Isabella ' is, technically, the painting of a marvellous youth, but compare its brilliant representation with Rossetti's ' The Girlhood ', and who can
deny that the latter, if not so well drawn, is nevertheless
more interesting, and touches a deeper recognition in us?
Hunt's ' Rienzi ' is not dramatic as it ought to be, because
the feeling is not focused anywhere, while the ' Lady of
Shalott ', in spite of every possible romantic cliché, lacks
the dream atmosphere which must have inspired the
painter in reading Tennyson's poem. Here Hunt was
carrying out both of the Pre-Raphaelite aims, not only the
detailed observation of nature, but also the serious invent-
ive thought. When he is content to do without some heroic
or poetic theme his detail makes his picture banal, as in
' Morning Prayer '. Yet all critics concur in saying that
the principal example by Rossetti of what may be called
the anecdotal type, the picture called ' Found ', is one of

his greatest works, and if completed would have been the greatest. In this picture a scene which may have been suggested by William Bell Scott's narrative poem, ' Mary Anne ', is shown with a power one looks for vainly in the poem. The theme of the poor and affianced girl who has been a rich man's cast-off mistress was as much in the air then as the theme of the unfaithful wife is to-day. Only a painter who was a great artist could take a dramatic moment from such a story and show us beauty without sentimentality or melodrama.

The greatest of the other Pre-Raphaelites, Millais, Hunt, and (though he was not a member of the P.R.B.) G. F. Watts, could descend with facility into the banal or sentimental. It might fairly be said that Millais's finest pictures, like his beautiful ' Ophelia ', are in the spirit of Rossetti's art rather than in that of ' Pre-Raphaelitism ': it is not so much the distinctively Pre-Raphaelite elements of ' Ophelia ' which make it a beautiful picture as the happy union of a peculiar imaginative atmosphere with good painting. Millais very easily became commonplace when the touch of true poetry went from his work. The virtue of Hunt's pictures is to be traced to his earnest sincerity and patience which softly shine through the best designs and often save them from the banality of misplaced detail. It seems as if the more skilful painters were all inferior to Rossetti as creators, and as if his imagination inspired them with a higher strain of poetry than that which was their wont, just as Shelley's personal contacts with Byron were reflected by a new subtlety in the latter's poetry. Deliberate obedience to a principle of revolt may have put them more in Rossetti's debt than they would otherwise have been, for it is certain that he was the least influenced in his work by any kind of system. Hunt, at least, seems to have partially confused attention to detail with truth, and to have forgotten the impossibility of absolute realism.[1]

[1] In his reminiscences he disclaimed realism as an object of the Pre-Raphaelites, but this sounds like wisdom after the event.

Their ' truth to nature ' was a good and useful slogan, but the impulse of reaction led them to identify it in practice with literalness. Prosper Mérimée, in describing the movement, illustrated the Pre-Raphaelite principle of truth to nature by explaining that, in painting a portrait it is not enough to represent the face and expression of the model; it is necessary to copy just as faithfully his boots, and if these have been re-soled, care must be taken to note this labour on the part of the cobbler. This may have been carrying the description a little too far—and in any case it is applicable to pictures by painters who were not ostensibly Pre-Raphaelites, such as the splendid ' Work ' by Ford Madox Brown, but it is essentially a just condemnation of the tendency to exchange ' sloshy ' truth-to-general-effect for detail insufficiently subordinated to artistic unity. Does it not, moreover, suggest a revolt in painting very similar to the Wordsworthian revolt in poetry fifty years before? Rossetti was the furthest from a false realism of all the chief Pre-Raphaelites, and if any evidence of this other than that of his paintings is needed, one has only to ask whether as a poet he is nearer to the critical Wordsworth or the critical Coleridge. It was on the question of a similar false realism that Wordsworth quarrelled with the profound Coleridge, who, as a critic, was compelled to disassociate himself from the extremist champion of ' natural ' diction.

Yet the emphasis would be wrongly placed if Rossetti's endeavour to see accurately were ignored. The picture ' Found ', for instance, shows a cobbled street of a market town at dawn, a small cart and a calf in it, in a rope-netting. The young man, dressed as a farm-worker in smock and gaiters, who was driving the cart, has come to the pavement edge and is trying to raise up a kneeling woman, who strives to turn her face from him in an agony of shame. He is the man she was once engaged to marry. The pen-and-ink studies were done in 1853, and the oil picture, uncompleted, in 1854. In September 1853 he is

writing from London to his mother at Frome and suddenly
refers to his intention of doing the painting:

I believe I shall be wanting to paint a brick wall, and a white heifer
tied to a cart going to market. Such things are I suppose to be had at
Frome, and it has occurred to me that I should like if possible to come
and paint them there. There is a cattle-market, is there not? Have you
ever seen such an article as the heifer in question, and have you or
Christina any recollection of an elegible and accessible brick wall? I
should want to get up and paint it early in the mornings, as the light
ought to be that of dawn. It should be not too countrified (yet beautiful in colour), as it is to represent a city-wall. A certain modicum of
moss would therefore be admissible, but no prodigicality of grass, weeds,
ivy, etc. Can you give any information on these heads?

At first sight this might seem to indicate an attitude
indistinguishable from that of the painter who toured Syria
for 'local colour'. Rossetti eventually painted the calf in
the cart while staying with Madox Brown in Finchley,
which was then more like a country village than the suburb
of London which it is now. But Holman Hunt's pursuit
of realism had a difference. Rossetti needed to see a calf
in a cart merely to draw these objects needed for his
composition, just as he went to Sevenoaks with Hunt on
one occasion to paint woodland as a background to a
picture which was never done. But almost any calf and
cart would have served his purpose. (If he mentioned a
heifer in his letter it was probably because the symbolic
sense of it appealed to him for such a picture as 'Found'.)
Now Hunt tells us that while he was in Jerusalem, after
travelling about Syria, he wanted a young white goat as a
model for his completion of 'The Temple'. An Arab
undertook to get one for him. 'Having until January
searched in vain, he delighted me after two or three days
by appearing with a model which was nigh perfect; the
price was a fancy one, the animal was tired with his
journey, and it was petted in every degree as a precious
possession, but the next day it died before I could do a
touch from it. I then had to send off two venturesome lads
for another, and in a week, in the middle of February,

they returned with a kid without a trace of brown or black on his coat, save for a patch on the off side. This animal served me to the end of my stay. . . .'[1]

It might be said that Rossetti, although he did not go travelling, was just as careful to get the actual objects he wanted to represent in his picture. But so far as this was a matter of taking special trouble or incurring unusual expense, Rossetti's acquirements were usually to gain a sensuous pleasure quite as much as for the sake of accuracy to facts. The special purchases, on which his expenditure was often lavish, of coloured cloths and blooms, for example, were not due to a pursuit of realism but to a taste for the sumptuous in *décor*. He would paint such flowers as roses and honeysuckles with a ' truth to nature ' which had been rare in English art before the time of the P.R.B., but it was not this kind of accuracy of observation which compelled Ruskin to admire the gorgeous beauty of the roses in the ' Venus Verticordia ', painted in the sixties, a picture of which he strongly disapproved.

More than a year before the intervention of Ruskin, the P.R.B.'s had been urged by Rossetti into collaborating to produce a magazine. The result was *The Germ*, which ran for only four numbers, and then died the natural death of such unworldly things, notwithstanding the judicious alteration of the title to *Art and Poetry* for the third and fourth numbers. *The Germ* affords us contemporary evidence of the deliberate aims of the Pre-Raphaelite group; it is also sufficient proof that whatever part Rossetti played, intentionally or unintentionally, in the Pre-Raphaelite innovations in painting, all of the so-called Pre-Raphaelite movement in literature is, purely and simply, due to his influence, whether as painter or as poet; his potent work produced definite effects in literature as the work of every powerful writer must do, sooner or later. If there is a peculiar and remarkable feature of Rossetti's influence, it is in the importance of the men whose work was affected by it.

[1] *Pre-Raphaelitism*, chap. xviii, by Holman Hunt.

The literary contents of *The Germ*, of permanent importance, consisted almost entirely of the seven poems contributed by Christina and the eleven by Dante Gabriel Rossetti, and the latter's fine prose pieces, ' Hand and Soul ' and ' An Autopsychology ' (afterwards entitled ' St. Agnes of Intercession '). Woolner's early poems, in the strain of the early Tennyson, ' My Beautiful Lady ' and ' Of my Lady in Death ' afford some useful evidence of the earnest mood of the group; being distinctly minor poetry they sound still the contemporary note more clearly than the Rossettis' poetry. The propaganda in *The Germ* is not impressive. The sonnet on the cover, by William Rossetti, the editor, is an abstract defence of independence in the service of truth rather than an explicit creed; it is specially addressed to potential critics who are told to ask ' Is this truth?' rather than to say ' So this is all!' when they find that someone is striving after honesty of thought instead of paraphrasing and mangling borrowed ideas. The anonymous announcement at the end of No. 1 concerning the aims of the magazine is very sketchy, and strengthens the feeling that the crystallizing of a mood into anything like a respectable set of principles was due to Ruskin's polemical defence in the following year. But the editorial proclamation does announce the intention in writings on ' Art ' to ' encourage and enforce an entire adherence to the simplicity of Nature ' (one can imagine Dante Gabriel reading his brother's script and putting ' and enforce ' in after ' encourage '!). An article on ' The Subject in Art ', by J. L. Tupper, the son of the magazine's friendly printer, affords evidence in confirmation of Holman Hunt's denial that Pre-Raphaelitism was a form of archaism. Tupper declared: ' we see that the antique, however successfully it may have been wrought, is not our model; for, according to that faith demanded at setting out, fine art delights us from its being the semblance of what in nature delights. Now, as the artist does not work by the instrumentality of rule and science, but mainly by an instinctive impulse, if he copy the antique, unable as he is to segregate the merely delectable matter, he must needs copy the whole, and thereby multiply models, which the casting-man can do equally well. . . .' This is, one must confess, a strange hotch-potch of half-baked ideas, and so is the greater part of the article from which it is extracted. The intention is not doubtful, in this particular passage, but one is driven back again to Ruskin for the voice of Pre-Raphaelitism. Ruskin's perceptive enthusiasm when he visited the centres of the true Pre-Raphaelite art in Italy has a curious counterpart in his self-criticism as a poet. Here his attitude, as in the case of the early Italian painters, anticipates that of the P.R.B. The letters he writes about his own early poems are, as E. T. Cook suggested,[1] more valuable than the poems. In one of these letters, written in 1845 to W. H. Harrison, an editor who had published a good deal of his verse, are some apt remarks about the imaginative realism of true poetry, and these remarks contain, prophetically, all the verity that could be found a couple of years later in the nursling ' Pre-Raphaelite ' creed. Harrison wrote piously to ask Ruskin what was ' the classical source of inspiration ' for a passage in ' The Last Song of Arion ':

> Farewell! but do not grieve: thy pain
> Would seek me where I sleep;
> Thy tears would pierce, like rushing rain,
> The stillness of the deep.

In reply, after confessing that he never had been vain of ' The Last Song of Arion ', and was ' now most heartily ashamed of it ', Ruskin wrote:

The fact is, that every thought in it—and it hasn't many—is so irretrievably well known and well used, that I am much surprised at any trouble being taken about their genealogy, as if I had been asked for a list of all the snuff-stained fingers which a dirty Scotch one-pound note —coming to pieces in mine from sheer age—might possibly have mouldered through. Nevertheless, I can very honestly say, respecting these same dirty notes, that I found them in my own purse without knowing how they came there; and I believe their very commonplaceness

[1] *Life*, vol. i, chap. iv.

arises from their being the genuine and natural expressions of true passion at any age of the world, rather than from their being borrowed by one writer from another . . .

I was about to say, that when I spoke of the feeling in question being common to all *ages* of the world, it was not among all *nations* that I suppose it to have been so, but only among those with whom some traditions of the Patriarchal or Mosaic dispensations had distinctly remained, or in modern times among Christians. Almost all true *ghost* feeling is, I believe, Christian ; but the most pure and beautiful expression of this particular one that I recollect is in the Border ballad—

'. . . The Bairnies grat;
The Mither, though under the mools, heard that.'

I conceive that nothing can beat the purity and precision and intensity of this poetic diction. The bringing the unimportant word to the end of the line when you are compelled to lay the right emphasis upon it by the rhyme; the straightforward unadorned simplicity of it; the quiet order of the natural words—how superior to my turgid piece of cold, degrading, and unnatural simile : 'Thy tears would pierce like *rushing rain*'—as if rain ever *did* pierce to a dead man's ear, or as if tears were no more to be counted of than protoxide of hydrogen, or as if a dying man would have thought of the tears being like anything but themselves, or as if a loving man would ever have compared his mistress's tears to a thunder-shower. . . .

Ruskin was the champion of artistic sincerity, and it was by the genuine feeling for his subjects that Rossetti had the best claim to be a force in Pre-Raphaelitism, but the admission makes it necessary to think of the P.R.B. as essentially a revival of romanticism in painting.

CHAPTER IX

THE EARLY ITALIAN POETS

'*An immense accession, even to one's means of understanding Dante's early life.*'—D. G. ROSSETTI.

THE TRANSLATIONS from the Italian were published first in 1861 under the title of *The Early Italian Poets*, Ruskin financing the venture. When the book had sold out the royalties paid Ruskin back his loan and left £9 over for the industrious translator. In 1874 the translations reappeared, with the title *Dante and His Circle*. In the first edition the arrangement was in two parts, the first a chronological collection of the poets preceding Dante. A second section contained poems by 'Dante and His Circle'. The later arrangement served to 'make more evident at a glance' the 'important relation to Dante' of the complete collection. Rossetti's preface shows that he saw the value and unusual character of the book, and also the limitations due to monotony of theme and obscurity of some of the poems. The obscurities of Cavalcanti are discussed in his letter to C. E. Norton, July 1858, when he sends Norton the proofs of Cavalcanti's poems. The obscurities, he assures his correspondent, 'are a thousand times more murky than in the original. One poem— No. 28—I have endeavoured to seem knowing about in the headings I have put, but must confess in private that I do not half understand it. And this applies to some others'. The poem is the one to which Rossetti supplied the heading 'He laments the presumptions and incontinence of his youth'. Regarding the unique value of his collection, he says that he has had to find out everything for himself, and 'I really feel it to be worth doing, as they

are an immense accession even to one's means of understanding Dante's early life, apart from their own poetical
interest'. It may be safely assumed that the work would
never have been carried through but for a passionate
interest in Dante alone.

The work of translating the early Italian poets taught
Rossetti many things, not always useful, in the formation
of his style, and for this reason as well as the intrinsic value
of the translations it is advisable to examine in some detail
Rossetti's earliest poetic work of importance.

The obscurities and difficult involutions in these translations do not need much searching for, and a good
example of the translator struggling to perform impossible
miracles is Pisano's canzone ' Of his Change through
Love '. The intellectual subtlety and technical sleight of
hand are here which drew from Coventry Patmore the
admiring remark: ' How I envy the iron muscle and
electric nerve which everywhere appears in your poetic
diction! ' and ' It seems to me to be the first time that a
translator has proved himself, by his translations alone,
to be a *great* poet '.[1] But this applies only to the translation
of Dante. With the inferior material only the dexterity of
the translator is apparent.

The first two strophes of Pisano's canzone are these:

> My lady, thy delightful high command,
>   Thy wisdom's great intent,
>   The worth which ever rules thee in thy sway
> (Whose righteousness of strength has ta'en in hand
>   Such full accomplishment
>   As height makes worthy of more height alway),
> Have granted to thy servant some poor due
>   Of thy perfection; who
> From them has gain'd a proper will so fix'd,
>   With other thought unmix'd,
> That nothing save thy service now impels
> His life, and his heart longs for nothing else.

---

[1] Quoted in *Memoir*, p. 215.

Beneath thy pleasure, lady mine, I am:
The circuit of thy will,
The force of all my life, to serve thee so:
Never but only this I think or name,
Nor ever can I fill
My heart with other joy that man may know.
And hence a sovereign blessedness I draw,
Who soon most clearly saw
That not alone my perfect pleasure is
In this my life-service;
But Love has made my soul with thine to touch
Till my heart feels unworthy of so much.

The long and tortured sentences in the complicated metrical scheme are not easy to read, and the effort of translating both the language and the form probably did Rossetti's style no little injury. In the second strophe the rhyme 'draw' and 'saw' is produced by an ingenious but otherwise unnecessary change of tense; the awkward placing of the relative 'who' is characteristic of this pseudo-archaic style adopted by Rossetti. The fourth strophe of the same poem concludes:

And so I do: and my delight is full,
Accepted for the servant of thy rule,

and the redundance of phrase in the last line is none the less perceived as redundance for all the cleverness with which the line is metrically filled out. In one of Rossetti's best sonnets of his maturity, 'The One Hope', which concludes *The House of Life*, the last line,

Not less nor more, but even that word alone,

shows that the poet had not lost the trick of providing, at a pinch, 'a mere filler to stop a vacancy'. The first line of the fifth strophe:

Without almost, I am all rapturous,

is unnecessarily obscure because of the strange use of 'almost', not to mention the unlucky clash with 'all', and the fall of the metrical stress on the second syllable of 'almost'.

Another mixed blessing which came to the poet through the exercise of his 'iron muscles' in translating was the helpful way of rhyming unaccented word-ends as if they were accented. An example is the rhyming of 'trembleth' with 'Death' in the song beginning 'Whatever while the thought comes over me' in *The New Life*. This kind of rhyme is not confined to Rossetti in English poetry, but it became an objectionable mannerism with him, no doubt because of the temptation to overwork it in the task of translating difficult rhyme schemes. When it is said, as A. C. Benson did say, that 'Rossetti's ear gave weak endings a certain emphasis which a pure-bred Englishman would hardly affix to them' one is justified in asking why Christina Rossetti was not subject to the same weakness. Her ear for Italian was much better than her brother's, and she remained throughout life much more at home in the language than he did. It would be easier to find such transferences of emphasis in the verse of unadulterated Englishmen like Swinburne and Shelley than in Christina Rossetti. In the translations from the Italian are many rhymes like 'minister—her', 'bring—marvelling', 'occasional—all', 'Salvation—son', which place beyond doubt the source of a mannerism which Buchanan parodied in:

> When winds do roar and rains do pour,
> Hard is the life of the sailor :
> He scarcely, as he reels, can tell
> The side-lights from the binnacle :
> He looketh on the wild water . . .

which William Rossetti said amused his brother.[1] In 'The Blessed Damozel', which is contemporary with the translations, these transferred stresses are used freely for rhyming, and with a sensitiveness of ear equalled by only the finest English poets. The decorative use of unusual words which also became typical of Rossetti's more ornate style may also probably be traced back, in part at least, to the use of words like 'consistory' when translating Dante.

[1] *Memoir*, p. 299.

[163]

Mainly, however, it was his researching among early romances and old English ballads which stocked him with ' stunning words '. And archaic English verse is of course the proper place to look for the idea adopted by later poets of rhyming on unaccented syllables.

There is a considerable variety of manners and metres in the work of the poets translated by Rossetti. Such a canzonetta as ' How he dreams of his Lady ', by Urbiciani, is a complete contrast to the floundering canzone by Pisano just quoted. The subject also is a reminder that dreams, whether real or feigned, are constantly occurring in these early Italian poems. Rossetti has a long note on Guido Orlandi's sonnet to Dante Da Maiano, ' He interprets the Dream related in the foregoing Sonnet '. There are three sonnets in a group by the two poets; the first, by Dante da Maiano, to Dante Alighieri, is a flippant explanation of the dream related in the first sonnet of the *Vita Nuova*. The second is also flippant, putting into the form of a dream a love-affair, and this is the subject of a rebuke by Orlandi. But trances, visions, and dreams are used with serious poetic intent also, though by none so finely as by Dante himself. The frequency of the dream in Rossetti's original work[1] may owe something to his observation of its employment by the poets he translated, especially by Dante. In the case of ' Hand and Soul ' and ' St. Agnes of Intercession ' there is no doubt of this.

For all that Pater called ' poetic anthropomorphism ' in Rossetti's poetry, the detailed personification of Love and Death and other abstractions, Rossetti found a model in these early Italian poets. The device, like that of the dream and the vision, is an important part of the *Vita Nuova*, and is sometimes carried to a pitch which is only sustained without bathos by the sincerity and great expressive power of the poet. After Love has appeared to him in a vision as a youth in white raiment, Dante resolves to ' make a

[1] See chap. xiv.

[164]

ditty ' about it, and he begins by addressing his own Song
as he would address a person:

> Song, 'tis my will that thou do seek out Love
> And go with him where my dear lady is;
> So that my cause, the which thy harmonies
> Do plead, his better speech may clearly prove . . .

So the ditty continues, being at once an address to
itself by the poet and also the message which he wishes to
communicate.

> With a sweet accent, when thou com'st to her,
> Begin thou in these words,
> First having craved a gracious audience :
> ' He who hath sent me as his messenger,
> Lady, thus much records,
> An' thou but suffer him, in his defence.
> Love, who comes with me, by thine influence
> Can make this man do as it liketh him:
> Wherefore, if this fault *is* or doth but *seem*
> Do thou conceive: for his heart cannot move '.

This, detached from its context, evidently comes to the
verge where the sublime and the ridiculous adjoin, and the
fact justifies the translator's resort to an archaic affectation.
In the prose commentary following the Song, Dante says:
' Some might contradict me, and say that they understand
not whom I address in the second person, seeing that the
ditty is merely the very words I am speaking. And therefore I say that this doubt I intend to solve and clear up in
this little book itself, at a more difficult passage, and then
let him understand who now doubts, or would now contradict as aforesaid '.

Later he describes another apparition of Love and again
represents Love as speaking to him. There follows now
the promised explanation of the personifying of impersonal
things. ' It might be here objected unto me (and even by
one worthy of controversy), that I have spoken of Love as
though it were a thing outward and visible: not only a
spiritual essence, but as a bodily substance also ', the poet
says, not quite meeting the merely rational objection that

Love is represented as a person. Dante's defence is that the old classical poets did it, but he hardly seems to realize the weakness of such a defence, for the old classical poets were not thinking of abstractions in a metaphysical sense. The 'sweet new style' of Italian rhyme and diction which, with his own *Vita Nuova*, triumphed over the convention of writing in Latin metre, should entitle the poet, he claims, to a licence at least equal to that of the Latin poets. 'That the Latin poets have done this, appears through Virgil, where he saith that Juno (to wit, a goddess hostile to the Trojans) spake unto Aeolus, master of the Winds ' . . . and that Aeolus replied. Again the inanimate thing is made to speak to the animate, while in Lucan the animate speaks to the inanimate, in Horace, as in Homer, man speaks to his own intelligence as to another person, while Ovid makes Love speak as a human being. But before this argument, Dante limits the use of Italian rhyming to matters concerning love, ' that mode of speech having been first used for the expression of love alone '. Rossetti regarded this as the reason why Dante put philosophical poems into the form of love poems: ' He liked writing in Italian rhyme rather than Latin metre; he thought Italian rhymes ought to be confined to love-poems; therefore whatever he wrote (at this age) had to take the form of a love-poem '. This carries us a little beyond the question of personification, but it is noteworthy that Dante's personification had a special fullness and subtlety owing to the metaphysical cast of his mind. His triumphant employment of the device is, to us, a better defence than his analogy with the older poets, though the early Italian poets did of course begin by imitating the device of the classical poets. Dante had to enlarge the scope of the device to serve a need for symbolizing a new vision of love. Rossetti adopted the device freely from Dante, and many of the *House of Life* sonnets written in his maturity show the trace of this discipleship.

The scope of the translated poems is wider in character

than the monotony of theme would suggest. It covered indeed rather more of the flippant and indecent than the youthful Rossetti, with one eye on Aunt Charlotte, could feel quite comfortable about. The collection, he remarked in his preface, 'includes now and then (though I believe in rare instances) matter which may not meet with universal approval; and whose introduction, needed as it is by the literary aim of my work, is I know inconsistent with the principles of pretty bookmaking'.

A quite pretty piece of paganism is the dialogue between a Lover and his Lady, by Ciullo D'Alcamo, which opened the original edition. The translator is not unsympathetic, although only the serious and more powerful Dante inspires him to his best efforts. In this dialogue it is clear that he found the metre and rhythm for 'The Blessed Damozel'. Each stanza without the final couplet is not merely formally similar to the 'Damozel' stanza, but moves in a similar rhythm. The alternating long and short verses with one thrice-used rhyme also sway the thought to and fro while progressing in the main direction of feeling. The comparison is the more noteworthy on account of the contrast of tone and, to a less extent, of theme, in the two poems. There is a great accession of poetic power in the original poem, and a freer use of the varying rhythmic pauses of thought. Most of the single verses[1] in the translated piece are without a pause, e.g.:

> Think not to fright me with thy nets
> And such like childish gear ;
> I am safe pent within the walls
> Of this strong castle here ;
> A boy before he is a man
> Could give me as much as fear.

And the rhythmic play induced by the pause, when it does occur in a verse, is comparatively ineffective. The last

[1] 'Verses' is used consistently here in the technical sense of 'lines', not the popular sense of 'stanzas'.

[167]

stanza shows a cruder versification than the 'Blessed Damozel', but an obviously similar rhythm:

> Now that this oath is sworn, sweet lord,
>   There is no need to speak:
> My heart, that was so strong before,
>   Now feels itself grow weak.
> If any of my words were harsh,
>   Thy pardon: I am meek
> Now, and will give thee entrance presently.
>   It is best so, sith so it was to be.

In the 'Blessed Damozel' the rhythmic pauses deviate from the metrical ones (the line-ends) as often as they coincide. The straightforward rhythm of

> When round his head the aureole clings,
>   And he is clothed in white,
> I'll take his hand and go with him
>   To the deep wells of light;
> We will step downward to a stream,
>   And bathe there in God's sight,

is gradually varied with more complicated effects gained from the caesura, which seems to hold the gaze a moment longer on profound images:

> It lies in Heaven, across the flood
>   Of ether, as a bridge.
> Beneath, the tides of day and night
>   With flame and darkness ridge
> The void, as low as where this earth
>   Spins like a fretful midge.

And:

> From the fixed place of Heaven she saw
>   Time like a pulse shake fierce
> Through all the worlds. Her gaze still strove
>   Within the gulf to pierce
> Its path, and now she spoke as when
>   The stars sang in their spheres.
>
> The sun was gone now; the curled moon
>   Was like a little feather
> Fluttering far down the gulf; and now
>   She spoke through the still weather.
> Her voice was like the voice the stars
>   Had when they sang together.

[168]

At this point it may be helpful to enquire how seriously one should take Rossetti's treatment of Leigh Hunt's remarks about ' The Blessed Damozel ' and other early poems. In 1848, it will be remembered, when Rossetti was feeling discouraged about his prospects as a painter, he sent a batch of verse in manuscript to Leigh Hunt and asked for advice. The parcel included translations from the Italians, the ' Blessed Damozel ', and probably ' Ave ' among other pieces. The translations seemed to Leigh Hunt to be ' harsh ', ' but when I came to the originals of your own, I recognized an unquestionable poet, thoughtful, imaginative, and with rare powers of expression. I hailed you such at once, without any misgiving; and beside your Dantesque heavens (without any hell to spoil them), admired the complete and genial round of your sympathies with humanity'. Writing to his Aunt Charlotte about this, he said: ' Where Hunt, in his kind letter, speaks of my " Dantesque heavens " he refers to one or two of the poems the scene of which is laid in the celestial regions, and which are written in a kind of Gothic manner which I suppose he is pleased to think belongs to the school of Dante '. Certain elements in both ' The Blessed Damozel ' and ' Ave ' are not to be explained by a ' Gothic manner '. The most interesting is the poet's attitude to the Virgin Mary. In ' The Blessed Damozel ', because the heroine of the piece is in the place of Beatrice, the Virgin is necessarily more exalted still and inaccessible. The ' Virgin Mother ' of the Paradiso (33) who is addressed by St. Bernard, she who is ' humbler and more exalted than any other creature ', is the same as ' the dear Mother ' in the ' Blessed Damozel '. Rossetti seems to have included more of the human side of the Virgin, which is caught by the early Italian painters rather than the poets. His sonnet for the ' Girlhood of the Virgin Mary ' is concerned entirely with that. In ' Ave ' is the double-sided aspect, to correspond with that of Dante's Paradiso, for there, besides the queendom of the Virgin her character of a friendly intermediary is realized. ' Ave ' is a remarkable poem to have been written by a youth who was not a Roman Catholic. In the first section the Virgin is addressed in her double character of

> Mother of the Fair Delight,
> Thou handmaid perfect in God's sight,

and also

> Thyself a woman-Trinity,—
> Being a daughter born to God,
> Mother of Christ from stall to rood,
> And wife unto the Holy Ghost,

therefore,

> Oh when our need is uttermost,
> Think that to such as death may strike
> Thou once wert sister sisterlike!
> Thou headstone of humanity,
> Groundstone of the great Mystery,
> Fashioned like us, yet more than we!

There follows a beautiful passage containing a picture which the poet afterwards put partly onto canvas. It contains also the statement that

> the sea
> Sighed further off eternally
> As human sorrow sighs in sleep.

When William Rossetti reminded him that the sea was not near enough to Nazareth to justify this, the poet retorted: ' I fear the sea must remain at Nazareth: you know an old painter would have made no bones if he wanted it for his background '. One wonders what the Pre-Raphaelite Holman Hunt would have said to this shameless ' early Christian ' indifference to facts! The poem concludes with another fine passage which reads like Dante translated into seventeenth-century ' metaphysical ' poetry:

> Soul, is it Faith, or Love, or Hope,
> That lets me see her standing up
> Where the light of the Throne is bright?
> Unto the left, unto the right,

The cherubim, succinct, conjoint,
Float inward to a golden point,
And from between the seraphim
The glory issues for a hymn.
O Mary Mother, be not loth
To listen,—thou whom the stars clothe,
Who seest and mayst not be seen!
Hear us at last, O Mary Queen!
Into our shadow bend thy face,
Bowing thee from the secret place,
O Mary Virgin, full of grace!

No other poet of the Victorian age, no other poet after the seventeenth century, except Francis Thompson and Gerard Hopkins, approached this magnificence in mystical religious poetry, where splendour of image is one with subtlety of perception. That it is only fragmentary is sufficiently accounted for by what truth was in Rossetti's repudiation of ' Dantesque heavens '. So long as he is inspired by the figure of the Virgin (or of Beatrice, which for him amounted to the same thing emotionally), he shares a feeling which is religious as well as aesthetic, with all the early Italian poets who were inspired by the refined Franciscan Maryolatry. The creative acceptance of the symbolism by poets and artists indicates not only an absence of sectarian antagonism to Roman Catholicism (and Rossetti, although he was not a Roman Catholic, was still less a Protestant) but also an introversion of mind in which the adoration of an ideal woman is the expression of a deep need of the soul. If Rossetti's poetry is not so rich as that of lesser poets in the mystical beauty which can be created with such an impulse, it should always be borne in mind that his genius spent half its energy in another medium, and if the Beatrice theme is essentially that of the Madonna, the total creative energy he spent on it in both painting and poetry is impressive. But just as he could not follow Dante into maturity of power, Rossetti, while deeply sympathetic to the mystical ideal he found in Dante, could not entirely absorb it, and preferred to romanticize the dream. How this came about

can be seen in following the lead given by the translations
he did from the German before approaching Dante.

The Italianate element in his work is not so much an
Italian background as a personal one. The figure of the
ideal divine Woman, the repressed paganism expressed in
torturing fears and hopes, the concrete hells and heavens,
appealed to him because something in him recognized
there an external reflection of itself. He might indeed be
regarded as less Italian than several English poets who
have sung of divine love in the mood of ecstasy induced by
a repression of the physical side of sex. The concentration
upon a Christian ideal of love in poetry like Crashaw's and
Francis Thompson's is at least quite as Italianate as any
ever written by Rossetti. Gerard Manley Hopkins, in the
nineteenth century, wrote a poem to ' The Blessed Virgin
compared to the Air we Breathe '. The following passage
is close to the Franciscan feeling of several early Italian
religious poets:

> This air, which, by Life's law,
> My lungs must draw and draw
> Now but breathe its praise,
> Minds me in many ways
> Of her who not only
> Gave God's infinity
> Dwindled to infancy
> Welcome in womb and breast,
> Birth, milk, and all the rest
> But mothers each new grace
> That does now reach our race—
> Mary Immaculate,
> Merely a woman, yet
> Great as no goddess's
> Was deemèd, dreamèd; who
> This one work has to do—
> Let all God's glory through,
> God's glory which would go
> Through her and from her flow
> Off, and no way but so.

CHAPTER X

DANTE AND THE DIVINE WOMAN

*' Supremely may be said absolutely or with respect to such
an one. None partaketh God supremely in the absolute sense,
but supremely with respect to himself. For each one partaketh
him so largely, not that he may not be partaken more, but that
he may not more partake him, because he may not advance
beyond, and is utterly content with that state which he hath.'*

BONAVENTURA.

IT IS an essential of any understanding of Rossetti
to realize that his lifelong feeling for mystery was
another aspect of the spiritual attitude or need revealed
in his ' early Christian ' phase as a painter and a poet.
That phase chronologically accompanied his Pre-Raphaelite beginnings as a painter, but had little to do with anything felt by the other P.R.B.'s except possibly the elevated
mood which gave to them a moral purpose in their revolutionary zeal. The fact that Rossetti's mother and sisters
were devoted members of the English High Church
reminds us of the deeply disturbed spiritual state of society
nearly a century ago. This disturbance was not confined
to England. It took various forms in Western Europe,
from political revolutions to religious and artistic revivals.
The poetic earthquake of the ' romantic revival ' seems in
retrospect but a phase of some deeper and more extensive
movement. Certainly the strange aesthetic change of outlook known as the Gothic Revival (which was in full
movement before Sir Walter Scott was heard of) did find
through the greatest member of the P.R.B. a peculiar
expression; in England perhaps its finest as it was almost
its latest expression. Moreover, certain developments of

the Gothic Revival were in harmony with that ecclesiastical return to features of early Christianity which produced the Oxford Movement. The revival of the mediaeval catholic spirit was largely an aesthetic one, though it involved a revival of faith freed from scientific or pseudo-scientific sophistication. If the Pre-Raphaelites are regarded as revolters against insincerity and lazy obedience to conventions in art, so may the Tractarians be regarded as fighting along almost parallel lines against the religious stagnation of the age. Christina Rossetti's poetry shows what this religious tendency meant to a poet and the extent to which her brother avoided the religious side of the experience. Although he nearly became one of the great mystical poets, earnestness in his poetry on religious themes more rarely becomes devotion than it does in Christina's; his ' Blessed Damozel ' is less truly religious than many of her ' secular ' and dreaming poems, though these may be indistinguishable in imagery from lyrical romanticism. A sidelight upon the religious controversies of the time is afforded by the incident of the libel action which Cardinal Newman won, brought against him by Dr. Achili, one of the ' various protestantizing Italians, most of them ex-Catholic priests'[1] who haunted Gabriele Rossetti's London home during his children's early years. While such Italian exiles were playing on Gabriele Rossetti's anti-papal convictions, prominent men in the English Church were turning towards Roman Catholicism. At the beginning of his career as a poet, which slightly antedates his first serious work as a painter, Rossetti with the suddenness of a conversion, discovered in Dante all the spiritual significance for himself which immaturity, and perhaps impatience with his father's eternal Dantesque commentaries, had hitherto prevented him realizing. He dismissed with a jest Leigh Hunt's impressionistic phrase ' Dantesque heavens ' for such work as ' The Blessed Damozel '; he was already aware of the profundity and intellectual

[1] *Memoir*, v.

austerity of the poet whose ' New Life ' was but a step
towards the *Divine Comedy*. Nevertheless, ' The Blessed
Damozel ' shows that in his earliest mood, which was
romantic rather than Dantesque, he was quickly ready to
absorb a fundamental idea from the early Italian poetry,
the idea of love spiritualized by longing, and of spiritual
states made concrete in plastic imagery. But he arrived
at this stage from a youthful admiration of the cruder
romance, not merely of Scott and Byron, but of M. G.
Lewis and Charles Maturin and Mrs. Wilde.

A consideration of this must be deferred because it leads
on to a succession of other subjects, whereas Rossetti's
Dantesque phase is more isolated, and practically ends early
in his career, the latest incident being the ' Beata Beatrix '
painting of 1863, which represents a reaching back to a
spiritual state which had flowered into the translations of
the early Italian poets and the pictures between ' The
Girlhood of Mary Virgin ' (1848) and ' Dante's Dream '
(1856). Careful studies for the ' Beata Beatrix ' were done
from 1859 to 1861. But nearly everything after 1856
which has a Dantesque theme is either a replica or an
elaboration of earlier versions or careful studies. The
' Dante's Dream ' of 1856 was a fine water-colour, which
Marillier describes as ' in certain points the most beautiful
version of the subject which afterwards served for Rossetti's
largest picture '[1] (which belongs to 1871). To quote again
from Marillier: ' Love arrayed in bright blue, instead of in
flame-red as later versions represent him, is leading a very
grave and sorrowful Dante up to the bier whereon in a
vision he saw his lady lie. Her maidens at head and at foot
are lowering or holding up a snowy pall, on which are
strewed symbolic sprigs of hawthorn bloom. Poppies of
death cover the floor. The scene is an interior, with open
vistas to right and left, showing the sunny city of Florence,
and the winding Arno. Certain features, such as the red
birds of love flying in and out at the openings and filling

[1] *Rossetti*, p. 72.

all the house, are absent in this earlier picture, which gains by a depth of feeling peculiarly its own, by entire freedom from affectation in the expression of the faces, and by the simple beauty of the recumbent Beatrice, with her golden hair.' At this time the painter had not yet gone to Oxford, where in 1859 he met Jane Burden, afterwards Mrs. William Morris, who served as the Beatrice of the large picture of 1871. The earlier Beatrice of 1856 was done from Mrs. James Hannay. William Sharp's opinion of the water-colour was not quite so favourable as Marillier's. Not only are the faces (except Dante's) less attractive than in the later picture, he says, but ' the live green colours of the two ladies lifting the canopy from Beatrice ' are ' in too strong a contrast with the blue of Love '.[1] It is not necessary to settle the question of preference; the earlier picture may be at least as good a piece of work as the later, which is enough to rob the later of originality. The significant fact is that after he was about thirty he almost ceased to originate designs with either Dantesque or what may conveniently be termed Catholic themes. And the Dantesque inspiration, which had first of all superseded the terror-romance, during the 1850's shared Rossetti's attention with other forms of romantic archaism. There is an early indication of divided attention in 1844 and again from 1848, that is to say, early in each phase, first the phase of Bürger's ' Lenore ' and then the Dantesque-Catholic divine Woman phase. In his 1844 translation of ' Lenore ', Rossetti deliberately altered ' pray to our Heavenly Father ' into ' utter an Ave Marie '. An examination of Marillier's chronology of his pictures shows that from 1848 to 1851, when he was painting the well-known ' Girlhood ' and ' Ecce Ancilla ', and the earliest Beatrice Salutation pictures (one pen-and-ink, one water-colour), he was also making designs from poems by Poe, Coleridge, and Browning, not to mention ' Gretchen and Mephistopheles in the Chapel ', from *Faust*.

[1] p. 142, Sharp.

DANTE AND THE DIVINE WOMAN

The alteration in Bürger's ' Lenore ' has made one commentator see ' an inclination to catholicize the atmosphere of the poem, which in the original is essentially protestant ', so that ' in his earliest works Rossetti displayed those Catholic sympathies which are entirely in harmony with the nature of Romanticism in literature and art '.[1] This is a dangerous generalization, but the suggestion of significance in Rossetti's alteration is valuable. It needs no argument to show that ' Romanticism ' is not necessarily an aspect of ' Catholicism ', because the very ballad Rossetti altered is a typical piece of terror-romanticism, and it is ' essentially protestant '. But there was probably a deeper personal cause, an intuitive choice of a goddess instead of a god, which is expressed throughout Rossetti's Dantesque phase, and this choice would of course favour Roman Catholic symbolism. It was the love of Dante for Beatrice which captured Rossetti's imagination, and Beatrice is a symbol for the same ideal as the Virgin Mary, the perfect and unearthly Woman. The quality of his translations from the Italian, particularly of Dante, is derived from Rossetti's kinship with the poet of the ' New Life ', which may be considered as the finest record in poetry of idealized passion. It is very characteristic of Rossetti's career that by his translation of the *Vita Nuova* he traversed spiritually (for he deeply felt Dante's inspiration) the field which he revisited in many of his finest early pictures and designs. No sensitive reader of Rossetti's version can doubt that as much emotional impulse went into it as could be found in his original poems of the same period.

The long poem on ' Dante at Verona ' was a pious testimony of the youthful poet's devotion, and indicates a painstaking study of Dante as he is revealed in the *Commedia* as well as the *Vita Nuova*. The poem was worked on during several years; it exhibits the poet's fine skill in

[1] L. A. Willoughby, *D. G. Rossetti and German Literature—a public lecture*, 1912.

verse and his power of mental concentration. These are
not the qualities which one first thinks of in reading his
passionate translation of the *Vita Nuova*. The labour expended upon the poem hardly fulfils the promise of the opening stanzas; perhaps the reason is in the third and fourth:

> Follow his feet's appointed way :—
>   But little light we find that clears
>   The darkness of the exiled years.
> Follow his spirit's journey :—nay,
>   What fires are blent, what winds are blown
>   On paths his feet may tread alone?
>
> Yet of the twofold life he led
>   In chainless thought and fettered will
>   Some glimpses reach us,—somewhat still
> Of the steep stairs and bitter bread,—
>   Of the soul's quest whose stern avow
>   For years had made him haggard now.

The two themes, ' Of Florence and of Beatrice ', were
difficult material for a poem extending to no less than
eighty-five six-line stanzas. The poet is labouring all the
while to subdue the anecdotal interests to the dominating
mood. Having written

> The soul could soar from earth's vain throng,
> And Heaven and Hell fulfil the song . . .

And:

> Therefore, the loftier rose the song
>   To touch the secret things of God,
>   The deeper pierced the hate that trod
> On base men's track who wrought the wrong;
>   Till the soul's effluence came to be
>   Its own exceeding agony,

the poet could only return at intervals to the same vision.
There was no spiritual progression possible: the poem just
goes on with incidents. All Rossetti's feeling was taken up
by the central idea. His imagination tended to manifest
itself in jets of brilliance: he was moved by one vision of
Dante, the undaunted exile whose love for Beatrice paid
the world's exile back with a more complete exile from his
own soul.

The question of the identity of Dante's Beatrice has

never been settled, nor that of the degree in which his love was at one with his feeling for a particular woman. Although the absolute sincerity of the lovely confession which he called 'The New Life' is above all doubt, there is no need to assume that Dante merely recorded a hopeless love for Bice Portinari, or some other young girl in Florence. The whole book is the creation of a powerfully repressed desire changed into aspiration. When the poet wrote it (just past his mid twenties, and married to a woman he did not respect), he was experiencing at the moment of creation a rapture of mystical contemplation; his mind, caught in the wind of emotion and winged with beauty, used a woman as a symbol for his adoration of ideal love. This book of the New Life alone would dispose of the assertion of a French critic,[1] and others, that the mystical element in Rossetti's work is of the North, and not Italian. It is impossible to make these geographical divisions either for mysticism or for the other elements to be traced in Rossetti's work.

It is a curious thing that while in one context criticism is found attributing Rossetti's mysticism to the North, in another—that of Dante Alighieri—it is apt to attribute a special feeling for dark mysteries to Dante's age and environment. Such generalizations are the results of historical perspective, which depends too much on personal vision. If 'the North' is to be objected to as an explanation of Rossetti's love of mysteries as also of his mysticism, the South also, represented by Dante, must be treated as similarly inadequate. In 1861, the year following his marriage, after making beautiful studies for 'Beata Beatrix', Rossetti wrote the sonnet:

DANTIS TENEBRAE
(In Memory of my Father)

And didst thou know indeed, when at the font
Together with thy name thou gav'st me his,
That also on thy son must Beatrice
Decline her eyes according to her wont,

---

[1] Edouard Rod: quoted in *Memoir*, p. 428.

DANTE GABRIEL ROSSETTI

Accepting me to be of those that haunt
  The vale of magical dark mysteries
  Where to the hills her poet's foot-track lies,
And wisdom's living fountain to his chaunt
Trembles in music? This is that steep land
  Where he that holds his journey stands at gaze
    Tow'rd sunset, when the clouds like a new height
Seem piled to climb. These things I understand:
  For here, where day still soothes my lifted face,
    On thy bowed head, my father, fell the night.

Thus in early maturity he seems about to pursue the arduous path followed by Dante, from the ' New Life ' to its accomplishment in the 'Divine Comedy'. In this sonnet Beatrice is already a kind of sybil, no longer solely the ideal of youthful love but the voice of divine wisdom. The measure of Rossetti's mind and temperament is indicated largely by what attracted him most in Dante. He never advanced further than the momentary reflection in this sonnet along the path of Dante. The full scope of the Florentine poet was beyond him. His deepest sympathy was with the Dante whose spiritual home was the Purgatory, but whose aspirations came to birth with the experience described in the ' New Life '. Although Dante's austere development led him away from distinction as an erotic poet, he is also the poet of the profane love of Paolo and Francesca, and the vivid passage in the *Inferno* (v, 112-136) inspired drawings by Rossetti in 1854 and 1855, to which he returned for the triptych painted in 1862. Rossetti would have understood the spiritual crisis, involving contrite repentance or conversion, which is indicated in the conclusion of the ' Purgatory '; but that passing through the dark valley which strengthened the aspiring poet of the New Life to become the epical poet of the Divine Comedy dismayed and for a time blinded the lesser man. Dante's Paradise was for him a subject for pictures in the ' early Christian ' style and something which in poetry could be ' written in a kind of Gothic manner '.

Carlyle said that in the Divine Comedy 'ten silent Christian centuries have found a voice', and indeed the historical significance of Dante's vision is not negligible. But it is necessary to insist that this is not an essential: the love of magical dark vales, the contemplation of sin, the agonies of remorse, the cleansing of repentance are universal experiences. In blending the individual lyrical cries of his contemporaries and of his youthful self into a vast scheme built up on an intellectual framework, Dante creates a concrete universe of human thought which transcends any historical period. Nevertheless, in reading the early Italian poets translated by Rossetti it is well to realize how the new ideal of love had come into poetry. The soul of a half-Christian Europe had been tortured with the gloomiest view of the corruption of human nature, the sinfulness of sexual desire, and even of procreation. There were violent alternations of ascetic severity and gross animalism. The Church authorities united in stressing the sordidness of this world. ' A characteristic and much read work of the twelfth century', says Federn,[1] 'was the treatise of Cardinal Lothar (afterwards Pope Innocent VII of the family which later on was called de Conti), *De contemptu mundi sive de miseria humanae conditionis* (" Of the Contempt of the World and the Miseries of the Human State "), which was soon translated into Italian by Bono Giamboni. It contains sentences like the following: " Man is composed of dirt and the most vulgar nutriments, while other things are made out of much nobler instruments, for the Sage says that the stars and planets are made of fire, spirits and winds of air, fishes and birds of water. . . . The trees produce leaves, blossoms and fruits out of themselves, men vermin and lice; the former produce wine and oil and balms, the latter excrements. The former produce sweetest odours, the latter abominable stench. . . . If thou wilt well think on it, woman conceives her son in the heat of lust, gives him birth in pain and sorrow, nourishes him with

[1] *Dante and his Time*, by Karl Federn, chap. 2.

fear and toil, and watches him with care and anxiety, all
this is just natural impulse. . . . The new-born boy says
' A ', the woman ' E ', which are both the sounds of woe
and pain, as many as there are born of Eve's race ".' Peter
Lombard, a very influential ecclesiastic author, wrote that
the joys of the blessed would be enhanced after the Judgment by the aspect of the damned in their pain.

The reader of Leigh Hunt's ' Critical Notice to Dante's
Life and Genius ', which serves as preface to the *Stories
from the Italian Poets*, will remember that Hunt could not
stomach Dante's Hell and Purgatory. Nevertheless,
Dante's pictures of punishment were no gloomier, and less
morbid, than the people of his time were familiar with.
And it was out of that vortex of conflicting fears and
hopes that the dynamic power of a new ideal developed.
The dying nightmares of paganism were the birth-
throes of the ideal of universal love and the doctrine of
universal equality. These ideas did more perhaps, as
Federn says, ' for the moral development of mankind than
any other element in human history. We generally forget
the hard and frightful cruelty of the ancient races when
we admire the splendour of their feats and accomplish-
ments.' In the creative process of art there was another
channel besides the social-political and religious for the
power of this new ideal. The poets and painters inevitably
were inspired by the new vision and contributed to it
renewed expressions. Elsewhere[1] I have sketched the
connection between the spiritual re-birth in Europe and its
consequences in art, especially in poetry.

The precursor and admired master of the poet of ' The
New Life ' was Guido Guinicelli, who belonged to a noble
family of Bologna and died in 1276. His famous canzone
of the Gentle Heart is an anticipatory poetic statement of
the ideal which inspired ' The New Life '. Guinicelli
himself represents a development of the refining process
which had been going on in Italian poetry from the time

[1] In *Francis Thompson*, chap. 9, 13, and 14.

of the chivalrous poetry of Sicily, in which the Provençal and German romantic exaltation of love became gradually imbued with the Christian spirit at the very time when the ecclesiastic fear-born detestation of woman was still most powerful. As the Italian poetry approaches Dante it displays a growing freedom and sensibility in translating the ecstasies of love, whether in the sweet and sensuous sonnets of Cino da Pistoja or the nobility of Guinicelli. The impetus which had made the humble Franciscans a revolutionary power had sprung out of the same need to express the new vision of love-inspired beauty. St. Francis's Hymn to the Sun has the very feeling of an address to Beatrice by Dante. Another Franciscan, Jacopone da Todi, wrote the beautiful *Stabat Mater Dolorosa*; another, Thomas of Celano, wrote the *Dies Irae*. So amid the ruins of the rich pagan antiquity such impulses in the European soul were finding expression, and at last needed only a Dante to sheave them all together. If the subject of the ' Divine Comedy ' is the whole world, the poem is none the less the story of Dante's own soul, though less personal a story than ' The New Life '.

' The New Life ' is the perfect expression of the sublime egoism of beauty-worshipping youth. With the intermediary symbol of the figure of Love, his Lord, the poet really identifies the imperishable part of himself. Beatrice is a kind of self-realization, a necessary symbol of an exalted beauty. The undoubtedly autobiographical element in the poem gives it depth of feeling, but this element might easily in the hands of a lesser poet have become a sentimental adoration of a woman who did not love him. Because the symbolic element is so powerful in the poem, his disciple Rossetti could easily enter into the experience recorded before any meeting with an actual Beatrice except his mother. There he had all the emotional impulse he needed. His fine translation into English of ' The New Life ' is eloquent of its power over his untried soul. When he completed it, he was, with less experience behind

him than Dante, casting the horoscope of his own inner
life:

> Beyond the sphere which spreads to widest space
>   Now soars the sigh that my heart sends above;
>   A new perception born of grieving Love
> Guideth it upward the untrodden ways.
> When it hath reached unto the end, and stays,
>   It sees a lady round whom splendours move
>   In homage; till, by the great light thereof
> Abashed, the pilgrim spirit stands at gaze.
> It sees her such, that when it tells me this
>   Which it hath seen, I understand it not,
>   It hath a speech so subtile and so fine.
> And yet I know its voice within my thought
>   Often remembereth me of Beatrice:
>   So that I understand it, ladies mine.

Rossetti's capacity for purely imaginary experience is
shown strikingly by the writings which we may call
Dantesque, done before he knew what it was to be in love
seriously, and before he had met and chosen Lizzie Siddal
—fatal error!—to be an attainable Beatrice.

'Hand and Soul' and 'St. Agnes of Intercession'
suggest by something in the style that they were attempts
to do what Charles Wells had done in his *Stories After
Nature*, which Rossetti much admired; but the essential
quality of these two unusual tales depends upon the poetic
imagination employed in making visions concrete. And
this is certainly guided by Dante's personification of
abstractions. There is an unmistakable similarity between
the account of the poet of the 'New Life' conversing with
Love, and the despondent artist, Chiaro, confronted with
his own Soul in the silence of his chamber, and being
comforted. In both stories by Rossetti there are also
purely romantic elements which have nothing to do with
Dante, and the same may be said of original early poems
like the 'Blessed Damozel' and 'The Portrait'. The
extraordinary depth of feeling which Rossetti could put
into 'St. Agnes of Intercession' and 'The Portrait'
caused many people to treat the story as an account of a

real picture, and ' The Portrait ' as an autobiographical
fragment referring to the ' Beata Beatrix ' which he painted
fifteen to sixteen years after writing the poem. In his
imaginative adventures Rossetti was always casting the
horoscope of his life like this. In the year 1851, soon after
he had met Lizzie Siddal, he made the first drawing of
' How they Met Themselves '.[1] This was a fresh treatment of the idea of the *doppelgänger* which occurs in a
beautiful stanza of ' The Portrait ':

> In painting her I shrined her face
> Mid mystic trees, where light falls in
> Hardly at all ; a covert place
> Where you might think to find a din
> Of doubtful talk, and a live flame
> Wandering, and many a shape whose name
> Not itself knoweth, and old dew,
> And your own footsteps meeting you,
> And all things going as they came.

The experience of the earthly paradise, from which Dante
moved towards the vision of the celestial paradise, came
for Rossetti after his imagination had hovered near the
celestial paradise, and his course was in the opposite
direction to Dante's. The artist drawing ' lovely Guggums '
day by day, and the poet who wrote:

> Because mine eyes can never have their fill
> Of looking at my lady's lovely face,
> I will so fix my gaze
> That I may become bless'd, beholding her,

were at their closest to each other. Before and after that
approach their orbits ran apart, though Rossetti's more
variable course brought him back towards Dante at times,
notably in 1869, the year which saw the writing of the
amazing ' Willowood ' sonnets in the *House of Life*.
' Willowood ' might have been written by the poet of
' The New Life '.

[1] Which he drew again during their honeymoon.

CHAPTER XI

THE 'FLESHLY' POET

— '*It is really very odd that people, friendly or unfriendly, will not let one be an artist, but must needs make one out a parson or a pimp.*'—SWINBURNE.

'*In the sex impulse man puts himself in the most personal relation with nature.*'—OUSPENSKY.

THE FORCES and scenes of non-human nature, such as winds and waters, sun and moon, forests and meadows, storm and stillness, are made to serve as metaphysical imagery by Rossetti much more than as pictorial description for its own sake. He was a visionary rather than a nature poet, and the natural was for him the necessary symbol of psychic realities. But there is a remarkable tendency in his poetry of human love to express natural desires in metaphysical or spiritual allegory. One hesitates to say imagery here, for spiritual imagery is a contradiction in terms. The gift for using natural imagery beautifully remains evident in his poetry of earthly love; which is love of woman, for him. In addition to this, however, he employs poetically and romantically, ideals of beauty, and some of the most ancient symbols of spiritual life, such as hell and heaven. He deliberately confuses physical life with psychic life because the most urgent experience he knew of love was that soul and body were not strictly to be separated. Why should he distinguish between them, if love of a woman's body set his heart on fire? As a love poet he is the poet of the heart on fire, but the delight in the visible beauty which made him also a painter of women provided the impulse to perception of the invisible beauty. He would never have been misled either morally or artistically, like Shelley, by idealism. Where Shelley wrote: 'There are some of us who have loved an Antigone before we visited this earth and must pursue through life that unregainable ideal', Rossetti wrote:

> O love, my love! if I no more should see
> Thyself, nor on the earth the shadow of thee,
>   Nor image of thine eyes in any spring,—
> How then should sound upon Life's darkening slope
> The ground-whirl of the perished leaves of Hope,
>   The wind of Death's imperishable wing?

And so, in the 'House of Life' sonnet following this:

> Lady, I fain would tell how evermore
> Thy soul I know not from thy body, nor
> Thee from myself, neither our love from God.

Rossetti's faults, moral and artistic, could spring only from accepting sensation as the first hint of beauty. Thus when he loved a gross and sensual woman like Fanny Schott because of her bodily beauty, he was preparing a disastrous division between his own flesh and spirit, and to restore the broken bridge between them he tried to join sensation and emotion in poetry of love. His love poetry, however, of 1869-1871 was not due to the old liaison but to a new love which permitted the 'concurrence of the soul'. Shelley tended to do precisely the opposite in poetry. If he fell in love unlawfully, he wrote 'Epipsychidion'. Swinburne's erotic poetry is again a reflection of personality quite different from either of the others. He was violent and lustful and unlawful in poetry because physically he was unable to obtain normal satisfaction. If Buchanan's attack on 'The Fleshly School of Poetry' had been merely stupid and sincere, he could not possibly have made Rossetti the principal accused, for Rossetti is quite Victorian in his strict morality in poetry, although bolder than all but Swinburne and Browning in representing realities which the Victorian preferred not to see.

Buchanan must easily have produced a strong prejudice

against Rossetti among the middle-class intelligent readers of his article who were unacquainted with the poet's work. His method of detaching lines here and there was especially effective as an act of warfare, though not of criticism, in Rossetti's case, because of the vivid imagery so deeply felt. In the dignified and crushing reply, called ' The Stealthy School of Criticism ', from Rossetti, which appeared in the *Athenaeum* soon after Buchanan's first attack had appeared in the *Contemporary Review*, the poet is forced to quote again, detached from its context, the lines quoted by Buchanan from ' Eden Bower ':

> What more prize than love to impel thee?
> Grip and lip my limbs as I tell thee!

and not even his explanation of the facts carefully omitted by Buchanan, that the embrace is only that of a snake-woman, and a snake could have dispelled the feeling of a proper-minded middle-class Victorian that the poet was ' unpleasant '. Rossetti could not have treated such a theme, combining the erotic and the demonological, in any less intense and vivid imagery than is to be found in ' Eden Bower ', but he could have chosen safer themes if he had been anxious to avoid the kind of criticism which only stimulated Swinburne to more splendid vituperation.

As with all his poems, Rossetti had taken much thought in the composition and revision of ' Eden Bower ' and ' Troy Town ', and he had no doubt of the artistic justification for his treatment of their themes. ' Eden Bower ' sprang out of his interest in the ' Lilith ' legend, which, as we have seen, he found early in life in his romantic reading. His translation of the lines on Lilith from *Faust* and his picture and sonnet on the theme lead up to the ballad-poem composed, with infinite difficulty, in 1869. None of his manuscripts in Mr. Wise's collection is more scored with alterations than that of ' Eden Bower '. The second stanza of the published version was an afterthought at the last minute. One stanza,[1] the third, will serve as an example

[1] Quoted in volume 8, *Catalogue of the Ashley Library*.

of the poet's persistence in revising. After various alterations, the first draft read:

> Low to the ear of the snake said Lilith:
>   Sing the bower in flower:
> 'With whom but thee should my shame take cover?
> When I was a snake I called thee my lover'.
>   Sing the day and the hour.

The second draft read:

> In the ear of the Snake said Lilith:——
>   (Eden Bower's in flower)
> 'Thou art left when the rest is over;
> I am a snake, do thou be my lover'.
>   (And it's O the day and the hour!)

Both of them are inferior to the printed version:

> In the ear of the Snake said Lilith:——
>   (*Sing Eden Bower!*)
> 'To thee I come when the rest is over;
> A snake was I when thou wast my lover . . . '

Only one refrain is put into each stanza of the published
poem.

Rossetti was enquiring for information about the
legend before doing the poem; for a theme like this, as
with his designs for pictures, he brooded over until his
imagination had grasped the conception which he could
recognize as the right one. There is great skill and justice
in the pregnant images; the brief stanzas and ominous
monotony of the rhythm are like the tolling of a bell, yet
the poem hardly succeeds in stirring the mind. Rossetti
seems to have hesitated between the demoniac and weird
element and the erotic feeling. If he had written a poem
on this theme fifteen years earlier it would almost certainly
have had a magic of atmosphere lacking in the present one.
'Troy Town' is more successful than 'Eden Bower', and
probably because the theme suited the poet better at the
time of writing. He corresponded about the legend involved in this also. James Thursfield, in writing (26th
October 1869) to him from Oxford about the ill-fated
mural paintings in the Union hall, answers his query: 'I

sent a few days ago to our common friend Tebbs a note on the subject of Helen's Cup, about which you were seeking information when I had the pleasure of dining at your house a short time ago. I am sorry the note is not more complete; but I cannot trace the story beyond Pliny, nor can I find any mention of the subject in Greek authors. The commentators on Pliny seem one and all to have over-looked the passage.' The legend was that Helen dedicated to Venus a cup that had been moulded upon her breast. In the first issue of the *Trial Book* preparatory to the pub-lished *Poems* of 1870, a footnote on page 1, under ' Troy Town ', appeared: 'Herodotus says that Helen offered in the temple of Venus a cup made in the likeness of her own bosom.' The note was omitted in the second *Trial Book* and, says Mr. Wise, never revived.[1]

The form of ' Troy Town ' suggests a ballad intention on the part of the poet, but the story is only reflected by anticipation in the refrain, and the poem is otherwise a lyrical reflection, but with a tremendous realization in it of the purely erotic feeling. Rossetti was very pleased with the poem, as well he might have been, for it is a master-piece of its kind. Certainly it is sensual; it is completely and beautifully sensual, and nothing in Swinburne's erotic verse can compare with it for perfection of expression.

Before the publication of the 1870 volume Rossetti's anxiety about public opinion or malicious reviewing had centred on ' Jenny ', which is a quite chaste dramatization of a young man's feelings and reflections when he stays all night in a fair young prostitute's room, and watches over her as she sleeps, tired out with the day's to-and-fro. It is typical of Rossetti's range of human sympathy, but there is a slightly disagreeable Victorian sentimentality about it too. Rossetti wrote on 11th April 1870 to C. E. Norton, from Robertsbridge, Suffolk, about the poem. His letter was partly a reply to an invitation from Norton and his wife to visit them at Florence. Rossetti promises to

[1] *Catalogue of the Ashley Library.*

send them a copy of his poems, the publication of which was imminent. 'Some friendly hands are already at work on reviews of it,' he says, 'Morris for *The Academy*—Swinburne for the *Fortnightly*—Stillman for an American paper—and many others. . . . I hope that when you get my book you will agree with me as to the justness of my including all it contains. I say this because there are a few things—and notably a poem called "Jenny"—which will raise objections in some quarters. I only know that they have been written neither recklessly nor aggressively (moods which I think are sure to result in the ruin of Art), but from a true impulse to deal with subjects which seem to me capable of being brought rightly within Art's province. Of my own position I feel sure, and so wait the final result without apprehension'. The same diffident attitude towards so enlightened a friend as Norton is revealed here as that which had deterred him from sending to his Aunt Charlotte a copy of *The Early Italian Poets*. One feels that his sensitive shrinking from the moral disapprobation of readers hardly justified his cheerful statement that he awaited the results of publication 'without apprehension'. Would that he had been insensitive to wrong-headed judgments, but on his own confession he had always some 'apprehension'. In 'The Stealthy School', when he comes to deal with Buchanan's quotation from 'Jenny', he says: 'Neither some thirteen years ago, when I wrote this poem, nor last year when I published it, did I fail to foresee impending charges of recklessness and aggressiveness, or to perceive that even among those who could really *read* the poem, and acquit me on these grounds, might still hold that the thought in it had better have dispensed with the situation which serves it for framework.'

The remainder of his careful remarks about 'Jenny' are an interesting self-criticism. He had considered how far it would be possible to treat the same theme 'from without', meaning, of course, in the form the poem had originally taken, of undramatic reflection. He had come to realize that the ' *inner* standing point ' was necessary, since ' the powers of art reverse the requirements of science '. This reads rather like a particular defence of romantic art as well as a general defence of all artistic perception. ' The heart of such a mystery as this must be plucked from the very world in which it beats or bleeds '; yes, but again under the general meaning is the sense that the knowledge must come from the poet's own heart. The ' young and thoughtful man of the world ', postulated by Rossetti as the only speaker from whose mouth the beauty and pity and questioning of the poem can come, is again himself. The very poems which Rossetti set out to defend against utterly baseless charges of immorality and vicious corruption are generally among the best examples of the virtue of sensuality in poetry.

The sensual aspect of eroticism is an important element of human experience and demands expression in art quite as insistently and justifiably as any other element. Rossetti, as all healthy people tend to do, passed through a specially sensual phase, in his quickly ripened maturity, after the death of his wife. With him it was more dangerous and difficult to control than with the majority of men, for he was temperamentally subject to irrational impulses of exceptional force. The dynamic power which had made him amazingly creative in poetry and painting began to break down the sublimating romantic symbolism and to seek more satisfaction in sensual delight. There was no sudden change, unless the shock of his wife's death hastened the dissolution of his self-repression. ' Jenny ' was re-written just before his marriage, but in 1869 began the triumphant renewal of poetic creation in which the erotic element comes to artistic fruition. Then were written the majority of his love sonnets in *The House of Life*, in which grieving memory only reinforces the joy of present possession, for only so could he give himself up, as he needed to give himself, to passionate love. The dead wife

has become a mothering spirit in his imagination. In
' The Stream's Secret', written in 1869 at Penkill, when he
was bringing himself to the decision to exhume the manuscripts buried in her grave, he asks the 'whispering water':

> Say, hath not Love leaned low
> This hour beside thy far well-head,
> And there through jealous hollowed fingers said
> The thing that most I long to know,—
> Murmuring with curls all dabbled in thy flow
> And washed lips rosy red?

And then:

> Shall Time not still endow
> One hour with life, and I and she
> Slake in one kiss the thirst of memory?
> Say, stream; lest Love should disavow
> Thy service, and the bird upon the bough
> Sing first to tell it me.

But his fantasy is in pursuit of more than the assurance
that the woman who loved him still loves. The stream,
which is his conscience, is bidden to withhold the vain
behest that his burning heart should cease to seek love.
He will have no rebuke: such would prove

> That thou dost ill expound the words of Love.

He is the man-child before the memory of the woman
who has died. He bids the stream to understand that she
had given him command in her compassionate love. She
' is far away now', and night hours do not bring to him
yet their reunion.

> Oh sweet her bending grace
> Then when I kneel beside her feet;
> And sweet her eyes o'erhanging heaven; and sweet
> The gathering folds of her embrace;
> And her fall'n hair at last shed round my face
> When breaths and tears shall meet.

> Beneath her sheltering hair,
> In the warm silence near her breast,
> Our kisses and our sobs shall sink to rest;
> As in some still trance made aware
> That day and night have wrought to fullness there
> And Love has built our nest.

[193]   N

The lovely stanzas, charged with tender memory and tenderer anticipation, are, with all the irrelevance of a child pursuing its desire, leading to his confession and his pleading for pity from the water that whispers with the voice of his conscience. The poem in its exquisite close is a sigh for reunion in death. Yet the sonnet, 'Farewell to the Glen ',[1] written at the same time, ends with:

> when an hour ago
> Thine echoes had but one man's sighs to bear
> And thy trees whispered what he feared to know.

The poet was already in love, and the conflict within him remained unresolved. The fantasy which made of the dead woman a mothering and forgiving spirit had not been powerful enough to bring peace to his divided soul. The terrible sonnet ' Vain Virtues ' followed; but still he must bring heaven down to his earth. The last communion of spirit is in the beautiful song-like sonnets entitled ' Willow-wood ', which are best described in the words Rossetti applied to the first one, from which the egregious Buchanan had quoted the final couplet. ' The sonnet describes a dream or trance of divided love momentarily re-united by the longing fancy; and in the imagery of the dream, the face of the beloved rises through deep dark waters to kiss the lover.'

In the same year the sonnets of passionate love begin to be written, and the passing of the barrier of memory, the hungry, forlorn, grasping for the present love, is eloquently expressed in ' The Love-Moon '.[2]

> When that dead face, bowered in the furthest years,
> Which once was all the life years held for thee,
> Can now scarce bid the tides of memory
> Cast on thy soul a little spray of tears,—
> How canst thou gaze into these eyes of hers
> Whom now thy heart delights in, and not see
> Within each orb Love's philtred euphrasy
> Make them of buried troth remembrancers?

---

[1] No. 84, *House of Life.*   [2] No. 37, *ibid.*

Nay, pitiful Love, nay, loving Pity! Well
    Thou knowest that in these twain I have confess'd
Two very voices of thy summoning bell.
    Nay, Master, shall not Death make manifest
In these the culminant changes which approve
The love-moon that must light my soul to Love?

'Life-in-Love', the sonnet preceding this in *The House of Life*, but written in 1870, in the middle of the erotic phase of the poet's creative period, is the record of complete reconcilement of present and past. The 'poor tress' of the sestet is almost certainly a reference to Lizzie's, taken with the manuscripts from the coffin because it came away with them. In reading these sonnets one is treading on sacred ground. No soul's diary ever touched more vital secrets of the heart.

Not in thy body is thy life at all,
    But in this lady's lips and hands and eyes;
    Through these she yields thee life that vivifies
What else were sorrow's servant and death's thrall.
Look on thyself without her, and recall
    The waste remembrance and forlorn surmise
    That lived but in a dead-drawn breath of sighs
O'er vanished hours and hours eventual.

Even so much life hath the poor tress of hair
    Which, stored apart, is all love hath to show
    For heart-beats and for fire-heats long ago;
Even so much life endures unknown, even where,
'Mid change the changeless nights environeth,
Lies all that golden hair undimmed in death.

Thereafter the course of passion is beautifully reflected in a big proportion of the *House of Life* sonnets in Part One, of which the ecstatic abandonment is indicated by some of the first lines; *e.g.*:

No. 28. What other woman could be loved like you,
    Or how of you should love possess his fill?
No. 26. Thou lovely and beloved, thou my love;
    Whose kiss seems still the first . . .
No. 18. Beauty like hers is genius.[1]

---

[1] The remark made many years before by Rossetti about Jane Burden (Mrs. Morris).

No. 27. Sometimes thou seem'st not as thyself alone,
But as the meaning of all things that are.
No. 34. Not I myself know all my love for thee.

But the first lines cannot suggest the sequent waves of emotion which culminate in each completed sonnet. Some of these sonnets, such as ' The Dark Glass ' (34), ' Severed Selves ' (40), ' Without Her ' (53), ' Lovesight ' (4), ' The Lovers' Walk ' (12), ' A Day of Love ' (16), ' Love-Sweetness ' (21), and ' Heart's Compass ' (27) are certainly among the finest poems of passionate love in the language. In such poetry Rossetti successfully united the sensual and the psychic elements of love. Some of the sonnets just mentioned as among the finest were special objects of Buchanan's contempt and disgust, but the two which roused most objection in the press were ' Nuptial Sleep ' (6a), and ' Supreme Surrender ' (7). The poet made verbal alterations in both before publication.

His anticipatory fear of public disapproval lends a peculiar interest to various emendations of ' fleshly ' poems. There was nothing accidental about the nature of the contents of the *Poems* of 1870. They had all been revised in the privately printed *Trial Books*, and the opinions of others, like William Rossetti and Swinburne, had been canvassed and carefully considered. ' Nuptial Sleep ' was one of the pieces which Rossetti realized to be dangerous. He asked his brother about it when sending the proofs, and William wrote back (24th August 1869) saying that the sonnet should go in ' even in a published form ' (the proofs under discussion were only for the privately printed test volume). The title then was ' Placatâ Venere ', and William says: ' I think you might *perhaps* reconsider the title, which appears to me a nearer approach to indecorum than anything in the sonnet itself '. Rossetti took the advice and called it ' Nuptial Sleep '. Mr. Wise quotes[1] from a long letter to his brother on the subject. ' About " Nuptial Sleep " ', Rossetti says, ' I enclose the proof

[1] Vol. 8, *Catalogue of the Ashley Library.*

before the last to ask you about the MS. alteration at the bottom, which is now in print. Above and below it I have written a further variation underlined. Do you think this or the present printed one best? I inclined to the printed one, "Chirped at each other". This is expressive of the lips kissing at each other as they lie apart. But is it clear, or, if clear, is it pleasant? Would it be better "kissed at each other", or, more likely, "moaned to each other"? Or does any other phrase occur to you? Or do you like it as it stands?' 'Chirped' was first changed into 'moaned', Mr. Wise points out, and this word stands in the first *Trial Book*. In the second *Trial Book* 'moaned' gave place to 'fawned', so in the published *Poems* of 1870 the last line of the octave had reached its final form:

Fawned on each other where they lay apart.

Rossetti's artistic absorption in intensely personal poetry was extraordinary, and it was this which enabled him to face publication, and yet which left him so open to injury in his deepest feelings when the poetry was unscrupulously bludgeoned and muddied with every scornful epithet, from 'very, very silly', to 'sickly animalism'. The story that Tennyson said 'Nuptial Sleep' was the filthiest thing he had ever read is picturesque but apparently apocryphal; but Charles Dickens, whose moral propriety was reserved for his writings, was a leader of the hue and cry. Because we can take a more disinterested view to-day, it is easy to under-rate the seriousness of the onslaught. It would have snuffed out the reputation of minor artists.

Rossetti's impersonal, artistic interest in his poems is illustrated by his discussion of many others, of which a few belonging to the same erotic mood may be glanced at here. The chief example of sensuality among his pictures painted in the 'women and flowers' period between 1863 and 1869 was the 'Venus Verticordia', an oil begun in 1864 and finished in 1868. At the same time he did a small water-colour, which, although rather sentimental and

luscious, is quite inoffensive—and that is more than one
can say for the oil, painted from a handsome cook whom
he stopped in the street one day. His prudish apprehen-
sions are revealed by the explanatory and apologetic
remarks he addressed to Rae, the buyer of the water-
colour. Both the ' Venus ' pictures are only half-length
nudes, and Rossetti got over the difficulty of avoiding both
drapery and full-length, by surrounding the figure waist-
high with flowers, honeysuckles in front and roses, like a
surrounding wall, in the background. Ruskin's antipathy
to the ' Venus ' oil caused the first serious strain in the
friendship of the two men, but even Ruskin eulogized the
sumptuous ' floral adjuncts '. Rossetti did only two full-
length nudes in his life, according to Marillier, and these
were pencil-drawings. The one which is reproduced by
Marillier is not pleasing, and seems wrong anatomically.
The sonnet for ' Venus Verticordia ' was written in 1868,
the year before Rossetti made the collection of poems
printed in *Trial Books*. Rossetti wrote first for the octave:

> She hath it in her hand to give to thee,
> Also within her heart to hold it back;
> She muses, with her eyes upon the track
> Of some dazed moth or honey-seeking bee.
> Haply, 'He is as one of these', saith she ;
> 'Now the sweet apple for his lips, alack'.
> But brings the dart to turn his midday black,
> With wandering for his feet perpetually.

As published the octave ran:

> She hath the apple in her hand for thee,
> Yet almost in her heart would hold it back ;
> She muses, with her eyes upon the track
> Of that which in thy spirit they can see.
> Haply, 'Behold, he is at peace', saith she ;
> 'Alas ! the apple for his lips,—the dart
> That follows its brief sweetness to his heart,—
> The wandering of his feet perpetually ' !

The improvements are towards making the sonnet a poem
independent of the picture. Writing to his brother,
Rossetti notes that the ' " Venus " sonnet has " She hath

the apple in " etc. Now " apple " is here placed awkwardly between two vowels, which makes the prosody dubious. Does any change suggest itself? ' The apple had been put into the opening line because without the picture ' it ' might have meant anything. Similarly the moth and bee are suggested by the picture but seem fortuitous in the verse. The alteration enables him to emphasize the gazing of Venus into the eyes of her worshipper. The fifth line again expresses the poet's thought independently of the picture—the original ' one of these ' means the moth or the bee carelessly lighting on the apple and the flowers. The sixth, seventh, and eighth lines are simply poetic improvements upon the original. A further notable improvement after the 1870 publication was made in the last line which, instead of

> And her grove glow with love-lit fires of Troy

became for the 1881 edition and after:

> And through her dark grove strike the light of Troy.

It is evident that alterations to such poems were usually for purely aesthetic reasons. Certainly Rossetti's feeling that ' chirped ' might not be ' pleasant ' assisted him to try again until he found ' fawned ' for the eighth line of ' Nuptial Sleep '; but ' fawned ' is poetically justified. Among the reasons for its rightness is that it shapes the lips just as the poet conceived of the lovers' mouths ' burnt red ' pouting in sleep. The opening three lines of this sonnet were also different before publication. Mr. Wise quotes[1] from the manuscript:

> So their lips drew asunder, with fierce smart,
> And like the last slow sudden rain-drops shed
> From sparkling eaves when the short storm has fled
> So singly flagged the pulses of each heart.

This is inferior to the published version, but the same vivid image which, like a Shakespearean metaphor, runs in front of the meaning and tells more than the poet says, is care-

[1] Vol. 9, *Catalogue of the Ashley Library.*

fully preserved but strengthened by omitting the word
'rain', thus slowing down the tempo with the long open
'are' before 'shed' and leaving the implicit idea clearer.
Another line which Rossetti discussed with his brother
was the last one of 'Parted Love' (46):

> And thy heart rends thee, and thy body endures.

'In the new sonnet "Parted Love"', he wrote, 'the last
line is declared by Scott to be too violent. Do you think
so? It occurs to me to say 'And thy feet stir not, and thy
body endures'. Do you like this better. It conveys the
sense of impotent retention, which is wanted, but that is
already conveyed in line seven.' No alteration was made,
fortunately. A rare example of alteration involving loss is
that which was made to the seventh line of 'Vain Virtues'
(No. 85). As a consequence of the abuse meted out to the
1870 volume, Rossetti tried to remove an occasional phrase
which had been objected to, and the sonnet 'Nuptial
Sleep' was altogether omitted from the 1881 edition. It is
a pity that when William Rossetti restored 'Nuptial
Sleep' to its place in *The House of Life* for the Collected
Works he did not restore at least this one original reading
of an altered line, if only in his admirable Notes. In 'Vain
Virtues' the poet is trying to suggest with the utmost
emphasis the horrible change which comes over virtues that
are proved to have been fair deeds 'which a soul's sin at
length could supersede'. He calls such a vain virtue the
'sorriest thing that enters Hell'. He likens them to virgins

> whom death's timely knell
> Might once have sainted; whom the fiends compel
> Together now, in snake-bound shuddering sheaves
> Of anguish, while the scorching bridegroom leaves
> Their refuse maidenhood abominable.

The emphasis of that is worthy of Shakespeare. But 'the
scorching bridegroom' was too much for the Victorian
era, so he altered the sonnet to read:

> while the pit's pollution leaves
> Their refuse maidenhood abominable.

SONNET XXVII IN 'THE HOUSE OF LIFE', ENTITLED 'HEART'S COMPASS'
WRITTEN 1871; FIRST PUBLISHED 1881

which is an exchange of a concrete and vividly dramatic image for a rhetorical phrase which adds somewhat to the consistency of the thought sequence, for it preserves the background of hell.

Rossetti's fine artistic sense saved him from ill effects of his ' fleshly ' feeling for imagery besides enabling him to make poetic alterations with wonderful tact. He certainly tended towards a sensuality of erotic feeling which, if translated too literally, would have weakened the art of his poetry. Perhaps a comparable case of a temperamental sensuousness betrayed at moments in expression is that of Keats's 'Endymion', which also was violently abused, mostly on quite unjustifiable grounds, by the press. The weakness to which Rossetti was artistically prone through his temperament is observable in the three unpublished sonnets written for *The House of Life*, all about 1869, which are quoted in Mr. Wise's Catalogue.[1] They are entitled ' At Last ', ' First Fire ', and ' Three-Fold Homage '.

' At Last ' is really another, poorer version of an argument already touched here and there in the published work, notably in ' The Love-Moon '; while the attitude to the beloved woman, as to a mother, which in ' The Stream's Secret ' is revealed in the invocation to the spirit of his dead wife, is here shown towards the woman who inspired the love sonnets of *The House of Life*. Here is the octave:

> Fate claimed hard toll from Love, and did not spare :
> Are the dues paid, and is all Love's at last ?
> Cling round me, sacred sweetness, hold me fast;
> Oh! as I kneel, enfold mine eyes even there
> Within thy breast; and to Love's deepest lair
> Of memory bid thy soul with mine retreat,
> And let our past years and our future meet
> In the warm darkness underneath thine hair.

' First Fire ', which, by its title, is associated with ' Last Fire ' in the *House of Life* is more frank and literal still, and it is lucky that Buchanan and Co. did not find it in the 1870 *Poems*! It is much inferior as a poem to sonnets like

[1] Vol. 9.

'Nuptial Sleep' and 'Supreme Surrender', which are themselves Rossetti's second best. The octave follows:

> This hour be her sweet body all my song,
>> Now the same heart-beat blends her gaze with mine,
>> One parted fire, Love's silent countersign:
> Her arms lie open, throbbing with their throng
> Of confluent pulses, bare and fair and strong:
> And her deep-freighted lips expect me now,
> Amid the clustering hair that shrines her brow
> Five kisses broad, her neck ten kisses long.

'Lo, Love! thy heaven of Beauty' exclaims the poet in the opening of the sestet, which reverts to his more characteristic blending of natural symbolic imagery. 'Three-Fold Homage', in which the poet asks

> Was I most born to paint your sovereign face,
>> Or most to sing it, or most to love it, dear?

is also inferior to the *House of Life* level, and is largely redundant in view of 'The Portrait' (10), where the poet-artist triumphs in the thought that henceforth they that would look on his beloved's beauty must come to him. But it must always be remembered that all the great poets could easily be attacked on the score of their worst work, or that which reveals most their faulty tendencies, just as, in Keats's observation, any man may be cut up on his worst side. If the whole body of Rossetti's erotic work, in poetry and painting, is considered, it is a wonderful contribution to controlled expression of eroticism; few men indeed have made so fine and beautiful a contribution.

CHAPTER XII

NATURAL IMAGERY

*' So one may lie and symbolize till one goes to sleep, and
that would be a symbol too perhaps.'*—D. G. ROSSETTI.

ACCORDING to several friends of his later years,
Rossetti displayed little active interest in scenery
or landscape. Watts-Dunton marked this in recalling
his first visit to Kelmscott manor house,[1] where he had
gone to see Rossetti concerning a legal affair of which he
had charge, the forging of Rossetti's name on a cheque by
a woman whom Rossetti was anxious not to prosecute.
Watts-Dunton reached Kelmscott late. It was a lovely
evening with a full moon rising. He approached the house
and noticed the lamplight shadow of Rossetti unmoving
against the blind. After some persuasion Rossetti was led
out for a walk to the moonlit weir. According to Watts-
Dunton he showed no sign of being impressed by the
beauty of the scene. The recollection of the incident
supplied Watts-Dunton with the text for a disquisition on
his favourite theme, that of the Vagabond Poet, of the
type of Borrow (and of Watts-Dunton, of course), who is
more concerned with living than writing, and who therefore at the cost of the final excellence in poetry allows
himself an unstinted communion with out-of-door life.
The chamber poet was the slave of his desire for expression
and tended to shut himself off from the finest sensory
experiences. The one was sedentary, the other an inveter-
ate wanderer. Watts-Dunton never satisfactorily proved
that to be a Vagabond Poet was necessarily to be a finer
nature poet. He himself was a sensitive recorder of the

[1] *Rossetti and Charles Wells.*

[203]

appearances and moods of nature in verse and prose, especially in 'Aylwin', which contains a character unmistakably resembling Rossetti, but when Rossetti's imaginative perception touches 'nature' the consequence is apt to be a line or two of imagery worth pages of his own descriptions.

In the appreciation of an outdoor scene Rossetti, though not often explicit, when he does write a description is unexcelled by Ruskin or any other man of his time. Typical of these little passages, written in an idle moment to some friend, is the following, in a letter to Brown (May 1854) from Hastings:

> The weather is generally splendid, though not so warm, at least indoors, as I had expected. I lie often on the cliffs, which are lazy themselves, all grown with grass and herbage, not athletic as at Dover, not gaunt as at North Shields. Sometimes through the summer mists the sea and sky are one; and, if you half shut your eyes, as of course you do, there is no swearing to the distant sail as boat or bird, while just under one's feet the near boats stand together immovable, as if their shadows clogged them and they would not come in after all, but loved to see the land. So one may lie and symbolize till one goes to sleep, and that would be a symbol too perhaps.[1]

When at the end of his life Rossetti accompanied Hall Caine on a visit to the Cumberland mountains and lakes, he seemed, according to the latter's testimony, to be quite untouched by the most romantic scenery. Probably Rossetti actually was indifferent to the sights and sounds which can give to many sensitive men a thrill of joy even long past the years of youth. It is in youth, if at all, that a man should know the inconceivable and inexplicable ecstasies that woods and streams, valleys and hills, sunlight and moonlight can awaken in us. The personal records of Rossetti's indifference to natural scenery all have reference to the period after his health had begun to fail, when nervous strain and insomnia were opposed by chloral and alcohol. The mind of the artist was then following its dangerously powerful tendency to turn in

[1] *Ruskin, Rossetti, Pre-Raphaelitism*, letter No. 3.

upon itself, avoiding fresh points of contact with the external world, and breaking the old Egyptian commandment: ' Consume not thy heart '. But external evidence of a poet's attitude to ' nature ' is never reliable indication of the processes of the imagination. A great poetic recorder of external beauty may, on some occasion which a spectator might expect to be a thrilling one for a poet, seem unresponsive and even philistine. This need not be due to self-consciousness in the company of those irritating individuals who regard aesthetic thrills as ' comme il faut ' on certain occasions, much as one might regard evening dress at the theatre (stalls). There is a good, and true, story of Tennyson setting out on a tour of Italy, which he of all Victorian poets should have found ' thrilling ' in the expectations of the class of aesthetic bore referred to. Well, perhaps Tennyson was being moved to the depths. The superficial facts, however, are that he failed to bring with him enough tobacco, his own particular tobacco, and after going from one likely shop to another in a famous Italian city which he had not yet looked at, the dismayed poet had to face the improbability of getting any more Bristol bird's-eye in that heathen land. He must see Italy without Bristol bird's-eye to smoke, or pack up his luggage and return to England. He packed up and came straight to London.

Rossetti's work is the test of his ability to observe. We know that his intimacy with the countryside during youth was limited to occasional visits in the holidays. But he was a painter as well as a poet, and much of accurate observation which he might have been able to manage without in poetry was essential to painting. Moreover, his early painting was influenced by a deliberate cultivation of an eye for beauty of detail. His earliest serious pictures, ' The Girlhood of Mary Virgin ', for instance, would afford a critic no adequate basis for an estimate of the Pre-Raphaelite Brotherhood's avowed intentions, yet it is reasonable to trace his care in the presentation of objects (although symbolic objects) as things sharply seen, to the Pre-Raphaelite ideal of ' truth to nature '. For some years Rossetti's hard work at the art of painting was necessarily a training in observation. He was born a visionary, but to some extent he was made an observer. That seems the best explanation of the wealth of what here is called ' natural imagery ' in his poetry. Even without any of his Pre-Raphaelite training, however, one might expect that the mind revealed in the poetry would have been keenly aware of the beautiful in non-human nature. The poet who wrote

> silent icicles
> Quietly shining to the quiet moon

was also a visionary, rather than a ' nature poet ', and so, too, was the author of the ' Ode to Autumn ', most marvellous of ' nature poetry '.

Rossetti in this respect is akin to Coleridge and Keats. Natural imagery was a rich and important element in the texture of his poetry, although this is predominantly visionary. It is already perfect in ' The Blessed Damozel ', which alone by its early date would show his leaning to symbolism rather than description. The descriptive elements of the poem are as perfect as the musical, yet the imagery is always symbolic even where the poet was not consciously doing more than present pictures to the imagination. This applies to illustrative phrasal similes such as 'waters stilled at even' and ' yellow like ripe corn ', as well as to the cosmic vistas seen ' from the fixed place of Heaven ' into the time-traversed gulf of space. But very soon afterwards he wrote light-heartedly in verse remarkable descriptions of things seen during that trip with Holman Hunt to the Continent in 1848, after the two youths had each just sold a picture.

In the Collected Works there are a series of verse jottings written much as one jots down impressions in a journal. The very opening of ' A Trip to Paris and Belgium ' would warn a reader that however spontaneous these

jottings, the writer can see and make others see. He looks
out of the train compartment window and notes:

> A constant keeping-past of shaken trees,
> And a bewildered glitter of loose road . . .
> Banks of bright growths, with single blades atop
> Against white sky. . . .

There are many vignette-like touches in the succeeding
lines:

> a constant sky
> Still with clear trees that let you see the wind;
> And snatches of the engine-smoke, by fits
> Tossed to the wind against the landscape, where
> Rooks stooping heave their wings upon the day.
>
> Brick walls we pass between, passed so at once
> That for the suddenness I cannot know
> Or what, or where begun, or where at end.
> Sometimes a station in grey quiet; whence,
> With a short gathered champing of pent sound,
> We are let out upon the air again.

All this was in the train from London to Folkestone. Then
from Boulogne to Amiens and Paris (the poet sub-titles
this metrical epistle to his brother—3 to 11 p.m.; 3rd class).
The scenery in the opening lines, to anyone who has taken
the same route from London, shows a curiously right
difference from that in the previous section:

> Strong extreme speed, that the brain hurries with,
> Further than trees, and hedges, and green grass
> Whitened by distance,—further than small pools
> Held among fields and gardens,—further than
> Haystacks and windmill-sails and roofs and herds,—
> The sea's last margin ceases at the sun.

Similarly, 'On the Road' from Paris to Brussels, yields
a verse letter with touches like these:

> The last lamps of the Paris Station move
> Slow with wide haloes past the clouded pane;
> The road in secret empty darkness.

At the moment after the sun has come out from clouds:

> And the sky has its blue floated with white,
> And crossed with falls of the sun's glory aslant
> To lay upon the waters of the world;

And from the road men stand with shaded eyes
To look ; and flowers in gardens have grown strong,
And our own shadows here within the coach
Are brighter; and all colour has more bloom.

The sonnet ' On the Road to Waterloo ' concludes:

Sometimes there is no country seen (for miles
You think) because of the near roadside path
Dense with long forest. Where the waters run
They have the sky sunk into them—a bath
Of still blue heat; and in their flow, at whiles,
There is a blinding vortex of the sun.

The lines ' Antwerp to Ghent ' are very good in giving
the impression of the water-seamed land. On the Scheldt:

We know we move
Because there is a floating at our eyes
Whatso they seek.

Then in the train, moonlight and running clouds and the
water everywhere—all seems running, but the water:

at whiles
Weak 'neath the film and heavy growth of reeds.
The country swims with motion.

Rossetti was capable of using natural imagery well in
description. It is true that in his poetry there is no greater
command of natural imagery than ' The Blessed Damozel '
reveals, but a sharper observation is employed when
occasion calls for it, and even when the poet is concerned
with ideas rather than objects a more powerful union of
facts and imagination is to be found in at least half of his
subsequent work, even in some poems which immediately
succeeded ' The Blessed Damozel '. ' The Bride's Prelude '
is examined elsewhere somewhat closely;[1] but here is one
more of the vividly realized pictures which help to sustain
the atmosphere of mental strain in the poem:

Her thought, long stagnant, stirred by speech,
    Gave her a sick recoil;
As, dip thy fingers through the green
That masks a pool,—where they have been
The naked depth is black beneath.

_____

[1] Pp. 269 and 279.

[208]

The periods of mental suspense in that still room where sister confesses to sister are marked by the stir of the outer world.

> A bird had out its song and ceased
> Ere the bride spoke. . . .

So the lover in ' A Last Confession ', parting from the girl who scorned him, at that stressful moment

> heard the sea
> Still trying hard to din into my ears
> Some speech it knew which still might change her heart.

Returning to ' The Bride's Prelude ':

> Although the lattice had dropped loose,
>   There was no wind; the heat
> Being so at rest that Amelotte
> Heard far beneath the plunge and float
> Of a hound swimming in the moat.

And as if that sound called up a vision of what lay far below outside in the sunshine, beyond the moat:

> Some minutes since, two rooks had toiled
>   Home to the nests that crowned
> Ancestral ash-trees. Through the glare
> Beating again, they seemed to tear
> With that thick caw the woof o' the air.
>
> But else, 'twas at the dead of noon
>   Absolute silence ; all,
> From the raised bridge and guarded sconce
> To green-clad places of pleasaùnce
> Where the long lake was white with swans.

It is superfluous to say that the writer of the sonnet ' For a Venetian Pastoral by Giorgione ' has a fondness for the imagery of fierce still radiance of sunshine, when

> beyond all depth away
> The heat lies silent at the brink of day.

The background landscapes in several of his pictures, like the ' Dante's Dream ' in both versions, show glimpses of life stilled beneath sunlight. The sonnet in *The House of Life* entitled ' Silent Noon ' (29) comes to mind. This is an English noon:

> The pasture gleams and glooms
> 'Neath billowing skies that scatter and amass.
> All round our nest, far as the eye can pass,
> Are golden kingcup fields with silver edge
> Where the cow-parsley skirts the hawthorn-hedge.
> 'Tis visible silence, still as the hour-glass.

The pictorial element is delicately shaped to the emotion of smiling peace which pervades the two lovers. The poet vividly realizes the imagery just because it is consonant with the lovers' mental state, where another poet, made rapturous by such a May-time scene, might drag in a memory of love-making to justify his pleasure in reproducing the natural imagery. Rossetti remembered the natural imagery when it suited the thought. The combination is wonderful. The sonnet concludes:

> Deep in the sun-searched growths the dragon-fly
> Hangs like a blue thread loosened from the sky:
> So this wing'd hour is dropt to us from above.
> Oh! clasp we to our hearts, for deathless dower,
> This close-companioned inarticulate hour
> When twofold silence was the song of love.

In a tumultuous mood the lover in ' A Last Confession ' remembers the dread moment when he and the girl came out of the Duomo at Monza, where she had prayed to a new Madonna who had her ' new thoughts '.

> Then silent to the soul I held my way:
> And from the fountains of the public place
> Unto the pigeon-haunted pinnacles,
> Bright wings and water winnowed the bright air.

Far-away brightness is suggested without description in ' The Staff and Scrip ':

> For him, the stream had never well'd
> In desert tracks malign
> So sweet; nor had he ever felt
> So faint in the sunshine
> Of Palestine.

Most of the natural scenes in Rossetti's verse are of

[210]

course English, and cloud shadows, foliage-chequered light, and mirroring waters glimmer and gloom everywhere. What an unforgettable image of wind-swung forest trees under sunlight is this!—

> through dark forest-boughs in flight
> The wind swoops onward brandishing the light. . . .[1]

As the sonnet in which this occurs was written in 1873 it is relevant to remark that Rossetti's later poetry, as it grows less visionary, more often entertains these imaginative descriptions. It is quite a mistaken impression that the natural imagery in *The House of Life* is chiefly in the sonnets which he wrote early in life. To begin with, these are but a small proportion of the whole sequence (only about one-seventh of the total), and they are distinguished by a visionary conception and atmosphere rather than any vividness of natural image. It is as though, having lost the earlier spontaneity, Rossetti brooded more on each poem and so struck out flashes of thought which are less hidden in the woven texture of the style. He is less tensely concentrated upon individual images in the earlier *House of Life* sonnets. ' Autumn Idleness ' (69) for instance:

> This sunlight shames November where he grieves
> In dead red leaves, and will not let him shun
> The day, though bough with bough be over-run.
> But with a blessing every glade receives
> High salutation; while from hillock-eaves
> The deer gaze calling, dappled white and dun,
> As if, being foresters of old, the sun
> Had marked them with the shade of forest-leaves.
>
> Here dawn to-day unveiled her magic glass;
> Here noon now gives the thirst and takes the dew;
> Till eve bring rest when other good things pass.
> And here the lost hours the lost hours renew
> While I still lead my shadow o'er the grass,
> Nor know, for longing, that which I should do.

That is not at all a typical Rossetti sonnet—it is too calm and smooth for him, who strove in maturity to

---

[1] 'Ardour and Memory', *House of Life* (64).

pack the sonnet with a Shakespearean concentration of thought.

In the earlier poetry the finest condensations (but of description, not thought) effected by image are in the more lyrical verse forms and in his ballad poems. Think of the things which are described in that one stanza of ' The Staff and Scrip ' telling of how the waiting Queen and her women see the soldiery returning after the victory. First the herald noise on the air, then the picture, then the thunderous turmoil—and in the midst of the commotion the bearers of the dead knight's bier:

> The first of all the rout was sound,
> The next were dust and flame,
> And then the horses shook the ground:
> And in the thick of them
> A still band came.

Condensation could go no further; but description of this kind is half-way to Rossetti's realization of dramatic crisis, in which he has no superior within the limits of narrative. Of scenery vividly and briefly sketched a fine example is in Part One of ' Rose Mary ', where the pictures seen by the girl looking into the beryl are described in a sequence. It is wild scenery, over ' moor and moss ' and mountain. There are many of the bleaker aspects of nature in *The House of Life*, where imagery of winter and early spring almost balances that of the more luscious months. An isolated sonnet on 'Winter' opens with the bald observation:

> How large that thrush looks on the bare thorn-tree!

One on ' Spring ' is a bucolic description which comes unexpectedly from Rossetti, though it was written as late as 1874. Only the concluding lines reveal unmistakably that the writer is the same as the poet of *The House of Life*. The essential spring feeling is in a stanza of ' Love's Nocturne ':

> Where in groves the gracile Spring
> Trembles, with mute orison.
> Confidently strengthening,
> Water's voice and wind's as one
> Shed an echo in the sun. . . .

[212]

A good example of bleak spring in *The House of Life* is the following:

> On these debateable borders of the year
>   Spring's foot half falters; scarce she yet may know
>   The leafless blackthorn-blossom from the snow;
> And through her bowers the wind's way still is clear.[1]

And from ' Last Fire ' again, the memory of winter:

> Many the days that Winter keeps in store,
>   Sunless throughout, or whose brief sun-glimpses
>   Scarce shed the heaped snow through the naked trees.

More involved in the metaphysical thought is this bleak picture:

> What of that hour at last, when for her sake
>   No wing may fly to me nor song may flow;
>   When wandering round my life unleaved, I know
> The bloodied feathers scattered in the brake,
> And think how she, far from me, with like eyes
> Sees through the untuneful bough the wingless skies?[2]

The dull grey of the day, not a winter day, recalled in ' The Portrait ', when the heat had turned to storm, is summed up in the line:

> The empty pastures blind with rain.

But the picture is brought in by the poet to suit the mood, for ' memory saddens those hours ', and it is to express mood as well as thought that Rossetti so often uses the imagery of wan waters and failing light. Nearly every image of ' Without Her ' [3] is a vivid picture and typical of Rossetti's preference for night or twilight imagery.

>   The blank grey
> There where the pool is blind of the moon's face. . . .

>   The tossed empty space
> Of cloud-rack when the moon has passed away.

> Steep ways and weary . . .
> Where the long cloud, the long wood's counterpart,
> Sheds doubled darkness up the labouring hill.

---

[1] ' Youth's Spring Tribute ', *House of Life* (14).
[2] ' Winged Hours ', *ibid.* (25).   [3] *Ibid.* (53).

Akin to this are:

> The ground-whirl of the perished leaves of Hope.[1]
> And as, when night's fair fires their queen surround,
> An emulous star too near the moon will ride,—
> Even so thy rays within her luminous bound
> Were traced no more. . . .[2]

> Since this day's sun of rapture filled the west
> And the light sweetened as the fire took leave. . . .[3]

Another fine sunset picture, though not English, is in ' Ave ' :

> For off the trees were as pale wands
> Against the fervid sky: the sea
> Sighed further off eternally
> As human sorrow sighs in sleep.

The poet was undisturbed when his brother pointed out that the sea was not near enough to Nazareth to be heard. He never allowed the sequences of superficial experience to upset the grouping of facts for artistic purpose. Those trees like pale wands in the lines just quoted might have been noticed on the journey from Paris to Brussels. Observing the effects of the sun breaking out of clouds, he wrote:

> And betwixt distant whitened poplar-stems
> Makes greener darkness.

Certainly the lines which end the ' London to Folkestone ' epistle:

> I was roused altogether, and looked out
> To where, upon the desolate verge of light,
> Yearned, pale and vast, the iron-coloured sea

were deliberately put into ' The Portrait ', stanza 10 of which concluded:

> And as I stood there suddenly,
>   All wan with traversing the night,
>   Upon the desolate verge of light
> Yearned loud the iron-bosomed sea.

---

[1] ' Lovesight ', *House of Life* (4).
[2] ' The Moonstar ', *ibid.* (29).
[3] ' Last Fire ', *ibid.* (30).

It is noteworthy that the new phrase ' the iron-bosomed sea ' is a masterly improvement for its special context in ' The Portrait '; the man there, sad, lonely, absent-minded, suddenly comes out of the forest close to the sea, and therefore hears its *booming*, suggested in the sound of *bosomed*. Again, in his state of mind, the man would have felt the sea's indifference to the grief which he had known since he last stood there. ' Iron-bosomed ' is therefore the right metaphor as well as the right sound. But in the original version 'coloured' was much better because it occurred in a mere description of the picture seen from the train window by the detached traveller, to whom, more-over, the sea was inaudible.

Perhaps the love of shadowy nocturnal scenes partly accounts for the poet's decided preference among daylight imagery, for massed foliage and for water, where many details are massed into some clear general effect. The beautiful pictures in ' Sunset Wings ' are typical—touch added to touch as in a picture:

> To-night this sunset spreads two golden wings
> Cleaving the western sky;
> Winged too with wind it is, and winnowings
> Of birds; as if the day's last hour in rings
> Of strenuous flight must die.

The sparingly used metaphors are made to link in one harmonious mesh of musical and shaken brightness, sky and birds and trees and the essence of sunset's dazzling peace.

> Sun-steeped in fire, the homeward pinions sway
> Above the dovecote-tops;
> And clouds of starlings, ere they rest with day,
> Sink, clamorous like mill-waters, at wild play,
> By turns in every copse.

> Each tree heart-deep the wrangling rout receives,
> Save for the whirr within,
> You could not tell the starlings from the leaves;
> Then one great puff of wings, and the swarm heaves
> Away with all its din.

[215]

This was written at Kelmscott in 1871, so that whatever impression was gained by Watts-Dunton of Rossetti's blindness to natural beauties, it could not have been generally true of the poet. Even here, however, the poet is not the light-hearted writer of those descriptions done on the continental tour in youth. The idea of Hope's hours ' in ever-eddying flight, to many a refuge ', and of Sorrow, whose pinions, folded on the heart, will not fly away, is the gist of the poem. ' Down Stream ', also written in 1871, in a punt on the Thames near Kelmscott, is in the same class of poem, mingling description and reflection with a lighter imaginative effort than is characteristic of Rossetti's later work. In writing to his mother Rossetti said: ' I doubt not you will note the intention to make the first half of each verse, expressing the landscape, tally with the second expressing the emotion, even to repetition of phrases '.

Running or still waters supply the poet with a wide range of imagery, and seem to serve his needs equally in sunlight or twilight. Sometimes the picture is independent of the hour:

> there in rings
> Whirl the foam-bewildered springs.

Speaking generally one might say that his daylight scenes are not often so deeply symbolic as in this couplet:

> As the cloud-foaming firmamental blue
> Rests on the blue line of a foamless sea,

which concludes perfectly the thought in ' The Lovers' Walk '.[1] But, as if to contradict any general argument, there is the playful sonnet ' A Match with the Moon ', which Keats would have enjoyed writing, in which the poet is content to dog ' the flying moon with similes '. It will hardly be disputed nevertheless that twilight imagery is more at home in Rossetti's imagination, except that with water, whether of forest pools or the sea, whether still or

[1] *House of Life* (12).

in commotion, Rossetti can find the symbols he needs
even without darkness. Darkness itself becomes an idea
suggested by any 'secret continuance sublime' such as
'the sea's listless chime ',[1] for

> The day is dark and the night
> To him that would search their heart,

and the contemplation of the macrocosm of nature reminds
this poet to ask

> Our past is clean forgot,
> Our present is and is not,
> Our future's a sealed seed-plot,
> And what betwixt them are we?[2]

The answer for him must come from the mouth of Love
or the hollow of Death.

[1] 'The Sea Limits.'   [2] 'The Cloud Confines.'

CHAPTER XIII

ROMANTIC ARCHAISM: SOME TRANS-
LATIONS AND PICTURES

' I have been reading all manner of old romaunts, to pitch upon stunning words for poetry.'—D. G. ROSSETTI.

THE TERM 'romantic archaism' is chosen as a convenient portmanteau phrase to include various aspects of Rossetti's work as painter and poet. These slightly varying aspects indicated by such labels as 'medieval-ism', 'romanticism', 'aestheticism' seem still to litter untidily the literature about Rossetti and his circles, the Pre-Raphaelites and the Oxford group. At the early stage of this literature, just after Rossetti's death, William Sharp endeavoured to stem the growing confusion by insisting that 'Pre-Raphaelitism' must be applied only to painting and had nothing to do with literature. For want of any generally recognized terms for certain tendencies in Victorian poetry, 'Pre-Raphaelitism' was used very freely and loosely not only for works of minor painters which flouted whatever definite principle there was in the intentions of the P.R.B., but for minor poetry also, especially of the kind characterized by tenuity of thought and richness of colour. It is not difficult to see that this came about through the increasing influence of painting and poetry by Rossetti, Burne-Jones, Swinburne, and Morris which, except for the frequent symbolism and strange atmospheric effects, had nothing in common with 'Rienzi', 'Christ in the Carpenter's Shop', 'Found', and 'The Last of England'.[1] There is no notable poem

[1] Although Brown was not officially a P.R.B., this fine picture is as Pre-Raphaelite in its truth to facts, bright colouring, and sincerity of feeling as the early works of either Hunt or Millais.

to mention in the company of these pictures as representative of the Pre-Raphaelite character, unless possibly Rossetti's ' Burden of Nineveh ', even if it is agreed that the term extends to literature by covering certain qualities which are not confined to plastic expression. In the pictures which may reasonably be described as Pre-Raphaelite there is often a quality of invention belonging rather to the literature of the period. In painting pictures that were like poems Rossetti was obeying and also encouraging a distinctly literary tendency in British art, and it is what may be called the romantic borrowings of the Pre-Raphaelite painters which make them, at their best (as in Millais's ' Ophelia '), akin to him.

An authority on the Pre-Raphaelite movement made a valiant effort to clear things up by declaring that ' Pre-Raphaelism was, of course, a return to Nature—it was nothing more and nothing less '.[1] I have already argued that it must have been both something more and something less than this, and that only one painter of any consequence can be described as a realist among those who announced their intention of studying ' nature '. This is Holman Hunt, whose most famous picture, ' The Light of the World ', suffices to show that his realism was confined to details and subservient to his invention and symbolism, which were romantic and personal. Of the later coterie at Oxford, in which Rossetti was again the mainspring, a coterie more literary than plastic, including Swinburne, Morris, and Burne-Jones, the same author wrote:

' They deepened, as it were, that particular channel of the romantic stream that Walter Scott had first caused to flow; they steeped themselves far more than he in the spirit of mediaevalism; they pursued it into France, into Italy, and even in Germany; they exhausted its tendencies until, in the case of William Morris, they became, in letters almost pre-mediaeval, and in aesthetics altogether

[1] Ford Madox Hueffer, *The Pre-Raphaelite Brotherhood.*

[219]

of the Renaissance. The upholders of this movement—which was not the Pre-Raphaelite movement—exhausted themselves, in fact, to think, to see, to feel, and to exhale Mediaevalism—and they were nicknamed the Aestheticists, just as, earlier, the small band of Realists had been called Pre-Raphaelite by a world that was anything but sympathetic '.

This playing with nouns and adjectives leaves matters as confused as ever, and it becomes necessary to take some fresh bearings.

Remembering the relation between Rossetti's Dantesque sympathies and the spirit of the age, attention is now called for to the earlier response to romantic literature in its cruder forms. It is instructive to find that Rossetti's earliest metrical composition worthy of inclusion in his Collected Works was a translation from the German romantic ballad of ' Lenore ' by Bürger, a ballad which had been translated into English several times after 1773, when it was written. Scott is supposed to have said that William Taylor's translation had made him a poet.[1] We have already seen that Rossetti's favourite early reading consisted largely of terror-romances and ballads of this type. His fondness for the Devil found in *Faust* made his first serious painting a failure. A juvenile composition, begun not later than 1841, *Sir Hugh the Heron, a Legendary Tale in Four Parts*, which was afterwards printed by grandfather Polidori, was founded on a story on Allan Cunningham's *Legends of Terror*. Another juvenile effort, belonging to 1843, entitled *Sorrentino*, brought in the Devil, and also showed that the author had been reading Hoffmann. As one of the books he read was *Peter Schlemihl*, by Chamisso, the story of a man without a shadow, one may recall Christina's destroyed prose-story *Folio Q*. In January 1861 Dante Gabriel wrote and asked her for it, so that he could show it to Macmillan. It dealt, in William

[1] But it was more probably the literary association with ' Monk ' Lewis in the compilation of *Tales of Wonder*.

Rossetti's words, 'with some supernatural matter—I think, a man whose doom it was not to get reflected in a looking-glass (a sort of alternative form, so far, of *Peter Schlemihl*'.[1] William thought it was the best story she ever wrote in prose, but someone suggested a moral problem which it seemed to raise, and Christina destroyed the manuscript. The nature of the story and this incident is enough to indicate an affinity of imagination between the brother and sister, however much in contrast their moral outlook might appear to be.

The 'Lenore' translation, however, is interesting for other reasons than that it was the poet's first attempt and bears the earliest date of all the poetry in his Collected Works. Taylor's translation was a very capable one, perhaps better than any of the other English versions, of which there were several, after its appearance in M. G. Lewis's *Tales of Wonder* in 1801, a book which the Rossetti brothers knew. Probably Walter Scott's version is the only other one ever read now. William Taylor of Norwich may not have been a poet, but he knew his job with a ballad which resembled one of the old English pieces in Percy's *Reliques* so much that in translation it seemed merely to take root again in native soil. The supposed original, in the form of a broadside, was entitled *The Suffolk Miracle: or, a Relation of a Young Man, who, a month after his death appeared to his sweet-heart, and carried her on horseback behind him for forty miles, in two hours, and was never seen after but in his grave.* Bürger denied having used this English version, and explained that his came from an old Low-Dutch ballad. It is interesting that there should have been at least two earlier versions of such a typical piece of terror-romance.

The inexperienced Rossetti is more sophisticated than Taylor in his diction and rhythm, and uses a double or eight-line stanza instead of the simple 4:3 quatrain, but he does not succeed so well as his predecessor in avoiding

[1] *Family Letters.*

[221]

monotony. He misses also one of the most telling effects in the description of the mad hurry of the demoniac horse and rider. His falsely romantic and pseudo-poetic language is especially unfortunate in this vital passage. Here is Taylor's:

All in her sarke, as there she lay,
   Upon his horse she sprung,
And with her lily hands so pale
   About her William clung.

And hurry-skurry forth they goe,
   Unheeding wet or drye;
And horse and rider snort and blow,
   And sparkling pebbles flye.

How swift the flood, the mead, the wood,
   Aright, aleft, are gone;
The bridges thunder as they pass,
   But earthly sowne is none.

Tramp, tramp, across the land they speed,
   Splash, splash, across the see:
—'Hurrah! the dead can ride apace!
   Dost feare to ride with mee?

The moon is brighte, and blue the nyghte,
   Dost quake the blast to stem?
Dost shudder, mayde, to seeke the dead?'—
   —'No, no, but what of them?

How glumlie sownes yon dirgye song,
   Night-ravens flappe the wing;
What knell doth slowlie toll ding dong
   The psalmes of death who sing?

It creeps, the swarthie funeral traine,
   The corse is on the beere:
Like croke of todes from lonely moores,
   The chaunt doth meet the eere.'—

—'Go, bear her corse when midnight's past,
   With song, and tear, and wayle;
I've gott my wife, I take her home,
   My howre of wedlocke hayl.

Lead forth, O clarke, the chaunting quire,
   To swell our nuptial song;
Come, preaste, and read the blessing soone,
   For bed, for bed we long.'—

[222]

The affectation of old spelling is quite apart from the
virtue of this clear, hard, swinging narration. The 'tramp,
tramp' and 'splash, splash' stanza has been justly admired,
and it recurs in the story of this mad ride by night. But
Rossetti quite missed it in his version. The following in his
translation is the same passage as the preceding by Taylor:

> She busked her well, and into the selle
>   She sprang with nimble haste,—
> And gently smiling, with a sweet beguiling,
>   Her white hands clasped his waist:—
> And hurry, hurry! ring, ring, ring!
> To and fro they sway and swing;
> Snorting and snuffing they skim the ground,
> And sparks spurt up, and the stones run round.
>
> Here to the right and there to the left
>   Flew fields of corn and clover,
> And the bridges flashed by the dazzled eye,
>   As rattling they thundered over.
> 'What ails my love? the moon shines bright:
> Bravely the dead men ride through the night.
> Is my love afraid of the quiet dead?'
> 'Ah! no;—let them sleep in their dusty bed!'
>
> On the breeze cool and soft what tune floats aloft,
>   While the crows wheel overhead?—
> Ding dong! ding dong! 'tis the sound, 'tis the song,—
>   'Room, room for the passing dead!'
> Slowly the funeral-train drew near,
> Bearing the coffin, bearing the bier;
> And the chime of their chaunt was hissing and harsh,
> Like the note of the bull-frog within the marsh.
>
> 'You bury your corpse at the dark midnight,
>   With hymns and bells and wailing;—
> But I bring home my youthful wife
>   To a bride-feast's rich-regaling.
> Come, chorister, come with thy choral throng,
> And solemnly sing me a marriage-song;
> Come, friar, come,—let the blessing be spoken,
> That the bride and the bridegroom's sweet rest be unbroken.'

The last line is a bowdlerization of:

> Komm, Pfaff', und sprich den Segen,
> Eh' wir zu Bett uns legen!

[223]

This and another example of Rossetti's prudishness, in translating ' Henry the Leper ', are pointed out by Mr. L. A. Willoughby.[1] The other example is in the translation of ' Henry the Leper ', which he did in 1846, from the twelfth-century Hartmann von Aue. He simply missed out the lines which tell how Henry, hearing the knife being whetted to take the life of the maid whose death is to be the price of his recovered health, peers through a crack in the wall and sees her lying bound naked on a slab. At this dramatic moment, the real climax of the story, Henry takes the decision that such a sacrifice shall not be made to cure his leprosy. Rossetti retains the situation, of course, but is forced to make the passage reflective instead of dramatic, and Henry the Leper looks on the maid only after his decision is taken and he is admitted to the mortuary. Considering that the translator was only eighteen years old, and very much under the Polidori female influence, which was inclined to carry piety and primness beyond the most exalted early Victorian standards, such a care for the proprieties of the most prudish reader does not seem surprising. We know how carefully he wrote to his mother to explain that the indecent book which his aunt had said he was seen reading was Shelley, and that he was reading Shelley for the most austere reasons! In ' Henry the Leper ' Rossetti again betrays a slight tendency to poetize instead of keeping to the hard and dramatic realism of the primitive story; he will lose some little homely touch, as when the farmer threatens his girl with a beating if she persists in offering her life as a sacrifice for the leper's health, but he is ready to dilute the story with his own imagery and reflection. The fact remains for all this that although a youth and still inexperienced as a writer, he made an English version of ' Henry the Leper ' which one would like to see more often equalled by translators into English of foreign or classical verse. Besides the translations from the Italian poets, his best

[1] *Dante Gabriel Rossetti and German Literature*, 1912.

things all show a strong sympathy for the most poetic
archaic literature, a part of which fed the stream of new-
old taste that in the eighteenth century broke out as the
' Gothic Revival '. He is supreme as a translator of Villon.
Even Swinburne would not attempt a version of ' The
Ballad of Dead Ladies ' after Rossetti had done his
miraculous version. If Swinburne had undertaken this
there would have been an interesting comparison of styles,
for Swinburne at his best was an excellent translator,
though less conscientious than Rossetti in transposing
sentences and fitting approximate equivalents for an
idiomatic or archaic phrase. In the ' Ballad of the Women
of Paris ', for instance, his refrain

There's no good girl's lip out of Paris

would hardly have satisfied Rossetti for

Il n'est bon bec que de Paris,

and neither would he so readily have added phrases like
' make their boast thereof ', and ' for the matter of love ',
which are not in the original, merely to finish off the lines
and rhymes. But this piece is not one of the best; and
Swinburne did not translate all of it (for it is a double
ballad) no doubt because, had he done so, there would have
been some more of those amusing asterisks which star his
version of ' The Fair Armouress '. Still, in reading the
translation of ' Les Regretz de la Belle Heaulmyere ', in
which Swinburne is doing his best, Rossetti's superiority
is manifest, for the English version is full of turns which
are Swinburnian mannerisms, such as

would God I were dead !
Would God I were well dead and slain !

quite alien to the original. Villon's style never seems to
waste words, even to get emphasis. When Rossetti adds a
phrase not in the original, it generally comes like an
inspiration, it seems to interpret. The emphatic poly-
syllable ' semblablement ' in

Semblablement ou est la Royne

[225]

would suggest to a translator who took the nearest literal equivalent within reach:

> Similarly where is the Queen.

But Rossetti makes it:

> And where, I pray you, is the Queen.

The well-known opening line of his version is another example of the skilful ingenuity which more than twenty years earlier (the Villon translations were done in 1869) he had devoted to the early Italian poets. Villon's line literally is, ' Tell me where and in what country ', and Rossetti's departure from literalness, ' Tell me now in what hidden way is ', is not a departure from the spirit of the original; neither is it, like Swinburne's ' would God I were dead ', a change of style. But the first two lines of the third stanza are as vicious as any changes made by the youthful translator of Bürger and Hartmann. The writer of

> White Queen Blanche, like a queen of lilies,
> With a voice like any mermaiden,—

was missing his opportunity, as he rarely does in his best translations. The original is either

> La Royne blanche comme ung lys
> Qui chantoit a voix de Sereine.
>
> (The Queen, white like a lily,
> Who sang with a siren's voice.)

or,

> La royne Blanche comme ung lys . . .
>
> (Queen Blanche (who was) like a lily . . .)

Neither ' Queen ' nor ' white ' is repeated by Villon, and ' queen of lilies ' is too pretty for his style. Faults like these are indicative of tendencies to faults in the translator's own style. ' Queen of lilies ' and ' any mermaiden ' are the equivalent of Swinburne's ' would God I were dead! Would God I were well dead and slain! ' In departing from Villon, and cheapening the original, though it may be but slightly, each reveals an individual weakness. The fact, however, that Swinburne, and also Morris, translated archaic poetry with deep sympathy, and, like Rossetti, through such translation actually made additions to English poetry, is enough to stress the romantic character of the Oxford group's tendencies. Theirs was a new series of adventures prompted by motives similar to Coleridge's and those of the poets who had succeeded Coleridge, including Keats, Shelley, and the youthful Tennyson and Browning. They were seeking that distance which lends enchantment, and according to the type and quality of their imagination they selected from old literature just as they selected from the closer environment of their own day such materials as it needed for the utmost vitality. Rossetti was not the less a conscientious translator on this account; no one has ever lived up to his own definition of the art of translating so fully as himself. In the Preface to *The Early Italian Poets* he wrote: ' The life-blood of rhythmical translation is this commandment,—that a good poem shall not be turned into a bad one. The only true motive for putting poetry into a fresh language must be to endow a fresh nation, as far as possible, with one more possession of beauty '. Literality should, he maintained, be secondary to this motive, but he was careful to distinguish ' literality ' from fidelity. Certainly he was well qualified to define the purpose of translation; not only is the quality of his translations rare, but so is the quantity. The section devoted to them in his Collected Works contains as much material as all the rest of his verse.

Much of that original verse is very close to some of the translations. There are instances of translations of archaic poems which might easily have been original. ' My Father's Close ', though it is a reincarnation of a certain type of old French song, is indistinguishable in style from much of Rossetti's own work. His great skill is best shown in a piece like ' John of Tours ', where he not only creates an English poem, but does it in a severely bald style which has been adopted for a special purpose. Any one who read ' John of Tours ' without having read other work of

Rossetti's except some of his ballads, would never suppose but that this was his own style:

John of Tours is back with peace,
But he comes home ill at ease.

' Good-morrow, mother.' ' Good-morrow, son;
Your wife has borne you a little one.'

' Go now, mother, go before,
Make my bed upon the floor ;

' Very low your foot must fall,
That my wife hear not at all.'

As it neared the midnight toll,
John of Tours gave up his soul.

' Tell me now, my mother dear,
What's the crying that I hear ? '

' Daughter, it's the children wake,
Crying with their teeth that ache.'

' Tell me though, my mother my dear,
What's the knocking that I hear ? '

' Daughter, it's the carpenter
Mending planks upon the stair.'

' Tell me too, my mother my dear,
What's the singing that I hear ? '

' Daughter, it's the priests in rows
Going round about our house.'

' Tell me then, my mother my dear,
What's the dress that I should wear ? '

' Daughter, any reds or blues,
But the black is most in use.'

' Nay, but say, my mother my dear,
Why do you fall weeping here ? '

' Oh ! the truth must be said,—
It's that John of Tours is dead.'

' Mother, let the sexton know
That the grave must be for two;

' Aye, and still have room to spare,
For you must shut the baby there.'

When translating verse by Francesco and Gaetano
Polidori, and according to William Rossetti, improving it,
he resorts to a Shelleyan diction:

> But most sublime of all, most holy,
> The unfathomable melancholy
> When winds are silent in their cells;
> When underneath the moon's calm light,
> And in the unalter'd snow which veils
> All height and depth—to look thereon,
> It seems throughout the solemn night
> As if the earth and sky were one.

The alterations of style are due to a sensitive feeling for
differing originals. In translating two lyrics from the nine-
teenth-century Italian of Tommaseo, where he has something finer to work on than the Polidori verse, his manner
is beautifully natural:

> Even as a child that weeps,
> Lulled by the love it keeps,
> My grief lies back and sleeps.
>
> Yes, it is Love bears up
> My soul on his spread wings,
> Which the days would else chafe out
> With their infinite harassings.
> To quicken it, he brings
> The inward look and mild
> That thy face wears, my child.
>
> As in a gilded room
> Shines 'mid the braveries
> Some wild-flower, by the bloom
> Of its delicate quietness
> Recalling the forest-trees
> In whose shadow it was,
> And the water and the green grass . . .

This is typical of his choice among modern poems when
he translates. It escapes modernity. With the slightest
change it would be indistinguishable from the work of the
archaic Italian poets. When he sent the translations (in
1874) to the *Athenaeum*, which had published an obituary
notice of Tommaseo, he wrote an accompanying letter.

In this he remarked that any countryman of Niccolò Tommaseo, reading his early lyrical poems, ' must have been struck by their not being chiefly concerned with public events and interests; inevitably a rare exception in those dark yearning days of the Italian Muse. Perhaps the two translated specimens which I offer of their delicate and romantic tone may not be unacceptable to some of your readers '. Certainly he was indicating here the reasons for his own preference. Fragmentary translations from Victor Hugo and Goethe are again escapes into the past. The translation of lines on Lilith from *Faust*:

> Hold thou thy heart against her shining hair,
> If, by thy fate, she spread it once for thee ;
> For, when she nets a young man in that snare,
> So twines she him he never may be free,

is merely a preparation for the sonnet ' Body's Beauty ' in *The House of Life*, written in 1867, the year following the translation. But the translation itself, as is often the case with Rossetti, expressed a previously formulated interest. The painting of Lady Lilith was done from Fanny Schott in 1864, though he was still doing something to it in 1866 or 1867, and in 1873 during his fit of revising and alteration, he got the picture back and repainted the head from a different model, producing a much inferior picture. In the same period of his painting—in 1865, to be exact— the 'Blue Bower' was done, in which the woman playing on the dulcimer is again Fanny Schott. But the ' Blue Bower ', an oil, is not merely an example of the sumptuous women-and-flowers phase of his work, for its romantic archaism recalls the mood of those earlier water-colours, ' The Blue Closet ', ' The Tune of Seven Towers ', and the Arthurian themes. So, following the hint of a translated fragment, one finds that Rossetti's painting in the Venus and Lilith period is also engaged with sudden glimpses of other regions far away. In 1860-61 he had done the beautiful pen-and-ink design of ' Love's Greeting ', intending it as a frontispiece for *The Early Italian*

Poets. In 1864 he did a water colour of the same theme, called ' Roman de la Rose ', where the figure of Love is again shown in a rose-garden overshadowing the kissing lovers with his sheltering wings. ' How Sir Galahad, Sir Bors, and Sir Percival received the Holy Grail ' is another unexpectedly romantic picture done in this period, a water-colour chiefly in red and gold. As early as 1850 Rossetti had translated some lines from ' The Roman de la Rose ', making a mistake, as his brother pointed out, in translating ' epousée ' as ' wife '. But the lines seem in retrospect another example of the weird anticipation of his future imaginative situation.

> Tender as dew her cheeks' warm life ;
> She was as simple as a wife,
> She was as white as lilies are.
> Her face was sweet and smooth and fair :
> Slender and very straight she was,
> And on her cheeks no paint might pass.
>
>   .   .   .   .
>
> Her fair hair was so long that it
> Shook, when she walked, about her feet :
> Eyes, nose, and mouth, were perfect art,
> Exceeding pain is at my heart
> When I remember me of her.

These lines, of little importance as a translation, would not be noteworthy in the work of a less abnormally imaginative artist, but they occur in Rossetti's career like other things he did, with a strangely ominous aspect. If the date attributed to them is correct, he probably had not met Lizzie Siddal when he wrote them. Two years after her death, he painted a picture with a title taking the mind back to them, but in theme recalling the sheltered lovers in ' Love's Greeting ', the picture done in the first year of his marriage. The only explanation of the absence of grief in the ' Roman de la Rose ' picture is that he could for periods while working at an idea banish the darker knowledge that was his. Usually he anticipated grief, and after the event tried to escape from memory until a strong resurgence of

[231]

old emotion captured his imagination. Those trips, as we may call them, in the sixties, towards the romantic scenes of his earlier adventurings, never carried him far. But his conscious attitude towards the pseudo-mediaeval trappings of poems and pictures done in the fifties with a depth of feeling which justified it all, had altered early in the sixties, although the tendency towards romantic archaism and mystery was not exhausted by any means.

In July 1858 he wrote a long letter to Professor C. E. Norton offering to give him ' Before the Battle ' in fulfilment of Norton's commission of £50. The picture, he tells Norton, ' represents a castle full of ladies who have been embroidering banners which are now being fastened to the spears by the Lady of the castle '. He thinks it is in colour one of the best things he has done, and adds ' these chivalric Froissartian themes are quite a passion of mine '. Norton agreed to take the picture and sent Rossetti the fee. Three and a half years later, in January 1862, Rossetti is writing apologetically to Norton for not answering letters and for not yet having despatched ' Before the Battle '. ' There is only one shadow of reason I can give for this', he says, 'namely, that I found it did not prove a favourite among my drawings with our mutual friend Ruskin, who had not seen it. . . . Nor will I disguise from you that, on mature consideration of the drawing, I myself think it rather ultra-mediaeval—it having been produced during a solitary stay in the country of some length, at a time when I was peculiarly nourishing myself with such impressions.' William Rossetti considered that this stay in the country must have been when the painter accompanied his fiancée Lizzie Siddal to Matlock in 1857. It was a late and over-elaborated expression of an interest which had flowered five or six years earlier in his verse as well as pictures, notably in the beautiful ' Staff and Scrip '. 'The Staff and Scrip' is a lyrical poem rather than a ballad, although, like the similarly rich coloured 'Bride's Prelude', it is the fruit of the romantic mood at its most poetic.

ROMANTIC ARCHAISM

Perhaps no letter of Rossetti's correspondence is better
known than the long one to his brother on 18th September
1849. William was at Ventnor, Isle of Wight, and the
chief part of the letter is to tell him of the progress made
with the projected magazine which was produced the
following January as *The Germ*. A series of remarks then
follows, indicating his recent reading.

I have done but little in any way, having wasted several days at the
Museum, where I have been reading up all manner of old romaunts,
to pitch upon stunning words for poetry. I have found several, and
also derived much enjoyment from the things themselves, some of which
are tremendously fine. I have copied out an exquisite little ballad,
quoted in the preface to one of the collections.

I bought the other day the original editions of the lyrical numbers of
the *Bells and Pomegranates*, which you remember contain variations;
also Horne's *Orion* (original edition) and *Death of Marlowe* ; also (for 5/-)
a translation, in two volumes, of the *Gesta Romanorum*—a book I had
long wished to possess. I was however rather disappointed having expected to find lots of glorious stories for poems. Four or five good ones
there are ; one of which (which I have entitled *The Scrip and Staff*) I
have considerably altered, and enclose for your opinion, together with
another plot of my own devising. Both of these I contemplate versify-
ing when free of existing nightmares.

It is noteworthy that the original of his poem ' The
Staff and Scrip ' has the background of chivalry, like the
Arthurian legends which he in common with other poets
of the age was to find full of poetic meat. The early
English tale which he found in the Museum is entitled
' The Bloody Shirt: of a Knight who restored a Princess
to her Kingdom, and of her gratitude to him '. This is the
title given to it by Madden, the editor of the Roxburghe
Club's edition. The original tale makes the Queen receive
a bloodied shirt from her victorious dead champion, not a
staff and scrip, and the knight obtains from her not only
a promise of love if he return victorious, having recovered
the Princess's inheritance, but also the undertaking that if
he is killed she will hang his bloodied shirt up where she
can see it, and weep each time she sees it, and when suitors
approach run to it for reminder of her dead knight and

[233]

admonishment to remain faithful to his memory. The essentials of the story are unaltered by Rossetti, but there is both an intensification and economy of expression and the addition of that *picturesque* dream quality which, for want of a more fitting term, may be described as the archaic mood. It is both a mood and a verbal craft which Rossetti had already found in Coleridge, Keats, and the Tennyson of 'The Lady of Shallot'. There is nothing of old English, nor, in truth, of the age of chivalry, in the pseudo-mediaevalism of poetry like this:

> The Queen sat idle by her loom;
> She heard the arras stir,
> And looked up sadly: through the room
> The sweetness sickened her
> Of musk and myrrh.
>
> Her women, standing two and two,
> In silence combed the fleece.
> The Pilgrim said, 'Peace be with you,
> Lady'; and bent his knees.
> She answered, 'Peace'.
>
> Her eyes were like the wave within;
> Like water-reed the poise
> Of her soft body, dainty thin;
> And like the water's noise
> Her plaintive voice.
>
> For him, the stream had never well'd
> In desert tracts malign
> So sweet; nor had he ever felt
> So faint in the sunshine
> Of Palestine.

Although Rossetti enclosed the prose story of 'The Staff and Scrip' in the letter to his brother, he did not, as just remarked, write the poem for at least another year. But in the same letter he says that he has added three stanzas to 'My Sister's Sleep', and the style of this poem, written first in 1847, shows, as do stanzas of 'The Staff and Scrip', a family likeness to that of 'The Blessed Damozel'. No one knew better than Rossetti the extent to which 'The Blessed Damozel' departed from the real early

Italian mood and manner; so probably would he have agreed as a matter of course that ' The Staff and Scrip ' and ' The Bride's Prelude ' belonged to a romantic no-man's-land in which his juniors, Swinburne and Morris, also stayed and disported themselves. But they were less creative in that dream-atmosphere than he. An indication of the distinction between his work and theirs may possibly be found in his deeper sympathy with the imaginative poet-painter, Blake.

CHAPTER XIV

DREAMWORLD

' Some thinking and some dreaming enter into all our mental procedures.'—J. JASTROW.

TWO DIFFERENT observations of Rossetti when writing about Blake in Gilchrist's *Life* show his attitude as a craftsman and his attitude as a dreamer towards the visionary. The first, concerning the imaginative artist's need of facts, of natural models, in completely carrying out the conceptions which he has elaborated imaginatively, is considered in connexion with Rossetti's painting.[1] It is not without reference to his poetry also, but the second, the emotional perception of Blake's experience, is that in which the poetic seeker thinks of ' his travels and adventures in the rich, strange, scarce-imaginable regions of romance '.[2] Here he is expressing an intuitive election. ' While any who can here find anything to love will be the poet-painter's welcome guests, still such a feast is spread first of all for those who can know at a glance that it is theirs and was meant for them; who can meet their host's eye with sympathy and recognition, even when he offers them the new strange fruits grown for himself in far-off gardens where he has dwelt alone, or pours for them the wines which he has learned to love in lands where they never travelled.'

Now the terms of this invitation to make acquaintance with the apocalyptic Blake would be most surprising from so good a critic as Rossetti, but for the personal element which he was not concerned to leave out of his amateur

---

[1] Chap. viii and xvii.
[2] Sub-title to *Henry Brocken* by Walter de la Mare.

critical surveys. It will be remembered how he contrived to bring into his discussion of Blake's influence two writers so unlike Blake, except in being neglected, as Charles Wells and Chatterton, and on account of ' the closest and most absolute resemblance to Blake's poetry ', an obscure book by Garth Wilkinson, the editor of Swedenborg in English. This volume was a collection of automatic writings entitled *Improvisations of the Spirit*. Rossetti's interest claims to be on account of the beauty of some of the pieces, sometimes remote and charming, sometimes grotesquely figurative, and ' startlingly akin to Blake's writings '. The book, he says, shared ' the general limbo of the modern " spiritualist " muse ' which ' in all other cases ' was deserved, thus implying his disbelief in the value of such productions. He says that the *Improvisations* are disjointed and often hopelessly obscure—' but then why be the polisher of poems for which a ghost, and not even your own ghost, is alone responsible ? ' Throughout his remarks on Blake's strangest pictures and eccentric mythology Rossetti is no more than just and usually detached, although in the 1880 edition of Gilchrist's *Life* he adds an eulogistic remark on Swinburne's *Critical Essay*, which has, he says, explored and expounded the Prophetic Books by creative intuition. As a poet-painter Rossetti could, of course, appreciate the workmanship and the imagination of Blake, especially the mixture of ' a subtle and exquisite reality ' with ' ideal grandeur ', and the esoteric lyrical pieces are recognized by him as both mystical and beautiful; but he shows less disposition than either his brother William or Swinburne to pursue Blake intellectually in the obscurities of a piece like ' The Mental Traveller '. In some notes to a selection from Blake he confesses to having been on the point of leaving out this poem, ' in spite of its high poetic beauty, as incomprehensible '.

The effect of such intellectual impatience with Blake is to emphasize the significance of Rossetti's emotional sympathy. Nearly all the notes were written for the 1863 edition of the recently deceased Gilchrist's *Life of Blake*. The reader may form a personal opinion whether an adventure into interpretation such as Rossetti risked in the case of the poem ' William Bond ' derived any motive from his own emotional experiences. Rossetti brings ' William Bond ' into conjunction with ' In a Myrtle Shade '. ' It is not long since there seemed to dawn on the present writer a meaning in this ballad not discovered before.' ' In a Myrtle Shade ', he reminds the reader, bears on marriage. ' William Bond ' may be William Blake, the bondman of the ' lovely myrtle tree ', for ' it is known that the shadow of jealousy, far from unfounded, fell on poor Catherine Blake's married life at one moment, and it has been stated that this jealousy culminated in a terrible and difficult crisis. We ourselves can well imagine that this ballad is but a literal relation, with such emotional actors, of some transfiguring trance and passion of mutual tears from which Blake arose no longer ' bond ' to his myrtle-tree, but with that love, purged of all drossier element, whose last death-bed accent was, " Kate, you have ever been an angel to me! " ' His own notes on Blake was the first work Rossetti attended to after Lizzie's death.

The purely personal or autobiographical interest in Blake is, however, not the most vital. From that day in his teens when Rossetti had bought from a British Museum official the Blake manuscript notebook with the ten shillings borrowed from his more provident brother, he had perceived in himself an imaginative kinship with Blake. The notes which he prepared, to help Gilchrist and then Gilchrist's widow, are necessarily a fragmentary record of his sympathy with Blake, and it is only by noting the prominence of certain aspects of such a sympathy that the link between the two poet-painters can be seen. The humour, both conscious and unconscious, in Blake, he can fully appreciate, and he can trace sadly the effects of Blake's persecution mania in the seer's work. But any sensitive editor can do likewise. So we come back to the tinge of unexpectedness in his description of the dream-like feast offered to the imagination by Blake. Discussing some of the work in more detail he often is moved to give the reader a verbal translation of Blake's pictures of lurid horizons behind lonely lovers on lonely hills; the dark sublimities of the Biblical themes, and the vitality of figures of women and of angels. In the last three designs for the Book of Job he ' would specially direct attention to the exquisite beauty of the female figures. Nothing proves more thoroughly how free was the spiritualism of Blake's art from any ascetic tinge. These women are given to us no less noble in body than in soul; large-eyed, and large-armed also; such as a man may love with all his life '.

If the reader is disposed to smile at this unusual sort of criticism of Blake, let him not forget that it is one of the truest things ever remarked about Blake as an artist. Rossetti perceived it merely because his own tremendous emotional power responded to Blake's. The essence of Blake, the secret of his creative energy and triumphs of expression over the gravest technical obstructions, is in his vast capacity for desire. His ' libido ', as modern psychology would say, is immense. This tremendous outward urge of the forces in his soul drove him to build up, for lack of sufficient traditional material in his intellectual acquirements, a whole universe of his own thought-forms and mythology. Keats's line

Huge cloudy symbols of a high Romance

is perfectly applicable to Blake's work, which externalizes the inner dream world of a very potent dreamer. Blake's failures were nearly always due to insufficient control of the power within him; most other creative workers' failures are generally due to weakening or misdirection of the impulsive inspiration. Rossetti's inspirational power is

not huge like Blake's, but it certainly was powerful enough
to make him ' see things ' that were not there; but whereas
Blake, besides quarrelling with the world, would use in a
confused poem such an externalization of his feelings as he
describes in the thistle that was also an old, old man,
Rossetti was far too sensible of the artistic proprieties to
find such safety valves for morbid intensity of emotional
conflict. Blake could both stamp on the thistle and write
about it, when his heart was boiling with rage against the
world. He could flaunt his most eccentric vision in the
face of smug commonsense, secure in his unbreakable
conviction of divine sanity. But Rossetti, after quarrelling
or being quarrelled with by his friends, had little outlet
except drugging and intoxicating, in which a sensual
mistress was perhaps even more effective and disastrous
than chloral and alcohol. In his work the morbid complications of his mind are merely hinted at, as in the distorted necks of women in his worst pictures (sometimes
the necks are almost phallic in their dreamlike formal
insistency). Usually his excess of imagination approaches
Blake's franker irrationality by finding in the work of
Dante, or in some picture of his own, the meanings of
ominous prophecy for himself. Never was a man's life
more influenced by his imagination than Rossetti's.

The mere occurrence and exploitation of dreams and
visions in the work of poet or painter does not *ipso facto*
indicate exceptional dynamic inspirational power. A
passing fashion, the popular acceptance of a romantic
tendency which has already flowered in the previous
generation, or even the unpopularity and comparative
eccentricity of dream subjects may stimulate an artist's
interest in them. The work containing such suggestive
signs must be examined for what it is worth ere the
demonic force put into it can be gauged. It happens to be
convenient and interesting to examine separately examples
of work having obviously dreamlike features; and it is
when we examine from this point of view the work of

poets often (and not without some reason) grouped together as expressing a particular aspect of their own age that any deep differences in their genius ought to be recognized. The writer of the invitation to feast with Blake on the fruits of those 'far-off gardens' was a native of Blake's dreamland in a sense which could not be applied to the two important Victorian poets Swinburne and Morris, who would seem at a first glance to be most securely in his company of all the poets of the Victorian age. As a matter of fact, Francis Thompson was nearer to Rossetti by divine right of temperament than either of these romanticists.

Poetry is necessarily an affirmation of faith. The faith of religion is belief based on moral feeling; the faith of poetry is belief based on imaginative feeling. Like all sweeping generalizations, this can be shown to make too clean a division, but it is convenient and true for most of the way that it goes. Swinburne's impulse lacked its full power until he found heroes and heroes' ideals to identify himself with. Morris also, though not so clearly, leaned toward the hero and the moral ideal, rather than to the heroine and her heavenly gardens. It may be added that Morris's archaic world was the easy creation of a kind of day-dreaming, having less profound and personal sources than Rossetti's, which no doubt coloured it. Rossetti's early work also coloured Tennyson's first maturity. The early Tennyson of 'The Lady of Shallot' was a direct inheritor from the English 'romantic revival', and as such was an early influence in Rossetti's and his sister Christina's work. Her 'Prince's Progress' is almost certainly inspired by Tennyson's 'Mariana of the Moated Grange', and the atmosphere of 'The Lady of Shallot' is reflected in a small magic mirror in her early lyrics in the mood of 'Dream Land'. Tennyson's magic in this realm is always less potent than either Christina's or her brother's, because he, too, was not thralled there like them, but after the first impulse merely played with the dream world and took therefrom some decorative scenes. In the *English Idylls and other Poems,* which came after the 'Lady of Shallot' group, it seems that he has read Rossetti's early poetry. One of the best stanzas in 'The Day Dream', stanza three of the section called 'The Sleeping Palace', reads like an inferior imitation of Rossetti's curious pauses and silences in 'My Sister's Sleep', a poem which appeared in *The Germ.*

> Roof-haunting martins warm their eggs:
> In these, in those the life is stay'd.
> The mantles from the golden pegs
> Droop sleepily: no sound is made,
> Not even of a gnat that sings.
> More like a picture seemeth all
> Than those old portraits of old kings,
> That watch the sleepers from the wall.

The fact is, although wholehearted admirers of Tennyson may dispute it, that with all his genuine gift and great skill, his mind ran into bogs of commonplace with a readiness almost as fatal as Millais's. What there was of the true romantic vein in Tennyson's work was eagerly appreciated by Rossetti, who at the end of his life, writing of a particular phase of it to Hall Caine, observed that Tennyson had 'the *weird* element . . . here and there in imagery, but there is no great success in the part it plays through his *Idylls.* The old Romaunt beats him there. The strongest instance of this feeling in Tennyson that I remember is in a few lines of 'The Palace of Art':

> And hollow breasts enclosing hearts of flame,
> And with dim-fretted foreheads all
> On corpses three months old at morn she came
> That stood against the wall.

I won't answer for the precise age of the corpses—perhaps I have staled them somewhat'. What Tennyson actually wrote was slightly different from Rossetti's memory of it, but he had not 'staled the corpses':

> But in dark corners of her palace stood
> Uncertain shapes; and unawares
> On white-eyed phantasms weeping tears of blood,
> And horrible nightmares,

And hollow shades enclosing hearts of flame,
  And, with dim fretted foreheads all,
On corpses three months old at noon she came,
  That stood against the wall.

Rossetti's 'breasts' showed an instinctive choice of a
concrete image where it was needed. Tennyson's 'shades',
though not so obviously as other instances, gives him
away. These 'horrible nightmares' are poetic pastiche,
a very little green dust of dreams to a jar of paste. Another
of the comparatively good stanzas of 'The Palace of Art'
was illustrated by Rossetti, and the picture was more
magical than the verses:

Or mythic Uther's deeply-wounded son
  In some fair space of sloping greens
Lay, dozing in the vale of Avalon,
  And watch'd by weeping queens.

Without the brilliant phrase-making, what would Tennyson's dreams of palaces and fair women have produced in
verse? What would the above stanza be without 'weeping
queens'? The useful Pre-Raphaelite 'slosh' is hardly
adequate here.

Tennyson's work nevertheless has an affinity, not always
superficial, to that of Swinburne, Morris, and the Rossettis,
and it is most clearly indicated by the frequency of the
dream motive. Whether working up a personal nightmare
in a 'Vision of Sin', or describing the dreams of a city
clerk and his wife who are awakened by a medicine bottle
falling on the floor,[1] he shows a conscious interest in the
working of the dreaming mind. But after 'The Lady of
Shallot' period he describes rather than evokes the dream.
Swinburne, in whose work dreams occur with still more
frequency, often uses them decoratively, but the authentic
quarter-tones dwindling into unheard melodies of dream
are heard in pieces like 'The Garden of Proserpine', a
title, by the way, which is remarkably characteristic of the
romantic pursuit of the dream. William Rossetti's

[1] 'Sea Dreams.'

[243]

observation was just, that in such rare music Swinburne may have remembered Christina Rossetti's haunting tunes.

There is at any rate no doubt that both Swinburne and Morris were inspired by Rossetti's early work, both painting and poetry. The 'Christmas Carol' in *Poems and Ballads*, first series, was, the poet declared, written after a water-colour with the same title painted by Rossetti in 1857 and exhibited in 1858 at Liverpool, in the same exhibition which contained the water-colour 'Dante's Dream'. In the picture there are three figures altogether, the central one being a woman with outspread billowing hair held up on either hand by two maids who are combing it. The lady contrives to play at the same time on a sort of spinet. Probably Swinburne wrote his poem from a memory of the picture because he supplies the queen with three damsels; he defines but also limits the mood of the picture:

> Three damsels in the queen's chamber,
> The queen's mouth was most fair;
> She spake a word of God's mother
> As the combs went in her hair.
> Mary that is of might,
> Bring us to thy Son's sight.

> They held the gold combs out from her,
> A span's length off her head;
> She sang this song of God's mother
> And of her bearing-bed.
> Mary most full of grace,
> Bring us to thy Son's face.

Unquestionably this poem is not in Swinburne's best manner, for the theme did not awaken in him the authentic feeling that Rossetti could charge it with. It is curious that two of the poems written by Morris which were inspired by early pictures of Rossetti also have for theme the playing of music by queenly women in a dream-tranced chamber. The pictures were 'The Blue Closet' and 'The Tune of Seven Towers', which were among the water-colours bought by Morris from the artist in 1857. In the closely filled space of the pictures there is again the decorative

symbolism and archaic musical instrument and costume.
'The Blue Closet' has four female figures, two of them
singing. Each of the two in the middle and slightly to
the front play on a clavichord. The right-hand one, who is
plucking at the strings and wears a crown, seems to have
been drawn from Christina Rossetti. The blue tiles of
floor and walls give the prevailing tone, but the two queenly
figures are dressed in crimson and grey, and red and green.
Archaic costume is still more in evidence in ' The Tune of
Seven Towers '. A lady plays on a flat string instrument,
presumably a sort of harpsichord, resting on her lap. A
man in green doublet and plumed hat, resembling the male
figure in ' How they Met Themselves ', sits close, leans
listening over the instrument. The lady is a portrait of
Lizzie Siddal, and the man's face is like a study from the
artist himself. The portraiture is therefore another link
with ' How they Met Themselves '. Symbolic and dream-
like details fill all the space of the picture. In the background, where a recess like another chamber is seen, a maid
leans through the aperture of a sliding panel and places a
sprig of orange on the bed. The rope from a belfry falls
along the lady's shoulder, and behind her stands another
maid, rapt and sorrowful in mien. This picture, painted a
few years before Rossetti's marriage, is almost as ominous
as the drawing of ' How they Met Themselves ' done on
his honeymoon. Such work, combining romantic archaism
of colour and detail with an atmosphere of weirdness, is
characteristic of his pictures after ' Ecce Ancilla Domini '
up to ' Beata Beatrix '. Morris was very sympathetic to
the work of this kind which Rossetti did between the ages
of about twenty-two to thirty-five. Sometimes, like the
pictures just mentioned, it was purely fantastic in character, at other times it borrowed more directly from legend
or history as in the ' Damsel of the Sanc Grael ', another
water-colour bought by Morris, and the ' Arthur's Tomb:
the Last Meeting of Lancelot and Guenevere ', which has
a counterpart in Morris's ' King Arthur's Tomb '. The

date of this last water-colour, 1854, shows the interest of
Rossetti in the *Morte D'Arthur* five years before the publication of Tennyson's *Idylls of the King*, though later than the
appearance of his first ' Morte D'Arthur ' poem. A comparison of Tennyson's and Morris's poems about the
death of Arthur shows that the clear and often haunting
imagery is Tennyson's and the deep feeling is Morris's.
Rossetti combined the passion and the dream imagery.
In the Arthurian vein Burne-Jones is Tennyson's plastic
equivalent. It was the purely fantastic in Rossetti's painting which found the happiest response in Morris's brief
poems of the type of ' Two Red Roses across the Moon '.
The equivalent of this poetry of dreamland was usually
more archaic in Swinburne, as in ' The King's Daughter ',
which is less detached from legendary context than ' Two
Red Roses Across the Moon '; though Swinburne, when
he chose, could do it as well as anybody, chanting a sestina
or a ballad of dreamland in a voice heavy with the pleasure
of secret song.

But that dreamy archaic and decorative mood which
Swinburne and Morris for a time gave themselves to,
which comes fitfully in Tennyson's work, and which a host
of lesser poets last century exploited, is not at all characteristic of Rossetti. There seems to be some popular confusion here of this precious style with ' pre-Raphaelitism '
and by association with Rossetti. Yet I do not know what,
except sheer fancifulness, could induce a writer to speak
as follows of Swinburne's career: ' Of the dim Bohemian
period after Oxford this much is sure: it saw a contest
between a restricted and, to his temperament, debilitating,
artistic influence, and the wide genial influence of unrestricted nature and open life. It was the Pre-Raphaelite
studio opposed by the sea. Rossetti led to the one, Watts-
Dunton and Landor's example to the other '.[1]

Swinburne had made himself the poet of the sea in his
early work. For him the contest was not between an

[1] *Swinburne and Landor*, by W. Brooks Drayton Henderson, 1918.

artistic influence and 'unrestricted nature' etc., but between dipsomania and Putney Heath. Rossetti did not make him intemperate. Pre-Raphaelite art was not in the least divorced from 'the sea' or any other phase of 'nature': it strove to be nearer to them. Mr. Henderson did not attempt to explain his use of 'debilitating'. Morris's and Swinburne's more sterile languors of musical emptiness were not found in Rossetti's work. Indeed, during the period of closest association with Rossetti they had only the finest of the latter's poetry to observe and admire, and there seems nothing 'debilitating' about 'The Blessed Damozel' or 'The Burden of Nineveh' or about the iron-muscled translations of the early Italians. Neither are the sensuous or sensual erotic elements of Rossetti's half-mystical poetry at all like Morris's frank pagan delight which produced:

> The bee-beset ripe-seeded grass
> Through which thy fine limbs first did pass;
> The purple-dusted butterfly
> First blown against thy quivering thigh,
> The first red rose that touched thy side,

in 'The Hill of Venus', which turned to impotent fever in Swinburne. Yet these poets were undoubtedly stimulated to their dreamy archaism by Rossetti, especially by the water-colours with archaic trappings which have just been referred to. That they may have been thus lured into a wasteful absorption of their genius for a time is possible but unlikely. How watchfully antagonistic Rossetti himself was to artistic softness in poetry is very well shown by his treatment of the early sonnet for the 'Venetian Pastoral' by Giorgione, which Swinburne not only admired enthusiastically but verbally imitated in some of the lines of 'At Eleusis'. Rossetti's criticism of his own sonnet indicates where he avoids the preciosities of Morris and Swinburne. When published in *The Germ* in 1850 it ended:

> Nor name this ever. Be it as it was,—
> Silence of heat and solemn poetry.

When his poems were being printed in 1869 and his brother

read the proofs of the privately printed *Trial Book*, the latter noticed the change of the conclusion of the sonnet into:

> Nor name this ever. Be it as it was,—
> Life touching lips with Immortality.

William expressed regret at losing the original last line for one which seemed too ideal an abstraction. The reply of the poet was: ' I remember you expressed a preference once before for the old line, which seems to me quite bad. " Solemn poetry " belongs to the class of phrase absolutely forbidden, I think, in poetry. It is intellectually incestuous —poetry seeking to beget its emotional offspring on its own identity. Whereas I see nothing too " ideal " in the present line. It gives only a momentary contact with the immortal which results from sensuous culmination, and is always a half-conscious element of it '.

Rossetti's austere severity is really surprising, for the banished line was certainly a good one, and ' solemn ' casts a shadow of meaning back to the midday heat of the whole picture and poem—heat and silence and stillness. Besides, poetry may sometimes be intellectually incestuous—it depends on the poet's dynamic energy whether the offspring is any good. But his self-criticism is true to the character of the work inspired by his dreaming mind, which supplied him with an exceptionally powerful impulse. This explains the authenticity of his romantic archaism and shows why refined virtuosity in the minor key of dream-desire is not a characteristic of Rossetti's work. Two of his earliest designs were, it is true, inspired by Coleridge's 'Genevieve' and Keats's ' La Belle Dame Sans Merci ', but he did not subsequently turn these into pictures, and his own poems with a dream-like atmosphere have a wider range of thought in them. The ' Blessed Damozel ' contains the extremely simple sensuousness of ' the gold bar of heaven ', and the metaphorical subtlety of

> From the fixed place of Heaven she saw
> Time like a pulse shake fierce
> Through all the worlds.

In ' Love's Nocturne ' the authentic inspiration is again impressively controlled and expressed with all the ability of the poet's intellect, so that the intelligence of the expression is apt to overshadow the exquisite justice of the style. The gathered wisdom of contemplative hours is united to the impulsive desire of the dream.

> Master of the murmuring courts
> Where the shapes of sleep convene!
> Lo! my spirit here exhorts
> All the powers of thy demesne
> For their aid to woo my queen.
> What reports
> Yield thy jealous courts unseen?
>
> Vaporous, unaccountable,
> Dreamworld lies forlorn of light,
> Hollow like a breathing shell.
> Ah! that from all dreams I might
> Choose one dream and guide its flight!
> I know well
> What her sleep should tell to-night.
>
> There the dreams are multitudes:
> Some whose buoyance waits not sleep,
> Deep within the August woods;
> Some that hum while rest may steep
> Weary labour laid a-heap;
> Interludes,
> Some, of grievous moods that weep.

Every line almost contains a verbal gem or a curious and searching thought. Swinburne would have sung all through a ballad of ' weary labour laid a-heap '—like the day's cast-off clothes—and of the dreams that are interludes between weeping sorrow. But the dream theme has illuminated the poet's mind in all its recesses, and he goes on discovering fields of knowledge in himself—in that world of dreams.

> Poets' fancies all are there:
> There the elf-girls flood with wings
> Valleys full of plaintive air;
> There breathe perfumes; there in rings
> ·Whirl the foam-bewildered springs;
> Siren there
> Winds her dizzy hair and sings.

DANTE GABRIEL ROSSETTI

From that world comes the mutual dream leading to bridal
union; there, too, are 'half-formed visions' that were
known in the womb, and also what we see when we reach
the gate of death. He knows that his own sleep is surren-
dered to a woman in whose eyes is the goal of his love.
Without her his dreams are hideous with fears. He wants
to know if dreams (as Hazlitt[1] might have told him) do in
some way mirror profoundly the self of the dreamer:

> Master, is it soothly said
> That, as echoes of man's speech
> Far in secret clefts are made,
> So do all men's bodies reach
> Shadows o'er thy sunken beach,—
> Shape or shade
> In those halls pourtrayed of each?

In the next two stanzas he imagines the separate existence
of his own phantom in the shadowy place. First, through
Love's good grace, he might

> Groping in the windy stair
> (Darkness and the breath of space
> Like loud waters everywhere),
> Meeting mine own image there
> Face to face,
> Send it from that place to her!

The intense pursuit of the exciting thought only stimulates
the subtle skill with which, inside those brackets, he
contrives to express unforgettably, in ten words, the
sensation of the awed soul leaving the body's accustomed
shelter. But not he can send himself so; he will ask Love:

> do thou
> Master, from thy shadow kind
> Call my body's phantom now:
> Bid it bear its face declin'd
> Till its flight her slumbers find,
> And her brow
> Feel its presence there like wind.

---

[1] In *The Plain Speaker*.

Where in groves the gracile Spring
Trembles, with mute orison
Confidently strengthening,
Water's voice and wind's as one
Shed an echo in the sun.
Soft as Spring,
Master, bid it sing and moan. . . .

Is the imagery and delicate adjustment of thought and
words not exquisite?

The poem becomes a little more reflective now, and as
in the idea of Love sending the dreamer's phantom to the
sleeping Beloved, Dante's ' New Life ' is recalled by some
succeeding lines. ' Song ' shall tell his secret, and say how
the alighting of her glance in his sleeping and waking
dreams marks the night-watches and the hours of day.
And then, another haunting image:

Suddenly her face is there:
So do mounting vapours wreathe
Subtle-scented transports where
The black firwood sets its teeth.
Part the boughs and look beneath,—
Lilies share
Secret waters there, and breathe.

In a new ecstasy of desire he invokes Love again, and asks
that his shadow may remain whispering over the Beloved's
sleep. But if another phantom should be there already?
And if she should hear that alien's words, and smile?
Shall his shade strive then, or fade unseen? Nay, how
should love's messenger strive with love—nay:

If thus, in her,
Sleep a wedded heart should show,—
Silent let mine image go,
Its old share
Of thy spell-bound air to know.

Then let his phantom give one more cold salute, at the
death of all his pining life of hope. But since Love's rule
is that of life, not death, as Adam ' with mingling breath '
woke beside his wife,

O Love, bring me so, for strife,
Force and faith. . . .

[251]

A peculiarity of Rossetti's poetry of dream is in its variety of content. His familiarity with dream landscape enables him to people the minds of characters treated dramatically. The psychological insight displayed in ' A Last Confession ', in the suggestion of the speaker's half-dream, half-hysteria, is profound and acute. It is really quite beyond Browning's capacity for reproducing such a state of mind: where the poet of ' A Last Confession ' lives into the drama, Browning would skilfully and sensitively analyse and interpret. The difference is due to Rossetti's freer communication with the mind's dark depths where passion creates dream phantasmagoria. How unexpected, in another way, is the sudden recital by the butcher who tells the story of ' The White Ship ', of his rush of dreaming memories when under water.

> These things and the like were heard and shown
> In a moment's trance 'neath the sea alone;
> And when I rose 'twas the sea did seem,
> And not these things, to be all a dream.

The use of the dream as a dramatic device, even as part of a sympathetic dramatic representation of experience is not so characteristic of Rossetti as it is of Tennyson. Rossetti writes best of dream in a subjective mood, as when he contemplates ' the soul's sphere of infinite images ' and ' that last wild pageant of the accumulated past that clangs and flashes for a drowning man '.[1] He takes the dream world seriously, not merely as an artistic device, but because it affords him more convincing material of reality than the world of daylight. When he maintains himself most securely in the world shared by the waking minds of others it is by his dramatic sense, a sympathy with elemental emotions, as in the ballads, and such poems as ' Jenny ' and ' A Last Confession ', where he is somewhat akin to Browning. Our dream world is more individual and private than the waking world, and therefore the poetry of dreaming is more egoistic than the dramatic poetry of human

[1] *House of Life* (62).

passions need be. Rossetti's dream world is ever intruding into his more personal poems, whatever the ostensible motive—which is nearly always love and desire or regret for a woman. It is in keeping with his cast of thought that when he writes a poem that runs like an accompaniment of human emotion to the sweet monotony of running and rippling water, it should be called ' The Stream's Secret ' and should show in half its imagery the reflected deeps of dreaming memory. The secret he would unriddle from the water's whispering is a secret of the grave, and beyond.

> O soul-sequestered face
> Far-off,—O were that night but now!
> So even beside that stream even I and thou
> Through thirsting lips should draw Love's grace,
> And in the zone of that supreme embrace
> Bind aching breast and brow.

Written during 1869 and 1870, begun at Penkhill, and completed at Robertsbridge, ' The Stream's Secret ' is close to the mood of the last sonnet of *The House of Life*, which also belongs to 1870. ' Love's Nocturne ', which was written in 1854 and may have been addressed to either Fanny Cornforth or Lizzie Siddal, completes the range of thought about the bodiless soul's journeys. There it was led by Love during the body's sleep to the Beloved. In ' The Stream's Secret ' the poet bends a flushed and urgent brow to the wordless whispering of water, pursuing now a desire that reaches past the grave, for this poem is occupied with the memory of his dead wife. But he can only question, and weep like a lost child, in pity of himself. In ' The One Hope ' the question has been transformed into a necessary belief that, as in dreams, so after death, the soul may travel free of the body and meet the Beloved.

But ' The One Hope ' is poetry of dream, rather than the poetry of mystical faith, in spite of its Dantesque vision. In all such poems Rossetti expresses a mystical perception, but it comes in rather as the creation of fantasy; it is not the constant background as, for instance, in Francis

Thompson's work. There are other sonnets in *The House of Life* written during the same period—notably Nos. 37 to 39, 'The Love Moon', 'The Morrow's Message', and 'Sleepless Dreams', in which past, present, and future are brought together in the moment of the mind's illumination, and always with similar symbolism referring to the union of Love. 'The Love Moon' faces the problem of his new love and its reconcilement with the memory of love. It is a reminder of another of those very curious imaginative anticipations of life which seam Rossetti's work with a darkly ominous streak. As a youth, when he competed with his brother in the writing of sonnets to fixed end-rhymes (an approach to automatic writing, since the mind has to seize the first images that occur to it), he wrote one called 'Another Love', in 1848. It is enough to quote it without comment:

> Of her I thought who now is gone so far:
>   And, the thought passing over, to fall thence
>   Was like a fall from spirit into sense
> Or from the heaven of heavens to sun and star.
> None other than Love's self ordained the bar
>   'Twixt her and me; so that if, going hence,
>   I met her, it could only seem a dense
> Film of the brain,—just nought, as phantoms are.
>
> Now when I passed your threshold and came in,
>   And glanced where you were sitting, and did see
>   Your tresses in these braids and your hands thus,—
> I knew that other figure, grieved and thin,
>   That seemed there, yea that was there, could not be,
>   Though like God's wrath it stood dividing us.

Several of the seriously written poems of later years reproduce the fantasy in these spontaneous lines. The chief imagery may be compared with that of the beautiful lyric 'Spheral Change', written in 1881 under the shadow of imminent death.

> . . . If only one might speak!—the one
>   Who never waits till I come near;
> But always seated all alone
>   As listening to the sunken air,
>   Is gone before I come to her. . .

DREAMWORLD

> O nearest, furthest! Can there be
> At length some hard-earned heart-won home,
> Where,—exile changed for sanctuary,—
> Our lot may fill indeed its sum,
> And you may wait and I may come?

This is a reminder of another of the later lyrics which are expressions of the same thought. 'Insomnia' has the music of dream as well as the fantasy:

> Thin are the night-skirts left behind
> By daybreak hours that onward creep,
> And thin, alas! the shred of sleep
> That wavers with the spirit's wind:
> But in half-dreams that shift and roll
> And still remember and forget,
> My soul this hour has drawn your soul
> A little nearer yet.

Sometimes Rossetti's dream imagery seems to have disturbed him too profoundly so that he could not make of certain favourite themes the poetry he conceived. No other explanation suffices for the prose fragments, 'The Philtre', 'The Orchard Pit', and 'The Doom of the Sirens'—which belong to the years 1869-1870—never being used as he intended. True, 'The Doom of the Sirens: a Lyrical Tragedy' was possibly too big an undertaking for him once he had passed the best of his health and inspiration. The prose sketch of it which appears in the Collected Works was a promise of something which would have rivalled Shelley's 'Prometheus Unbound'. The story in its dramatic situations and scenery is beautifully adapted to Rossetti's genius, and the synopsis he wrote is very like an account of day dreaming. If only Rossetti's mind had not been divided between poetry and painting he might have greatly enriched his poetic work by following some of the possibilities which opened before him in such archaic settings for his dream world as the Siren's Rock, an abandoned Oracle of the grove, revivified and terrible Sirens, and a newly married Christian Prince withal, who must triumph over them spiritually

[255]

though he succumb to the doom of death. Had Rossetti pursued this path he could not have failed to re-enter the ancient world of Artemidorus. He might have united, with strange and beautiful consequences, the pagan mind which recognized the giver of dreams as a god, and that archaic, mediaeval world in which he found the mysteries of cruder superstition. When poetry was still largely a function of religion, the Greeks recognized several dream gods, though Hermes was chief. Such products of poetic imagination were quickly absorbed in religious beliefs. To the figures of Morpheus and Ikelos were added Phobetor the Terrifyer (who assumed animal shapes as well as human) and Phantasos (who represented inanimate things), and a regular cult grew up of the God of Dreams co-existent with the cult of the God of Sleep. So developed the mantic art and the custom of holy incubation. Dream oracles became a flourishing industry, and certainly the memory of them persisted in the Middle Ages and coloured the imagination of Europe. Rossetti's archaic pictures and ballads show that he needed rather more material to choose from. Among pictures his 'Proserpine' and 'Astarte Syriaca' and 'Pandora' are the most successful plastic expressions of such visions with an ancient background. Whatever more he might have done with them, like 'How they Met Themselves', would have been impoverished, as his weird ballad stories are, by lack of traditional atmosphere to fill in the dark spaces penetrated by his dreaming mind. I think something of this is suggested by the finished prose fragment 'The Orchard Pit', which is closely akin to Poe's fantastic tales, though the imagery is typical of Rossetti's imagination: the pit, filled with men's corpses, the screens of foliage, the fair siren in the fork of the moonlit apple tree who lures men by her song and kills them by her apple. The narrator dreams of the dell because he is doomed to die there. The apple trees there 'are like others, and have childish memories connected with them, though I was taught to shun the place'. The doomed man, like the Prince in 'The Doom of the Sirens', is loved by a good woman, the innocent and protective, mothering influence, who nevertheless unconsciously assists the fulfilment of the doom.

'One day at table my love offered me an apple. And as I took it she laughed, and said, "Do not eat, it is the fruit of the Siren's dell". And I laughed and ate: and at the heart of the apple was a red stain like a woman's mouth; and as I bit I could feel a kiss upon my lips.'

The story concludes as the record of the narrator's dream of 'how the end will come'. He descends the moonlit slopes of the dell, pushing through the thick apple trees which are loaded, though it is autumn, with both fruit and blossom. At last 'looking far down' he sees a white hand holding out an apple and hears the first notes of the Siren's song. He finally breaks away from his Love who has followed in vain attempt to restrain him. As the Siren's song came clearer to his ears, it sounded first 'Come to Love'. Then 'Come to Life'. Then 'Come to Death'. 'The Orchard Pit' is not merely an invented story, it is too true a reflection of Rossetti's dreaming mind, which carried him along that ever inward-turning path whose source is a human womb and whose destination finds the counterpart of that lost home at last in the dark, quiet tomb. Hence comes that mood in *The House of Life* clearly voiced in 'The Heart of the Night':

> From child to youth; from youth to arduous man;
> From lethargy to fever of the heart;
> From faithful life to dream-dowered days apart;
> From trust to doubt; from doubt to brink of ban;—
> Thus much of change in one swift cycle ran
> Till now. Alas, the soul!—how soon must she
> Accept her primal immortality,—
> The flesh resume its dust whence it began?

The sonnet ends in a prayer for salvation through work from the Siren's doom of nescience. Between the writing of 'The Orchard Pit' and 'The Heart of the Night' Rossetti had made that attempt in the summer of 1872

to kill himself by laudanum. That was a desperate pursuit
of easy peace through a sudden accession of energy to the
regressive tendency of his mind towards its earliest
memories. We know that the dream imagery strengthened
into action because of his disordered nervous system and
the shock it could not sustain of attacks on his *amour-
propre* from the outside world, but his work shows that
these facts were merely incidental accompaniments of his
spiritual career. Because of his ill-health the strokes of external events could precipitate a disaster in his life, but
otherwise they account for scarcely anything in that dream-
world whose gleaming shadows seem to charge his poems
and many of his pictures with an illumination which makes
sunlight as but shadow and, sometimes, a goblin of the
very sun.

CHAPTER XV

BALLAD-POEMS AND NARRATIVES

'*Here undeluding dreams abide.*'—WALTER DE LA MARE.

'*Truth in art seems to me to stand at a fixed centre, midway between its two antagonists—Fact and Phantasm.*'—
SAMUEL PALMER.

WITHOUT trying to settle the disputed question as to whether any written poem can be called a ballad at all, some basis for judging Rossetti's ballad-poems is afforded by comparisons with recognized traditional balladry. For convenience the following pieces by Rossetti may be grouped together as narrative poems with varying degrees of ballad character: 'Dennis Shand', 'Stratton Water', 'Sister Helen', 'Rose Mary', 'The King's Tragedy', 'The White Ship', 'Troy Town', 'Eden Bower', 'The Staff and Scrip'. 'The Blessed Damozel' also has affinities with this group, but on account of its lyrical and pictorial qualities it is rightly outside, and nearer to narratives with lyrical reflection like 'The Bride's Prelude' and 'Jenny'. The difficulty of making such varied poems fit into any classification is evident in the diversity of this company, for among Rossetti's narrative poems are 'Dante at Verona' and 'A Last Confession'. Even among the nine just grouped as ballad-poems there is a wide range of essential poetic power, formal character, and of mood. 'Dennis Shand', which Rossetti himself excluded from his published poems, because, as he explained to Hall Caine, 'it deals trivially with a base amour', is as close to the construction and manner of the old ballad as any piece he wrote. It opens on the eve of the conclusion of an episode, casting a glance at preceding events and leading straight up to the climax, the return of the betrayed husband. It is certainly trivial as a poem, but this may account for its formal success. Rossetti was not forced to complicate the story, which is as simple as the traditional ballad stanza used for it. But of course it lacks the emotional climax of the best ballads. The climax here is also anti-climax; the returned lord's good-natured remarks in reply to his wife's lies dissolve the ballad motive in an ironic smile, behind which is a suspicion of disgust. 'The Staff and Scrip', which is a beautiful poem, is a lyrical narrative, nearer to 'The Blessed Damozel' than might be realized at once, because of the very dramatic opening:

'Who rules these lands?' the Pilgrim said.
  'Stranger, Queen Blanchelys.'
'And who has thus harried them?' he said.
  'It was Duke Luke did this:
    God's ban be his!'

The Pilgrim said: 'Where is your house?
  I'll rest there, with your will.'
'You've but to climb these blackened boughs
  And you'll see it over the hill,
    For it burns still.'

'Which road, to seek your Queen?' said he.
  'Nay, nay, but with some wound
You'll fly back hither, it may be,
  And by your blood i' the ground
    My place be found.'

That claims the highest praise as dramatic narrative, and it might have been the opening of a tremendous ballad, but the intensity of the poetry quickly takes the poem out of its ballad character so soon as the preliminary action gives place to the lyrical-pictorial description. The atmosphere is suddenly rarified and exotic, and after the description of the scene within the arras discovered by the Pilgrim, the poet becomes purely lyrical to describe the Queen whose 'eyes were like the wave within' and the

Pilgrim Knight's recognition of her as the haunter of his dreams. The narrative quickly becomes dramatic and passionate again as it covers the departure of the Knight to battle; the suspense of the women, and the woeful victory. Then the poem becomes more retrospective, telling of the Queen's long years of grief, yet ' a Queen's life ' surrounded by the cares and trivial pleasures of others. But above the bed she sleeps in are the staff and scrip which the Knight had left in her keeping in case of his death in the fight which restored her dominion. The first night her grief shook the staff and scrip hanging there. Each year after ' the wind that shed the leaf ' shook them again. Then, in the following stanza, is a dramatic touch rather too subtle for the ballad proper:

> And once she woke with a clear mind
> That letters writ to calm
> Her soul lay in the scrip; to find
> Only a torpid balm
> And dust of palm.

After a Queen's life, ' a Queen's death '. The unity of the ballad's single theme is again broken here, for ' the lists are set in Heaven to-day ', and a moving climax, in the present tense, makes all the preceding story like an intro-duction to the celestial triumph of the united lovers. God pays at last the Pilgrim the ' wage He owed ' of ' imperishable peace '. Except that the scene is set in heaven the eve of this denouement would mark the beginning of a separate ballad story. The ' Staff and Scrip ' is a fine poem, but it is better not to apply to it any standard of method or of shape which belongs to the kind of archaic literature adapted by Rossetti for his own creative pleasure.

On the score of dramatic quality ' Sister Helen ' will bear comparison with any ballad, and it is structurally a ballad indeed. The original version of 1851 was more simple but less powerful than the final version, and it is interesting to note that Rossetti's masterly alterations tended to change its ballad character by complicating the psychology.[1] Eight new stanzas involving a new incident, Rossetti wrote to Hall Caine, were being added. 'Your hair is on end, I know, but if you heard the stanzas, they would smooth if not curl it. The gain is immense.' The fourth line of the third stanza from the end, which originally ran:

But Keith of Ewern's sadder still,

had previously been altered, for the 1870 edition, to:

But he and I are sadder still,

which was a revolutionary change, because Sister Helen loses her witch character and becomes a woman; instead of fiendish pleasure in her revenge against the man who has betrayed her, she tortures herself while burning the waxen effigy of her former lover. This intensifies the dramatic suspense which in true ballad style is slowly developed by the refrains, and by the repeated pleas for mercy for the dying man, which are each followed by her bitter refusal. Rossetti's most important addition was consequential to the idea of making the dying man a three days' bridegroom. The bride 'is the last pleader', in Rossetti's words,[2] 'as vainly as the others, and with a yet more exulting development of vengeance in the forsaken witch'. The final stanza, when the effigy is burnt and the bridegroom is dead,

'Ah! what white thing at the door has cross'd?
Sister Helen?
Ah! what is this that sighs in the frost?'
'A soul that's lost as mine is lost,
Little brother!'
(O Mother, Mary Mother,
Lost, lost, all lost, between Hell and Heaven.)

expresses the original idea, that Sister Helen's demoniac vengeance was bought only at the price of her own soul. There seems to be no justification for describing this as

[1] A detailed account of the discussion between Rossetti and Sir Hall Caine of the changes made in 'Sister Helen' is given in the latter's *Recollections of Rossetti*, chap. 4. [2] *Ibid.*

'a departure from the scheme that forms the underplot
of Goethe's *Faust*',[1] for it is the point of closest resemblance
to an otherwise very different theme. The question is not
Faust's motive, whether love of knowledge or hatred of it,
but whether he could obtain an unlawful desire without
paying the price of his true self. That was the price paid
by Sister Helen. Rossetti's poem is too rich in truth to be
a ballad in the sense that his translation of 'John of Tours'
can be called a ballad. The verbal nuances are also of
course too fine for the bald ballad style which concerns
itself with stating facts only, not shades of meaning.

In 'Stratton Water' the traditional device of incre-
mental repetition is employed as accurately and effectively
as in 'Sister Helen'; moreover, 'Stratton Water' is in the
usual ballad stanza, and in language as close as the poet
could get to the old simple diction without the ill-advised
exploitation of many archaic words. The theme is again
that of a betrayed woman, but the betrayal has been due to
treachery. Lord Sands finds Janet, whom he had been
told was dead, in the throes of imminent child-bearing,
lying helpless by the rising Stratton flood. Mutual
explanations follow in the approved ballad style. She
refuses to enter his castle or meet his mother's eye until
she is wed. Rossetti skilfully avoids bathos by introducing
a comical touch in describing the fetching of Father John,
and the perilous journey to the flooded kirk-yard. Lord
Sands succeeds in lifting the distressed woman inside the
just parted kirk-yard gate.

> But woe's my heart for Father John
> And the saints he clamoured to !
> There's never a saint but Christopher
> Might hale such buttocks through !

Nevertheless all went well, and the story ends with:

> Now make the white bed warm and soft
> And greet the merry morn ;
> The night the mother should have died,
> The young son shall be born.

---

[1] *Ibid.*, chap. 2.

[263]

The piece is neither more nor less serious, in the artistic sense, than ' Dennis Shand '. It was written in 1854, at a time when Rossetti was working at mediaeval themes for pictures, and writing but little poetry.

The only other notable poems done in the same year were ' Sudden Light ' and ' Love's Nocturne ', apart from two sonnets. Not an unproductive year judged by ordinary standards, and better than some of his later years, but certainly well below Rossetti's average rate of poetic production in the good years. A study of the dates of composition given by his brother in the Collected Works leads to the conclusion that he put less feeling into verse when he was writing little than when he crowded the poems into a rich period of time. This would be explained by his absorption in creative effort, which was deepest when his mind was tuned to the deeper inspiration. While he was young he enjoyed a ready communication with the subconscious impulses, but this had to be recovered by continually more difficult preparation as he approached his complex maturity. The difficulty was felt first in his poetic creation because of the loss of facility resulting from disuse of the verbal medium. He had very little to learn in verbal craft; but in painting, which the need for money forced him to practise with more continuity, he was learning until past his maturity. After that, as he told Sir Hall Caine, he painted by rule, knowing exactly by what means to gain any effect he sought. After ' The Day Dream ' and ' Proserpine ' summit his art failed because the old force was not there to be expressed through the experienced technique. His remaining genius found in poetry the link with its own former achievements. That portion of his poetry which appears in the form of narrative reappears at intervals throughout his life, in youth, in maturity, and in the final phase when he could do no more in painting artistically comparable to ' The White Ship ', ' The King's Tragedy ', and certain brief poems belonging to these years.

At least two of the ballad poems belonging to Rossetti's maturity of life could be guessed at if we were not supplied with the dates, which are connected with the publication of the 1870 volume of *Poems*. They are 'Troy Town' and 'Eden Bower'. The other is 'Rose Mary', which has more affinity with the earlier interest in weird mysteries. His dabbling in spiritualism during the 1860's was a practical expression of that instinctive fearful curiosity about the dark unknown, and it left him convinced of unknown realities but extremely repugnant to any further contact with them. Poetry still offered a safe expression of the mixture in his mind of superstition and mysticism. Thus it is that 'Rose Mary' came to be written in 1871, after the final and emotionally most expensive conquest of his hidden fears; the exhumation of his poems from his wife's grave in 1869 had been succeeded by a burst of wonderful creative activity stimulated by the prospective 1870 volume and then continuing by its own momentum for a while after the publication. The contemplative 'Cloud Confines' belongs to the same year as 'Rose Mary'. A mature mind—at least as mature as Rossetti's mind ever was—had control of a mature craft. The weakest element in 'Rose Mary' was the Beryl-Songs, inserted about 1879 through a discussion of the poem with Watts-Dunton. Unfortunately, the poet's principle in composing them was to show how much he could force the word 'beryl' to serve as a rhyme! If he had written the Songs at his highest level, or even at the level of 'Rose Mary', which is almost equal to his finest work, they would no doubt have had a tremendous refrain effect. The story of this poem, which is quite appropriate in character to the ballad form, is again too complicated for a ballad proper. The brainwork in the poem would have sufficed to produce a whole 'geste' of primitive ballads. It has to be read through more than once before it can be intellectually mastered sufficiently for a realization of its power and unity. The feeling for mystery is not so spontaneous, and there is a less refined subtlety of atmosphere than in earlier and slighter poems. The mere mass of the poem might be held enough to account for this: not even Coleridge could have tackled a weird ballad on these lines and maintained a word-created atmosphere to match the subject, as he did in ‘ Christabel ’ and ‘ The Ancient Mariner ’. For sustained poetic power this long and condensed narrative poem has rarely been equalled. Comparisons on the score of length alone give it an unusual character among poems so closely woven of a single incident. In its three parts it has respectively 56, 59, and 51 five-line stanzas, so that without counting the beryl songs at the end of each part, it has 830 lines. Comparison of length with diffuse poems covering many incidents or characters, such as Spenser, Shelley, and Swinburne wrote, has no value. Shakespeare’s ‘ Lucrece ’ has 264 seven-line stanzas, a total of 1,848 lines. It is difficult to think of other poets’ narratives which may be compared with ‘ Rose Mary ’ as examples of power sustained; for anything like Shelley’s ‘ Revolt of Islam ’ belongs to a different order of composition. His ‘ Witch of Atlas ’ is more comparable, and so is Keats’s ‘ Lamia ’. Browning is too talkative. Among later work, more than one of Mr. Gordon Bottomley’s lyrical dramas around a central incident, such as ‘ The Riding to Lithend ’, is close enough to such a narrative as ‘ Rose Mary ’ to contribute an element of perspective.

The complicated beauty of ‘ Rose Mary ’ must have been drawn from a great emotional fund; the power of the story is due to the constant flashing out of the poet’s imagination. The plot is simple and ingenious; it answers to all primitive requirements, though probably only a part of it would have been used for a real ballad. A resemblance to ‘ The Bride’s Prelude ’ is in the central character’s situation of concealed guilt, but the story is quite different, being concerned with the old idea that only the pure may read the future in the crystal or spelled stone. A young girl, affianced to a knight, is bidden to look into the beryl by her mother, who overnight has performed the necessary rites so that, as she tells her daughter, 'the spell lacks nothing but your eyes'. The girl is to look and see what will hap to the man she is going to marry. The mother has heard rumours that on the morrow when he rides to Holy Cross for a shrift before his marriage, he is to be ambushed by enemies. The frightened Rose Mary, who has read the stone ere now for her mother, is loth to read it this time for herself:

> O mother mine if I should not see!

she explains, but is reassured by her mother, who suspects no danger. The girl does see, but the vivid scenes disclosed to her are a false picture of the morrow. Rose Mary, unknown to her mother, is not a maiden, so that the evil spirits which only 'a Christian's sin' could enable to re-enter the magic stone, have deceived her. The warning to the knight will prove ineffective. Part Two is the dialogue between mother and daughter, after the girl's confession that she bears 'a rose that Mary weeps upon'. Rose Mary does not yet know the fullness of her disaster.

> Yet O my heart, thy shame has a mate
> Who will not leave thee desolate.
> Shame for shame, yea and sin for sin:
> Yet peace at length may our poor souls win
> If love for love be found therein.

Only the mother realizes, for she it was who gave the vain warning.

> The mother looked on the daughter still
> As on a hurt thing that's yet to kill . . .

And

> Closely locked, they clung without speech,
> And the mirrored souls shook each to each.

She asks Rose Mary,

> Your heart held fast its secret sin:
> How think you, child, that I read therein?

[267]

The girl says she had not wondered about her mother's guess, and has to be told how the old 'accurst powers' whose 'heart is the ruined house of lies' seal sinful eyes or show truth by contraries.

> Daughter, daughter, remember you
> That cloud in the hills by Holycleugh?
> 'Twas a Hell-screen hiding truth away:
> There, not i' the vale, the ambush lay,
> And thence was the dead borne home to-day.

The primitive ballad would be content with this for a climax, only perhaps adding that the girl swoons or dies under the news. But Rossetti adds eloquent stanza to eloquent stanza.

> Deep the flood and heavy the shock
> When sea meets sea in the riven rock:
> But calm is the pulse that shakes the sea
> To the prisoned tide of doom set free
> In the breaking heart of Rose Mary.
>
> Once she sprang as the heifer springs
> With the wolf's teeth at its red heart-strings.
> First 'twas fire in her breast and brain,
> And then scarce hers but the whole world's pain,
> As she gave one shriek and sank again.
>
> In the hair dark-waved the face lay white
> As the moon lies in the lap of night;
> And as night through which no moon may dart
> Lies on a pool in the woods apart,
> So lay the swoon on the weary heart.

But Part Two after this develops a second dramatic crisis. The dead man is brought into the house while the girl is still in a swoon, and the mother kneels by the corpse and addresses it. Then she notices in its breast a blood-stained packet, glued to a gay broidered fragment shredded by some spear-thrust. The mother's heart is faint with pity as she draws it open, thinking it a pledge from her daughter. But it is from another woman, whose lover the dead man was, and who also looked forward to approaching marriage. Part Three begins with Rose Mary's recovery from her swoon. The poet brings back the image of whelming sea water which he had used in the middle of Part Two to suggest the mental disturbance which ended in oblivion. The further suggestion of night-shadowed water is also picked up again, by the image of dawn gleaming over waters wild all through the night.

> A swoon that breaks is the whelming wave
> When help comes late but still can save.
> With all blind throes is the instant rife,—
> Hurtling clangour and clouds at strife,—
> The breath of death, but the kiss of life.
>
> The night lay deep on Rose Mary's heart,
> For her swoon was death's kind counterpart:
> The dawn broke dim on Rose Mary's soul,—
> No hill-crown's heavenly aureole,
> But a white gleam on a sunken shoal.

Rossetti is always sensitive and vivid in describing a mental crisis. The dramatic effect of ' The Bride's Prelude ' is almost entirely due to the repeated suggestions of the tension of suspense and effort between the minds of the two sisters while the elder is making her confession. Aloÿse pauses in her confession to look at Amelotte, who is kneeling, silent,

> the gold hair upon her back
> Quite still in all its threads.

For Amelotte, with her face hidden in her hands,

> That listening without sight had grown
> To stealthy dread; and now
> That the one sound she had to mark
> Left her alone too, she was stark
> Afraid, as children in the dark.
>
> Her fingers felt her temples beat;
> Then came that brain-sickness
> Which thinks to scream, and murmureth;
> And pent between her hands, the breath
> Was damp against her face like death.
>
> Her arms both fell at once; but when
> She gasped upon the light,
> Her sense returned.

[269]

DANTE GABRIEL ROSSETTI

The crises in 'Rose Mary' are not so perfectly done as this; the writing is more elaborate and laboured, but the sureness of perception is there. Rose Mary gradually felt her own sighs again rolling over her heart, as the far travelled wind that has swept the wold 'Beats out its breath in the last torn tree'.

> She knew she had waded bosom-deep
> Along death's bank in the sedge of sleep,

but all else was clouded; though dread phantoms wailed past in her soul and to her lips still came the murmur of her mother's and her lover's name. The state of her mind is then put into one stanza:

> How to ask, and what thing to know?
> She might not stay and she dared not go.
> From fires unseen these smoke-clouds curled;
> But where did the hidden curse lie furled?
> And how to seek through the weary world?

She wanders abstracted through the house; but meaningless are all the sights that meet her eyes. The dread memories of 'Death and sorrow and sin and shame' are suddenly let loose when her gaze falls upon the Beryl-stone. Then

> The dead hours seemed to wax and wane,
> And burned till all was known again.

At last, dumb, white-faced and stern, she takes down the sword of her father, who had brought that 'bitter gift' of the Beryl-stone from Palestine.

> 'O ye, three times accurst', she said,
> 'By whom this stone is tenanted!
> Lo! here ye came by a strong sin's might;
> Yet a sinner's hand that's weak to smite
> Shall send you hence ere the day be night.

> 'This hour a clear voice bade me know
> My hand shall work your overthrow:
> Another thing in mine ear it spake,—
> With the broken spell my life shall break.
> I thank Thee, God, for the dear death's sake!

[270]

'And he Thy heavenly minister
Who swayed erewhile this spell-bound sphere,—
My parting soul let him haste to greet,
And none but he be guide for my feet
To where Thy rest is made complete.'

While her thoughts still run lovingly on the man who had died in betrayal of her she addresses to him her promises of their meeting in Heaven,

And O my love, if our souls are three,
O thine and mine shall the third soul be,—
One threefold love eternally.

Her eyes were soft as she spoke apart,
And the lips smiled to the broken heart.

At last with her father's sword she cleaves the Beryl and dies in the explosion of pent-up force which destroys also the house that was her home. The poem ends with the address of a spirit voice bidding her come, 'for thy bitter love's sake blest', to her heavenly guerdon.

Although, with 'Dante at Verona' and 'A Last Confession' (and in lesser degree 'Jenny') in mind, one must not say that Rossetti's deep understanding of human hearts is due to an exclusive sympathy with women, it is nevertheless remarkable how often he makes the drama centre in a woman's heart. This is the case with all but one of the ballad-poems, 'The White Ship', for although 'The King's Tragedy' has King James for undeniable hero, the centre of interest is the witch-woman's boding knowledge of his danger, Kate Barlass's heroic and vain sacrifice, and the Queen's love and courage—all vain to save him.

'The King's Tragedy', because it is less powerfully poetic, accentuates the tendencies shown in 'Rose Mary' to diffusion and confusion of purpose. There is less excuse for illustrative similes which hamper the story, and the imagery is not remarkably telling. Moreover, the asides are in the retrospective narrative of Catherine Douglas herself, who is supposed to be recounting to a group of girls how in her own youth she earned the name of Kate

[271]

Barlass, when she barred the door with her arm against the murderers of James the First of Scotland. Rossetti's feeling for dramatic irony is once more evident in the description of the feast in hall at which sat some of the sworn traitors to the King. A stanza like the following, however, is neither ballad nor poetry:

> But the wine is bright at the goblet's brim
>   Though the poison lurk beneath;
> And the apples still are red on the tree
>   Within whose shade may the adder be
>   That shall turn thy life to death.

This is also an impossible comment for the narrator to indulge in, looking far back at the events. There follows an excellent passage describing how later in the evening the King played chess with a knight who was a firm friend, and of the endeavour to make good cheer, though the Queen and her maid Catherine are oppressed. Kate asks the King to sing for the Queen the song he made in love of her when he was a prisoner at Windsor, and Rossetti then adapts some stanzas from ' The King's Quair ' for the song of the King. The impending doom is made darker by the love of the royal couple; ' her smiling lips and her tear-bright eyes ' at the song's end, and when he kissed her:

> And her true face was a rosy red,
>   The very red of the rose
> That couched on the happy garden-bed,
>   In the summer sunlight glows.

> And all the wondrous things of love
>   That sang so sweet through the song
> Were in the look that met in their eyes,
>   And the look was deep and long.

> 'Twas then a knock came at the outer gate,
>   And the usher sought the King.
> ' The woman you met by the Scotish Sea,
>   My Liege, would tell you a thing . . . '

The King says it is late, and the morrow will do as well. The poem after this very finely maintains the cumulative suspense as the action moves towards the final horror.

The voice of the wise woman who had seen the King's wraith and warned him twice already is heard below the window of the royal chamber that fateful night. Her warning, she cries, is now too late.

> ' Last night at mid-watch, by Aberdour,
>   When the moon was dead in the skies,
> O king, in a death-light of thine own
>   I saw thy shape arise.
>
> ' And in full season, as erst I said,
>   The doom had gained its growth;
> And the shroud had risen above thy neck
>   And covered thine eyes and mouth.
>
> ' And no moon woke, but the pale dawn broke,
>   And still thy soul stood there;
> And I thought its silence cried to my soul
>   As the first rays crowned its hair . . .'

Immediately after the woman had spoken comes the tread of the armed traitors. The ensuing excitement and swift action is admirably treated by Rossetti, who indeed seems never to fail when he is forced to ' get on with it ', but even here the attention is mainly concentrated on the sensations of the Queen and her maid, who is recalling the scene of the murder. A sort of epilogue follows, in which the Queen's vengeance on her husband-lover's assassins is described with the true pagan spirit of the feud. The Queen kept vigil by his bier and would not have the corpse buried until she has heard the news from Catherine Douglas of the gradual capture and death by torture of all the murderers. The Queen

> bent to her dead King James,
> And in the cold ear with fire-drawn breath
>   She spoke the traitors' names.

When all the dreadful news had been told ' she kissed the lips of her lord '.

> And then she said ' My King, they are dead !'
>   And she knelt on the chapel-floor,
> And whispered low with a strange proud smile,—
>   ' James, James, they suffered more !'

[273]

S

But then the emotional reaction—it is typical of Rossetti's intuition to show that next:

> Last she stood up to her queenly height,
>   But she shook like an autumn leaf,
> As though the fire wherein she burned
> Then left her body, and all were turned
>   To winter of life-long grief.

> And ' O James ! ' she said,—' My James ! ' she said,—
>   ' Alas for the woful thing,
> That a poet true and a friend of man,
> In desperate days of bale and ban,
>   Should needs be born a King ! '

It will be noticed that sympathy with the exalted ruler is also typical of Rossetti's story. It is clearly seen in the treatment of the Queen in ' The Staff and Scrip ', and again here. His kings are kingly, his queens queenly, and they are always true lovers. Even in ' The White Ship ', which is narrated by a more humble eye-witness than Catherine Douglas, the ruth of the ruthless King at the death of his lawless son Prince Henry is the centre of the dramatic interest. And poor Berold, the butcher of Rouen, who was the only survivor from the wrecked ship, confesses that the good-for-nothing Prince lost his life by ordering the boat to return and save his sister. 'The White Ship ' was written between 1878 and 1880, just before ' The King's Tragedy ', and it is, within its lesser compass, one of the poet's most successful narratives, largely on account of its simplicity. Seemingly the telling of the story by the mouth of the poor butcher was a gain from the point of view of narrative alone. The two other ballad-poems, ' Eden Bower ' and ' Troy Town ', which belong to 1869, are more conveniently considered in the next chapter, but it is to be noted that the employment of the refrain in each of them is a striking feature and yet quite fails to lend either piece the semblance of a true ballad, for no ballad can be so personal in style and so esoteric in metaphor. Rossetti's ballad-poems, taken as a whole, are akin to ballads in their dramatic quality, and often in

[274]

structure; they also deal generally with the right themes, of supernatural powers, of human treachery and passionate love. The deep sympathy of the poet with women's emotions is also truly akin to the ancient ballad. But some faults and some poetic virtues of Rossetti—his over-elaboration, and his psychological subtlety, his too plentiful metaphor and his finest and unforgettable images—are all alien to balladry. It is enough perhaps that after Coleridge and Keats he is easily the chief creator of what we have been calling ballad-poems in the nineteenth century, and if he does not quite touch the heights of ' La Belle Dame Sans Merci ', ' The Ancient Mariner ', and ' Christabel ', the total creative energy represented by his contribution to the stock of such poetry is very much more than that of Coleridge and Keats combined.

CHAPTER XVI

ROMANTIC ARCHAISM: IMAGINATIVE FULFILMENT

' In mystical sensations all men feel definitely something in common, having a similar meaning and connection one with another.'—OUSPENSKY.

' If you will behold your own self and the outer world, and what is taking place therein, you will find that you, with regard to your external being, are that external world.'—BOEHME.

THE RAVEN shadows of romance again brought a sombre depth to poetry when Rossetti, stimulated by crude melodramas as well as the romantic beauty of Coleridge and Keats, found in that no-man's-land a spiritual home.

The universal symbolism which we think of as romantic, mediaeval, archaic, supernatural, may serve a double purpose in literature. It can be chosen by a writer as an aid to imagination, a stimulus to visionary thought. Just as a poet in a certain mood may find inspiration through solitude or in some natural scene like a mountain tarn, an oriental desert, a wild seashore, so he may stimulate into partial consciousness his dream-life by filling his mental gaze with pageantries that are as much stuff of dreams as historical facts. Things like draughty old halls, barn-like ' castles ', old paintings, arras curtains, primitive musical instruments, border forays, bloodthirsty quarrelling for stolen land or a stolen woman, witches and wizards, and magic stones can take on a new life in an atmosphere which allows the imagination to escape from the commonplace. So, too, old poems become furniture of the ever renewed dream-world which is the dynamic source of new creations. It has been implied already that artists like Tennyson, Burne-Jones, Swinburne (until he found ' Freedom ' and Landor), and Morris tend to exploit romantic archaism in this way, gaining fitfully the intoxication they need to revive the visionary faculty of the mind. It has also been suggested that Rossetti is nearer than such artists as these to the type of Blake, whose eccentric images are unavoidable results of inadequately controlled vision. Rossetti's eccentricity was unfortunately almost entirely kept out of his art, and made all the deeper a disturbance in his life, but it remains true that he is far less dependent than most artists on curious mental furniture as a stimulus to imagination. This makes the romantic element in his work all the more interesting. It has the profundity of image which is found in the greatest romantic poets of last century; here he joins the company of Coleridge, Keats and Shelley, and Edgar Allan Poe.[1]

For the other purpose which is fulfilled by the romantic element in creative work is to afford a necessary outlet for inspiration. Thus, clearly, the two purposes are but different aspects of the one imaginative process by which the private dream-world of the mind can be externalized and made intelligible to other dreamers. The tendency of the poet who resorts to archaic *décor* and to mystery as a stimulus to an imagination not sufficiently hostile to the world will always be towards preciosity and sterility. When he escapes from this extreme he may, like Tennyson, run into bogs of commonplace and ill-founded idealism, or like Morris and Swinburne, find other furniture of the mind, though not before demonstrating the exhaustion of the romantic vein. Rossetti compels us to pay special attention to romantic archaism because it was so essential to his imaginative creation.

The potent imagination will find what it wants in diverse kinds of ' romance ', from crude melodrama to beautiful artistic creations like ' The Ancient Mariner '.

[1] Whose stature cannot be estimated by ignoring his prose.

Usually the mind's inclinations will be revealed first in a taste for the cruder literature, because, as with Rossetti, reading opens the doors to violent imaginative pleasures long before the mind is critical. Rossetti's best romantic work was done in early maturity, hot on that youthful debauch among the ghosts and demons, the moonlit forests, the phosphorescent cadavers, haunted rooms, magnetic eyes, and magically vital portraits of the 'Gothic Revival'. The flood of romantic melodrama in English literature, from Horace Walpole's 'Mysterious Mother' to the saturnine Byronic hero, was augmented by many translations. One of the most interesting of such tributory works which belong to the early nineteenth century was Carlyle's *German Romance: Specimens of its Chief Authors.* This appeared in four volumes in 1827. Carlyle had already translated *Wilhelm Meister,* and there was by 1841 Filmore's translation of *Faust* for the youthful Rossettis. Hoffmann's weird tales would probably have reached Rossetti through two French translations, but Carlyle had included in his collection the one with the Lamia theme ('The Golden Pot'), about a student who leaves his fiancée and becomes the prey of a snake woman. This Lamia (or Serpentina, as Hoffmann calls her) is a close relative of Rossetti's Siren, and of Lilith, the enemy of Mother Eve. Rossetti's treatment of these has been referred to, and we can look for other themes of romantic terror and mystery which his mind appropriated.

Two of such will strike the reader at once—the power of magic and the ominous wraith. The reality of the wraith or 'double' which to behold is to read the death sentence of the person whose phantasm so appears, must be a very old belief; but the amount of interest the idea attracted in the nineteenth century was extraordinary, and no doubt came from the new thrill of the unknown provided by the romantic movement signalized in the previous century by *Ossian,* Percy's *Reliques, The Castle of Otranto,* Chatterton, and then the 'Monk' Lewis school. Catherine Crow's

Night Side of Nature, an interesting survey of dream omens, apparitions, and the like, contained many cases, of varying credibility, of the *doppelgänger,* as it was called in Germany. Theodore Watts-Dunton's sonnet ' Foreshadowings: the Stars in the River'[1] was much admired by Rossetti as an original presentation of the theme which he himself had pictured in ' How they Met Themselves '. In ' The Bride's Prelude ' are several vivid images of the mind's hidden deeps, but the poet's nearest approach to the underlying idea of the double is the dramatic intuition of the bride's surprise at herself. During the days of her concealed guilt, she feared every glance directed to her:

> Yet I grew curious of my shame,
> And sometimes in the church,
> On hearing such a sin rebuked,
> Have held my girdle-glass unhooked
> To see how such a woman looked.

And describing the shock of realization when she first met her virgin sister after her own sinning:

> That year the convent yielded thee
> Back to our home ; and thou
> Then knew'st not how I shuddered cold
> To kiss thee, seeming to enfold
> To my changed heart myself of old.

There is some deep affinity between the belief in ' doubles ' and the state of divided personality which in the extreme pathological condition results from the conflict of diverging emotions. The feeling of ' possession ' is a stage along this road. Rossetti's powerful intellect coped with this feeling very successfully in his work; he was able to elaborate the most conflicting desires, as he does in the three sonnets entitled ' The Choice ',[2] and he continually externalized the imaginative confrontation of self, as in ' Lost Days ',[3] which with him is always—as with all true romantics— imbued with a feeling, more or less explicit, of sin. ' A Superscription '[4] is another presentation of a similar idea:

[1] In *The Coming of Love.* [2] Nos. 71-73, *House of Life.*
[3] *Ibid.,* 86. [4] *Ibid.,* 97.

Look in my face; my name is Might-have-been;
  I am also called No-more, Too-late, Farewell;
  Unto thine ear I hold the dead-sea shell
Cast up thy Life's foam-fretted feet between;
Unto thine eyes the glass where that is seen
  Which had Life's form and Love's, but by my spell
  Is now a shaken shadow intolerable,
Of ultimate things unuttered the frail screen.

Mark me, how still I am! But should there dart
  One moment through thy soul the soft surprise
  Of that winged Peace which lulls the breath of sighs—
Then shalt thou see me smile, and turn apart
Thy visage to mine ambush at thy heart
  Sleepless with cold commemorative eyes.

This sonnet is followed by the one entitled ' He and I '
in which the definite image of the soul's other, opposite,
self supplies the pervading theme of the poem. Other
instances,[1] especially in *The House of Life*, occur of
Protean reappearances of the same idea. The Medusa
theme, as Rossetti treated it in the dramatic design
' Aspecta Medusa ', which he did for a picture never
painted (owing to disagreement with the prospective
purchaser about the treatment of the subject), is a near
relative of the phantasmal ' double '. The lines which he
wrote for this drawing are most suggestive, and quite
outside the probable scope of any other Victorian poet's
ideas provoked by the Greek myth:

Andromeda, by Perseus saved and wed,
Hankered each day to see the Gorgon's head:
Till o'er a fount he held it, bade her lean,
And mirrored in the wave was safely seen
That death she lived by.
                              Let not thine eyes know
Any forbidden thing itself, although
It once should save as well as kill: but be
Its shadow upon life enough for thee.

---

[1] 'Love's Nocturne', examined in the previous chapter, is really at one
with these in its treatment of the phantasm.

What a theme for a poem is suggested by these few casual lines, and how characteristic of Rossetti's mind divided between the desire and the fear of the ghoul-haunted region! But the best known instance of the *doppelgänger* belief is in 'The Portrait', which was mostly written during the Dantesque and Early-Christian phase of about 1847. This piece was originally inscribed 'On Mary's Portrait, which I painted six years ago '—a purely fanciful legend, although the depth of feeling in the poem convinced many people that it had an autobiographical reference to ' Beata Beatrix '.[1]

Now both ' The Portrait ' and ' A Superscription ' bring together the phantom double and the idea of magic, which is usually associated by Rossetti with a portrait, and especially with the vision of a woman's eyes. Both the mirror and the portrait are ancient furniture of romantic terror, and they are continually being appropriated by poets for authentic creations of art. The mirror is with Rossetti either dark, still water, as in ' Willowood ' and ' Aspecta Medusa ', or the soul's memory, which is a glass reflecting future as well as past. The portrait inevitably serves his imagination in painting as well as poetry. Without the ecstatic belief in the potency of such a symbol he could never have painted immortal portraits—for such they are—like ' Beata Beatrix ' and ' Proserpine '. He has adapted the old ideas to his own needs, just as Edgar Allen Poe did. But Rossetti, for all his indifference to theories, seems always uncannily wise in his fantasies. Look at the opening lines of ' The Portrait ':

> This is her picture as she was:
> It seems a thing to wonder on,
> As though mine image in the glass
> Should tarry when myself am gone.

Who could summarize more cogently the complete range of feeling and fantasy which has found so many expressions between Poe's ' The Oval Portrait ' and Oscar Wilde's

[1] See page 279, where the *doppelgänger* stanza is quoted.

' Picture of Dorian Gray'? The magic which in the melo-drama of Maturin's ' Melmoth the Wanderer' charges a portrait with magnetic vitality is refined and deepened into exquisite poetry:

> Here with her face doth memory sit
>   Meanwhile, and wait the day's decline,
> Till other eyes shall look from it,
>   Eyes of the spirit's Palestine,
> Even than the old gaze tenderer:
> While hopes and aims long lost with her
>   Stand round her image side by side,
>   Like tombs of pilgrims that have died
> About the Holy Sepulchre.

The affinity between the poet of this ' Portrait' and that fictive painter Chiaro in ' Hand and Soul' hardly needs commenting upon. Once more Rossetti seemed imagin-atively to anticipate experience when he wrote about Chiaro, who, out of his agony, has a vision of a beautiful woman, who is his own soul. She bids him use all his art to paint her while she stands before him, and he paints. ' While he worked, his face grew solemn with knowledge.' The narrator describes how he found this inspired picture in the Pitti Gallery at Florence, and says that in one corner of the canvas the words *Manus Animam pinxit* (' the in-spired hand ') appeared as signature. Archaism does not falsify Rossetti's art as poet or painter because he truly was inspired. That is to say the profound elemental aspirations of the soul which have created the universal symbols and themes of ' romance ' found their appropriate shapes in those old visions, and reanimated them.

How much at home Rossetti found himself amid the shadows cast by the unknown is more easily realized per-haps in those poems which do not seem to borrow any of the superficial stage-property of romance. Not only in sonnets of *The House of Life* such as have been referred to, or the flashes of dazzling darkness in a love poem like ' Love's Nocturne ', but in other pieces of the most miscellaneous kind—even trifles like ' The Mirror ' or serious contemplation like ' The Cloud Confines '—and best of all in the profoundly macabre gloom of ' The Card Dealer '. This queer and impressive poem was written in 1849, only two years after ' The Blessed Damozel ', the metre of which is used, but with a startlingly different effect. The extraordinary tendency of Rossetti's mind to divide itself between conflicting opposites could not be better exemplified, for at this time he had just painted ' The Girlhood of Mary Virgin ' and was preparing to paint ' Ecce Ancilla Domini ', both of which are unsurpassed by all but the finest of his pictures for depth of feeling. And most of the sonnets for pictures connected by date with ' The Card-Dealer ' are on definitely religious, Christian themes. When ' The Card Dealer ' was published in the *Athenaeum* in 1852, Rossetti added a note that it was written from a picture by Theodore von Holst, which ' represents a beautiful woman, richly dressed, who is sitting at a lamp-lit table, dealing out cards, with a peculiar fixedness of expression '. But the poem was revised and a few phrases definitely applying to Rossetti's reading of the picture were dropped out. What had happened, of course, was that the picture called ' Open Sesame ' to his mind. The poem disclosed, as a consequence, lives its own secretly rooted life.

> Could you not drink her gaze like wine ?
>   Yet though its splendour swoon
> Into the silence languidly
>   As a tune within a tune,
> Those eyes unravel the coiled night
>   And know the stars at noon.

From this initial vision of mystery in the woman's gaze the poet is lifted out of the world where card-playing has associations of any social or moral convention. The very cards, ' smooth polished silent things ', as ' her fingers let them softly through ', are suddenly charged with hypnotic power as they reflect ' in swift light shadowings ' the colours of ' the great eyes of her rings '. ' Whom plays she with ? ' With all of us, ' bless'd or bann'd ',

> We play together, she and we,
> Within a vain strange land.

Her cards are

> The heart, that doth but crave
> More, having fed ; the diamond,
> Skilled to make base seem brave ;
> The club, for smiting in the dark ;
> The spade, to dig a grave.
>
> And do you ask what game she plays ?
> With me 'tis lost or won . . .

She plays with all ; while we see the card that falls, she knows the one to follow it.

> Her game in thy tongue is called Life,
> As ebbs thy daily breath :
> When she shall speak, thou'lt learn her tongue
> And know she calls it Death.

There is no immaturity in this startling poem by a lad twenty-one years old who had already made for himself a secure place among English poets with an equally romantic poem about the Christian heaven. Wonder flags from overwork in the examination of Rossetti's creative career.

Whenever an artist uses archaic themes and romantic trappings with the justification of genius, his selection of material has much the same personal significance as the entire absence or the recurring presence of universal imagery in a person's dreams. One of the most common themes of romance, the opposition of good and evil in the figures of two opposed types of women, is used freely by Rossetti. Another theme, just as frequent in the romantic imagination, that of incest, he completely avoids, notwithstanding the example of Byron and Shelley. He also hardly uses at all the idea of the lonely wanderer or forlorn knight, which appears so frequently in poetry and melodrama, from the time of Marlowe—indeed, from Spenser —throughout English literature. The hero may be burdened with sin (Faust, the Wandering Jew, Lucifer, Manfred, Cain, the Knight of Horsel) or a suffering champion of an idea (Hamlet, Prometheus, Alastor, Gebir, Usheen, Arthur), but he is always a personal symbol to his creators. In view of the prose stories, ' Hand and Soul ' and ' St. Agnes of Intercession ', it is not possible to say that Rossetti ignored this theme, for the artist hero in each is clearly related to the knights and champions of beauty. In both of these instances, however, this is a motive subsidiary to the motives of the fantastic or mystic transference of self into an object, and the magic vitality of a portrait. And since the portrait theme counts for so much in Rossetti's imagination, let us note that his insistence on women's eyes is part of it. Elsewhere[1] I had occasion to remark that Francis Thompson, another woman worshipper, showed a curious affinity with Crashaw in his recurrent images of eyes. For Thompson the eyes of woman are as gates of paradise, opened doors of birth and of death, vistas of eternity.

Rossetti's feeling for the expression of a woman's eyes is one of the most striking features of his painting, shown first in the pictures drawn from his sister Christina, and then most conspicuously in those done from Lizzie Siddal and Mrs. Morris, though Miss Mackenzie (' The Beloved ') was another model for an important example. Miss Wilding, the model for ' Sibylla Palmifera ', also served him so, though (if one may judge from a reproduction) the result is not comparable with the finest examples, in spite of the gaze being drawn so surely to the woman's eyes. The sonnet for this picture proves where lay the centre of Rossetti's imagery.[2] Nearly all the octave is spent on the gaze of ' Soul's Beauty ':

> Under the arch of Life, where love and death,
> Terror and mystery guard her shrine, I saw
> Beauty enthroned; and though her gaze struck awe,
> I drew it in as simply as my breath.

---

[1] *Francis Thompson*, chapter 4, ' His Imaginative Type '.
[2] No. 77, *House of Life*.

> Hers are the eyes which over and beneath,
> The sky and sea bend on thee,—which can draw,
> By sea or sky or woman, to one law,
> The allotted bondman of her palm and wreath.

The strange sapience of Rossetti in using images is shown here once more. Arch and vaulted sky and sea or pool are all images with a similar emotional value, and here linked with women's eyes, for this Lady Beauty is the Divine Woman once more, the Queen of Heaven and the Queen of Hell. It is not mere accident that this sonnet begins with the image of the arch of Life, while 'The Monochord ',[1] which described the sense of imminent death by absorption of the self into a larger unit, begins: ' Is it this sky's vast vault ' and concludes with ' devious coverts ' (= groves, or just covered-in dark places). The alterations which Rossetti made to ' The Blessed Damozel's' eyes are interesting. In *The Germ*:

> Her blue grave eyes were deeper much
> Than a deep water even.

In the *Oxford and Cambridge Magazine*:

> Her eyes knew more of rest and shade
> Than waters stilled at even.

In the *Poems* of 1870 and the subsequent editions:

> Her eyes were deeper than the depth
> Of waters stilled at even.

While the suggestion of depth and darkness, as of a pool, is retained, the original likeness to the sky or to sky-reflecting water is abandoned in favour of increased suggestion of soft and deep gloom. The final version indeed is an immense increase of depth to the image, and the reader's ability to appreciate the sensitive certainty of Rossetti's touch in altering until he got that final version is a good test of a general sympathy with his imagination. The two earlier versions are both attractive and the second

[1] No. 79, *House of Life.*

one is quite as good as the third merely on the score of poetic expression. But the third is truer to Rossetti without loss of poetic beauty. It is curious that one of Rossetti's most beautiful images, which is very near to the underlying idea of woman's eyes:

> Secret somewhere on this earth
> Unpermitted Eden lies,

occurred in a stanza of the manuscript version of ' Love's Nocturne ' which the poet omitted from the published versions.

Enough has been said to show the affinity between Rossetti and the type of poet represented by the author of ' The Mistress of Vision ', who wrote:

> But woe's me, and woe's me,
> For the secrets of her eyes !
> In my visions fearfully
> They are ever shown to be
> As fringèd pools, whereof each lies
> Pallid-dark beneath the skies . . .
>
> Many changes rise on
> Their phantasmal mysteries.
> They grow to an horizon
> Where earth and heaven meet . . .

In his freer metrical scheme Thompson also falls into Rossetti's repeating rhythm of:

> Still-eyed, deep-eyed, ah how dear !
> Master, Lord
> In her name implor'd, O hear !

Thompson's metrical scheme in ' The Mistress of Vision ' suddenly changes a beat in stanza 13, and uses a similar effect at the succeeding stanza-ends. The final line of each has the value of two of Rossetti's four-beat lines:

> Mourn, O mourn !
> For the vine have we the spine ? Is this all the Heaven allows ?

The imaginative validity for Rossetti of the face and especially eyes of woman may be demonstrated by one more example, from the prose story ' Hand and Soul ', which has exceptionally clear marks of its autobiographical character. Out of his agonizing contemplation of himself the painter Chiaro arouses to a vision. He suddenly ' found awe within him, and held his head bowed, without stirring '.[1] That secluded room to which he had retreated from the noisy outside world is one with the dream-tranced rooms occupied by fair women in Rossetti's early water-colours. It is one with many a still, secret garden. ' The warmth of the air was not shaken; but there seemed a pulse in the light, and a living freshness, like rain. The silence was a painful music, that made the blood ache in his temples; and he lifted his face and his deep eyes.'

Then he beholds the apparition of the woman who has come to comfort and inspire him. Her eyes are as his.

' It seemed that the first thoughts he had ever known were given him as at first from her eyes, and he knew her hair to be the golden veil through which he beheld his dreams. . . . She did not move closer towards him, but he felt her to be as much with him as his breath.'

She was the image of his own soul. The Divine Woman always is that to her creator; but once more Rossetti's knowledge is so strangely explicit. The boundaries between the realm of fearful superstition and mystical insight are often brought by him, as here, very close together. A little step away from the mystical to the romantic, and we have his other prose story of ' St. Agnes of Intercession ', in which besides the portrait and the ' double ' themes, is a masterly description of the narrator's dreaming. Another step towards the merely romantic, and with the design of ' How they Met Themselves ' we are on the very borders of the weird in terror-romances.

---

[1] ' The Mistress of Vision ' begins :

> Secret was the garden :
> Set i' the pathless awe
> Where no star its breath can draw.
> Life, that is its warden,
> Sits behind the fosse of death. Mine eyes saw not, and I saw.

Rossetti's triumph in the region of romance is none the less genuinely temperamental and imaginative although his archaic work sometimes lacks the rightness of successful artistic achievement. As may be seen from the examination of his ballad-poems, Rossetti can and does fail sometimes, but the failure is due rather to maladjustment of technical means. In the ballad of ' The King's Tragedy ' the effect which ought to be produced by this tale in verse is not spoilt by his introduction of the witch woman who saw the king's wraith and thereby prophesied his doom. The supernatural and the archaic elements are the best parts of the ballad. ' Rose Mary ', although an astonishing production in mid-nineteenth century, is far from being a perfect work of art; but again its failure is not like the failures in the romantic archaism of Swinburne, Morris, and Tennyson: it is not due to inadequate imaginative feeling for the rationally incredible, but rather to wrong technical methods, especially the over-elaboration to which the poet was prone. Yet, with all such faults, these long, lovingly-wrought, and heavy ballads by Rossetti might with some justice be accepted in the way that he accepted Browning's ' Sordello ':

> ' Sordello's story ', the Sphinx yawned and said,
>   ' Who would has heard.' Is that enough? Who could,
>   'Twere not amiss to add, has understood :
> Who understood perhaps has profited.
> For my part I could tell a tale instead
>   Of one who, dreaming of no likelihood
>   Even that the ' Book ' was going to end for good,
> Turned the last page and lo the book was read.

A suitable conclusion to which seems to be some of the ' Verses to John Tupper ':

> Though as to NATURE Jack,
> (Poor dear old hack !)
> Touching sky, sun, stone, stick, and stack,
> I guess I'm half a quack ;
> For whom ten lines of Browning whack
> The whole of the Zodiac.

There was in Browning also the necessary dynamic

[289]   T

urge of emotion to justify most of the archaic *décor* he used, and Rossetti's sympathy certainly sprang from a recognition of this. Browning's early anonymous 'Pauline' was found by Rossetti as a youth when reading in the British Museum library, and hailed by him enthusiastically as the work of Browning. Yet 'Pauline' is not obviously typical of Browning, who would gladly have suppressed it when his collected works were published, and one might say that Rossetti as a poet does not obviously resemble Browning. The two men are, however, deeply akin, and 'Pauline' helps to show how this is. Browning's mother's practical piety and his father's keen interest in art and literature were formative influences comparable in character and depth to the parental influences of Rossetti's youth. It is true that Browning's passionate energy gradually found an expression very different from Rossetti's, but his talents, after all, were very different, and so was his life. It is only in the elemental emotions and certain clear sympathies between the men's intuitions which bring them and their work into close relationship. 'Pauline' was hailed so gladly by the young Rossetti because it was a piece of unguarded youthful egoism, an adolescent confession of dream desires similar to Rossetti's, and of course it betrayed also Browning's early enthusiasm for Shelley. It is easy to understand why the mature moralist who wrote the Epilogue to 'Asolando' should feel uneasy when he re-read what he had written at the age of twenty-one (only a year or two older than Rossetti was at the time of his discovery of 'Pauline'). Apart from the technical immaturity, there was a spiritual immaturity which the author of 'The Blessed Damozel' had already left behind:

> As life wanes, all its care and strife and toil
> Seem strangely valueless . . .

Other passages reveal a soul akin to Rossetti, although their naive egotism would not have been possible to the latter's more certain aesthetic sense. Browning had not

yet adopted the dramatic device to veil the emotional
egoism in his poems, so that his story here is a frank
confession of adolescent dreaming, and of aspiration to the
divine woman who has come to concentrate and direct
his purposes. The evil influence of the Lilith type is also
described and opposed to that of Pauline. But a fuller
comparison of the two poets' temperaments belongs to
another chapter.[1] Rossetti's designs and pictures for some
of Browning's poems, such as 'Taurello's First Sight
of Fortune' (from 'Sordello'), 'Hist! said Kate the
Queen' (from 'Pippa Passes'), and 'The Laboratory'
were among his earliest work and place Browning second
only to Dante among the poets whom Rossetti illustrated
(for Malory occupies the position of a whole literary phase
rather than of a personal genius).

The truth is that Browning, although a purposeful
moralist was less afraid than Rossetti of flouting the Victorian feeling for ideals of conduct and belief; when his
adventurous mind fastened upon the drama of evil power
opposed to unarmed innocence he wrote with a surprising disregard of the prevailing attitude of the age. 'The
Ring and the Book' is more anti-Victorian than any work
by Rossetti. But even W. B. Scott, at least in his earlier
phase, seems to move more freely towards the macabre
and dionysian spirit of romance than Rossetti ever could.
Had Scott been a finer poet than he was (though he certainly is not negligible) his 'Witch's Ballad' might have
made him as dangerous as a charge of moral dynamite to
the Tennysonian plaster nobility. Rossetti's sister Christina, whose 'Goblin Market' seems to have derived an
impulse from the 'Witch's Ballad', was really less
oppressed aesthetically than he by the moral outlook
reflected in the work of the great Victorians. This was
probably due to her deeper simplicity and also to the
greater scope she found, in devotional writings, for the
expression of religious feeling. Once he had exhausted the

[1] See p. 308 *et seq.*

Dantesque phase Rossetti really lacked an adequate outlet for the religious feeling which accompanied the romantic urge toward the mysterious and the fearful. Here may be another partial explanation, in addition to the technical faults, of an incompleteness about his success in the so-called ballads. This does not prevent Rossetti being the most powerful romantic poet of the Victorian age, for his ballads are but one aspect of his imaginative temper, and these ballads, whatever their lack, possess certain romantic virtues more completely than any other poet's in the age of sentimental reason.

CHAPTER XVII

STYLE AND CONTENT, AND CONCLUSION

'*To learn to suffer and to learn to die, this is the gymnastic of Eternity, the noviciate of immortal life.*'—ELIPHAS LÉVI.

'*Emotion is always justified by time, thought hardly ever. It can only bring us back to emotion.*'—W. B. YEATS.

'*The truth is that we travel on a journey that was accomplished before we set out.*'—XENOS CLARK.

AN OPPRESSIVE quantity of facts about Rossetti's work is available. It is extremely difficult to avoid the appearance of burking anything significant in order to simplify the argument, and also to avoid a tiresome repetition of information plentifully supplied in William Rossetti's edition of the literary *Works* and H. C. Marillier's *Chronological List* of the pictorial works. But if the preceding chapters have not quite failed in developing an intelligent attitude towards Rossetti, the amount of mere information also packed into them should clear the ground now. Rossetti's career may be summarized briefly. It is divisible into two main periods. The division is marked by the death of Rossetti's wife on the merely biographical side, and the painting of ' Beata Beatrix ' in 1863 on the creative side. By the age of twenty-five (*i.e.*, in 1854) he had completed all his best writing in the first period; but did not complete the same period in pictorial work until 1863, after which—indeed slightly overlapping the date—begins immediately the second pictorial period which continues for ten years (except for three stragglers of importance). The second period of poetic creation did not set in for about fifteen years after the closing of the first. It starts properly in 1869 and finishes early in 1872 (in the spring of which year Buchanan's pamphlet on the 'Fleshly School' was published). There was a poetic aftermath in the last years, which began just after the last important picture—'Astarte Syriaca'—was done in 1877. A rough selection of the most important items will give a bird's-eye view of the course of Rossetti's creativeness:

PERIOD ONE

(a) Poetry: The translations from the Italians—especially 'The New Life'; 'Henry the Leper' (from early German); 'Ave'; 'My Sister's Sleep'; 'Blessed Damozel'; 'Bride's Prelude'; 'A Last Confession'; 'Retro me, Sathana!' (*House of Life*, 90); 'The Card Dealer'; 'For a Venetian Pastoral by Giorgione'; 'On Refusal of Aid Between Nations'; 'The Staff and Scrip'; 'Love's Nocturne'; 'The Sea-Limits'; 'The Burden of Nineveh'; 'Stratton Water'; 'Sister Helen'; 'The Woodspurge'; 'Sudden Light'. Prose: 'Hand and Soul'; 'St. Agnes of Intercession'.

(b) Pictorial: Designs for romantic subjects from Goethe, Keats, Coleridge, Browning, Poe; 'The Laboratory' (from Browning); 'Maids of Elfen Mere' (Allingham); Dantesque themes;[1] Arthurian themes in Malory; 'early Christian' themes, *e.g.*: 'Girlhood of Mary Virgin'; 'Ecce Ancilla Domini'; 'Passover in the Holy Family'; 'The Seed of David'. Miscellaneous: 'St. Cecilia'; 'The Blue Closet'; 'Tune of Seven Towers'; 'A Christmas Carol'; 'My Lady Greensleeves'; 'Before the Battle'; 'King René's Honeymoon' (the water-colour); 'St. George and the Dragon'; 'St. George and the Princess Sabra'; 'Heart of the Night, or Mariana in the Moated Grange'; 'Love's Greeting'; 'How they Met Themselves'; 'Cassandra'; 'Aspecta Medusa'; 'Found'.

[1] Including the original 'Dante's Dream', 1856.

STYLE AND CONTENT, AND CONCLUSION

The predominating character of Period One, (*a*) and (*b*), is romantic archaism. Now for

PERIOD TWO

(*a*) Pictures: 'Bocca Baciata' (1859); 'Regina Cordium' (Lizzie); 'Regina Cordium' (Miss Wilding); 'Fazio's Mistress, or Aurelia'; 'Lady Lilith'; 'Venus Verticordia' (oil); 'Venus Verticordia' (water-colour); 'Monna Pomona'; 'Monna Vanna'; 'The Beloved'; 'Sibylla Palmifera'; 'Joli Cœur'; 'Rosa Triplex'; 'Mrs. William Morris'; 'Pandora'; 'Water-Willow'; 'Proserpine' (1873-1877); 'Mnemosyne' (1876); 'Astarte Syriaca' (1877).

(*b*) Poetry: Two-thirds of the *House of Life* sonnets; 'Jenny'; 'The Stream's Secret'; 'Troy Town'; 'Eden Bower'; 'The Cloud Confines'; 'Sunset Wings'; 'Insomnia' (1881); 'Spheral Change' (1881); 'The White Ship' (1878-80); 'The King's Tragedy' (1881); and 'Rose Mary'. Prose: 'The Orchard Pit'; 'The Doom of the Sirens'.

Period Two, taken as a whole, is distinguished by eroticism, often expressed with great sensual feeling, and the contemplation of human destiny.

The characteristics of most importance which are strong in both periods are (*a*) intuitive feeling for the drama of the individual heart, especially of women; (*b*) an awareness of mystery, which shifts from mysticism to mere romanticism. In so far as (*b*) is a characteristic of Period Two it forms the chief thread of continuity with Period One, therefore it, and not eroticism or archaism, must be regarded as the prevailing feature of Rossetti's creative work. But, as we have seen, it is really at the root of romantic archaism. The romantic element is perhaps stronger than the mystical in the poetry of both periods, but the archaic is almost completely abandoned in the later work, no doubt because the artist's range of conceptions was fixed and he did not

[295]

need any more furniture for his imagination. I think in the later pictures the mystical vision is more prominent than the romantic atmosphere, and this development is accompanied by the maximum sensuous decoration, which had already been reached in the gorgeous oil paintings— ' The Beloved ' and ' Monna Vanna '—belonging to the most erotic phase. The course of the art towards a mysticism which includes the erotic element can be followed in the pictures of Period Two; it is reflected in poetry by the predominant character of *The House of Life*, but in the verbal medium Rossetti was able to express ideas more freely, and so there is more romantic thought (or lyricism) and less mysticism than in pictures like ' Proserpine ' and ' Mnemosyne ', though the erotic element is notable in both the plastic and poetic expressions.

An example of what I mean by distinguishing between ' mere romanticism ' and mysticism is shown by the greatest individual poem (not counting *The House of Life*) which Rossetti wrote in Period Two: ' Rose Mary '. ' Rose Mary ' might have become as purely a decorative story in beautiful poetry as Keats's youthful ' Eve of St. Agnes ', so far as mystical vision is concerned. It is more profound than that because Rossetti could not help pouring into it the great energy of his mature mind; and of course it is highly dramatic also. But the intensest fusion of passion and thought does not lead to any vision of reality comparable with that which is expressed in the early prose story of ' Hand and Soul '. The most beautiful stanzas in ' Rose Mary ' are produced when the poet is purely poet—that is to say, is wielding a verbal magic to convey intangible atmosphere, as when he tells us of what happens when ' Rose Mary ' looks into the beryl held by her mother:

> Even as she spoke, they two were 'ware
> Of music-notes that fell through the air;
> A chiming shower of strange device,
> Drop echoing drop, once, twice, and thrice,
> As rain may fall in Paradise.

And before this, when he is merely describing the magic beryl stone: ' Shaped it was to a shadowy sphere ':

> With shuddering light 'twas stirred and strewn
> Like the cloud-nest of the wading moon :
> Freaked it was as the bubble's ball,
> Rainbow-hued through a misty pall
> Like the middle light of the waterfall.
>
> Shadows dwelt in its teeming girth
> Of the known and unknown things of earth....

In such imagery Rossetti's mind can command a consummate technique of expression. So, near the end of Part One, when the mother, after taking a last look at the beryl, puts it back in her robe, the poetry ceases to be fine poetry of action, and becomes again a subtle song of unspeakable things:

> The flickering shades were dusk and dun
> And the lights throbbed faint in unison
> Like a high heart when a race is run.
>
> As the globe slid to its silken gloom,
> Once more a music rained through the room ;
> Low it splashed like a sweet star-spray,
> And sobbed like tears at the heart of May,
> And died as laughter dies away.

The imagery of moon and water, already referred to,[1] which enabled the poet to picture the girl's swooning mind is embodied in a diction just as perfect, but the dream-atmosphere necessarily begins to dissipate each time the poem approaches the tragic drama of the story. In the last scene, in Part Three, where the attention is again centred upon the beryl stone, the weird and ominous feeling again possesses the words, though this merges into the human tragedy of the girl who is going to destroy the beryl with her father's sword though she must die. The diction of ' Rose Mary ' is a reason for care in identifying the gorgeous and decorative quality of Rossetti's style with his later development. ' Rose Mary ', although it belongs to the second period, is less decorative than some

[1] In chapter xv.

of the finest early poems, like 'The Bride's Prelude',
and no more loaded than the brief early piece, 'The
Card Dealer', in which is a similar magic of subtly
ominous atmosphere. 'The Card Dealer', in not being
archaic except in its sense of mystery, is more exception-
able among the poetry of the first period than 'Rose
Mary' in the second. The markedly romantic themes of
the later period are all of them less ornamented as well as
less archaic in treatment than the best of the earlier poems,
like 'The Staff and Scrip' and 'The Bride's Prelude'.
The exception is 'Sister Helen', which is almost as
unadorned as the late ballad-poems, 'The White Ship'
and 'The King's Tragedy'. The perfectly simple diction
of the translated 'John of Tours' is also in the second
period, but, like the early ballad 'Stratton Water', it may
be disregarded as an indication of tendency since it is a
deliberately imitated style. There is little unconscious
imitation of other poets' styles with Rossetti, less than
in the work of most great poets. A rare suggestion of
Tennyson or Shakespeare, and a few resemblances to
Browning, usually so evident—as in 'A Last Confession'
—that they must have been deliberate experiments, like
the resemblances to bald ballad style.

Rossetti's imagery, as already noticed, is strongly
personal, and in its most intense expressions confined in
range to a few universal symbols. The nearest he could
come to this in the pictures was by obeying an intuitive
choice of favourite colours, bits of jewellery and furniture,
and other objects—such as cups, chalices, ewers, the apple,
certain musical instruments, crowded interiors (mostly
early) with outlets to the distant world, sheltering wings
which (as in 'Love's Greeting') sometimes reveal their
unconscious symbolism of the mother's body. The
imagery of the early pictures, mostly water-colours, is
richer in symbolism than the later oils. A comparison of
the stylistic quality of the two pictorial periods seems at
first sight to offer a much surer ground than the poetry

for the generalization that the ornamental—occasionally tending to the florid—in Rossetti's style is a special feature of his later development. But examine the rich oil paintings ' Monna Vanna ' and ' The Beloved ', which show Rossetti's use of a Venetian wealth of colour. Can they truly be described as overloaded, over rich? Is it the sensuous delight in the visible world which is inadequately expressed (for an overstressing of the ornamental would result in an expressive weakness), or is it some shortcoming either of composition or mere draughtsmanship which seems to give those glowing colours and the concentrated feeling of the whole picture a somehow imperfectly triumphant form? Composition and drawing in a painting may be compared with metrical skill and clearness of language in a poem. They are not the unique and essential, not the inspirational force which gives vitality, but their technical inadequacy may seriously interfere with the expression. In other words the inspiration is weakened, for that which is not expressed in art does not exist; the idea of silent poets belongs to philosophy or psychology, not to aesthetics. But there is a considerable range of personal response to differing though equally fine works of art, and the concentrated narrowness of Rossetti's later pictorial range of ideas would alone be sufficient to account for a partial failure of appreciation in many intelligent people. If he cannot paint a woman, with or without mystery of soul, he must find compensation in stressing a romantic or mystical idea. The fine design of ' The Question ' (or ' The Sphinx ') is remarkable among his works for its male figures. The breasts of the living sphinx make her extravagantly female, it is true, and the looming yet hollow darkness from which she seems to confront the dying youth and the urgent, questioning man, also stresses her female character. The unspoken answer, known to the female sphinx, is that Love and Death are one. Men reach her and her meaning before the figure of ancient Time, for Time cannot die until the last man arrives at that destination simultaneously with him. Rossetti's pictures of female beauty can be regarded as images of the Sphinx. The male figures are out of the picture, but one male figure is always confronting her; it is the artist.

Before finding the counterpart of the painter's vision in the poet's, the comparison of the style of the second pictorial period with the first will help in the similar comparison of the poetry, which is less clearly divided. The later pictures may strike one as more ornamental in style than the earlier, because the medium is different. The earlier are nearly all water-colours; the later, oils. There is more formal restraint in the earlier, chiefly because the artist had less control of the necessary technique. A little drawing had often to go a long way— hence the simple straight lines, as of costume. Also the design is usually more complicated with objects. Rossetti limited himself to three-quarter length single figures in the later work and so gained greater freedom in composition. In the earlier he wants to crowd poetic ideas, instead of the single half-mystical idea of the fleshly paradise, into each picture. Instead of the face of a woman, he has to crowd a closed space with dream symbols. The more ' romantic ' the water-colour the more crowded it seems to be, but at the heart of the dream-tranced room is love, the cause of the dream. Rossetti's Arthurian pictures and designs would give one the impression that Malory was a great erotic poet like Dante instead of a romancer idealizing chivalry. Superficially simple in style, the water-colours are really supremely rich in sensuous ornamentation. The effect of oil painting which the depth and harmonies of his water-colours give has often been noted; it is as noticeable as the suggestion of water-colour in the pure lustre of his oil painting. Thus the principal difference between the work of the two periods is surely less a difference of richness than a difference of language. The variety of crowded symbols in the earlier makes up for lack of technical freedom gained in the later partly through experience and partly by simplifying the former complexity of symbolism and forms.

In Rossetti's poetry the style does not change much either; neither does the content, for his command of technique in poetry was adequate to begin with; indeed, it is more adequate to what he has to express in the first period than in the second, and so here and there we can discover in the second period of the poetry the insistence on separate images and phrases which is a fair parallel to the earnest complexity of the water-colours. Only the chronological order of the change is reversed; but it is not nearly so complete a change in the poetry as in the pictorial work. It is indeed confined mostly to certain poems in which the erotic feeling is too strong for the medium, and produces a slight over-insistence on the imitative function of verbal music.

In chapter xi I suggested that Rossetti after several alterations decided on ' fawned ' in the eighth line of ' Nuptial Sleep ' because it made the mouth shape as he imagined the lovers' lips pouting after their last kiss. Such imitative language if akin to onomatopœia. Sound imitation is not the only imitative function of language which contributes to the so-called magical element in poetry, but it shows more obviously than any other the *physical* basis of verbal expression. No one can fail to see why words like *plop, hiss, boom, shriek* are expressive. Nor why certain collocations of consonants and vowels add to the dictionary meaning of words an expressiveness which has a physical (*i.e.,* sensual) basis. Why, for instance, to give two examples,[1] the following makes us almost hear the bubbling and feel the vibrating of the witches' cauldron:

> For a charm of powerful *trouble,*
> Like a hell-broth *boil* and *bubble.*
> *All. Double, double toil* and *trouble,*
> Fire burn and *caldron bubble,*

[1] Suggested by Edwin Guest's *History of English Rhythms,* book i, chap. ii.

And this is the sound and appearance of waters imitated in the larynx and mouth:

> Fountains, and ye that *warble* as ye *flow*,
> *Melodious murmurs, warbling* tune his praise.[1]

This gives pleasure, and so does Shakespeare's Witches' song, although the poet has given a free play to his feeling for the sensuous reality; but if an equally sensuous diction is used to express erotic sensuality, whatever the argument of the poet—that is to say, however much he insists that ' all the passionate and just delights of the body ' are ' as naught if not ennobled by the concurrence of the soul at all times ',[2] since it is easier to express physical sensation than spiritual aspiration with the tremendous force of sensuous imitation of which language is capable, the sensual imagery will attract an unjust proportion of the reader's attention. Take the last line of the beautiful singing sonnet ' I sat with Love upon a woodside well ':

> And as I stooped, her own lips rising there
> Bubbled with brimming kisses at my mouth.

It almost turns the sonnet into a kiss. Rossetti was logically right in complaining that Buchanan seemed to regard it as the poet's ' absurd bubble-and-squeak notion of a kiss '; perhaps in a way he was aesthetically quite right also, since only a very insensitive reader could reach the last line before being moved by the sighing emotion of the poem. All the same, because of the tremendous reinforcement of sensuous imitation, the last line overwhelms the expressiveness of all the others, much as a sudden physical contact might disturb a train of thought. In the couplet which Rossetti takes from ' Eden Bower ', again because Buchanan lighted on it, the over-powerful expressiveness is the reason why it was useful to an enemy:

> Grip and lip my limbs as I tell thee!

Swinburne's wildest bites and reddest blood do not weigh on the reader's attention so heavily, for the sensuous feeling

[1] *Paradise Lost*, v, p. 195.   [2] *The Stealthy School of Criticism.*

A POCKET NOTE-BOOK KEPT BY ROSSETTI
(*By courtesy of the owner, Mr. Thomas J. Wise*)

is not there. Rossetti's most sensuous diction is quite justifiable as poetic expression, indeed it is occasionally a superb example of magical creation in words, but it upsets the artistic balance of many poems, and therefore by its very forcefulness becomes a defect of style. The examples of erotic imagery are easiest to detect, but these are not the only examples of an excess of feeling, which is the sign of a range of thought inadequate for the poet's imaginative force.

The concentration of thought and feeling causes Rossetti to weight every part of many a poem—to crowd it, as he crowds the earlier pictures. Sometimes the weightiness is impressive, as in the best stanzas of ' The Burden of Nineveh ', but in the same poem the style can be alternately right and wrong, and this is indeed a flaw in several of Rossetti's otherwise great poems. The two opening stanzas of ' The Burden of Nineveh ' exhibit this curious unadaptability of manner. The first is too heavy for the content:

> In our Museum galleries
> To-day I lingered o'er the prize
> Dead Greece vouchsafes to living eyes,—
> Her Art for ever in fresh wise
>   From hour to hour rejoicing me.
> Sighing I turned at last to win
> Once more the London dirt and din;
> And as I made the swing-door spin
> And issued, they were hoisting in
>   A wingèd beast from Nineveh.

But the second immediately justifies the form:

> A human face the creature wore,
> And hoofs behind and hoofs before,
> And flanks with dark runes fretted o'er.
> 'Twas bull, 'twas mitred Minotaur,
>   A dead disbowelled mystery:
> The mummy of a buried faith
> Stark from the charnel without scathe,
> Its wings stood for the light to bathe,—
> Such fossil cerements as might swathe
>   The very corpse of Nineveh.

The poem taken as a whole is a little too heavy because its twenty stanzas are like separate footsteps of that gigantic bull. The poet has countered the strong self-containing tendency of the stanza by offsetting the emphatic rhymes with a weak, assonantal feminine rhyme that is like a refrain; but although his technical skill is admirable the poem struggles to a satisfactory conclusion, and then it leaves a feeling of having been drawn out to a length unsustained by the central idea. This is an effect of other of the longer poems of Rossetti which is the more curious because of the evident condensation of language. But in fact the condensation of language is a clue to the weakness. Rossetti's imagination tended to seize too intimately the images which came in the train of the principal conception, and the reader is forced to shift the focus of the mind from one vista to another; the culmination of realization is delayed and then slightly dissipated by the overweighted unity of the poem. So it is that Rossetti's stanzas are greater achievements sometimes than his poems, and why also a compact form like the sonnet awaited a master in him. His concentration of thought when it is swept along by an undeviating rush of emotion through the compass of a sonnet produces perfection of form. Without the sonnet's strict plot his intensity is most valuable to the poem (except in the briefest lyrical pieces) when he is expressing his contemplative view of life and the images are not too luring for his imagination. He could beat Browning and Tennyson in writing didactic thought into true poetry, though he did it so rarely. ' The Cloud Confines ', for example, although it does not contain his most beautiful poetry, shows an artistic justice which poems filled with rarer treasures often lack. It is lyrical and packed with contemplative ideas. The endeavour to extend the outlet for his mind by a wider range of ideas was imperfectly successful, but it is often evident in his poetry. A sign of his unexpressed philosophical interest is the curious and remarkable ' Soothsay ', which one hesitates to call a poem, since it has no centre; it is a series of six-line stanzas charged with reflection. It just grew. Originally, when Rossetti showed it to Scott, it consisted of three stanzas. The third stanza then differed from the third stanza in the *Works*. Scott quoted it as follows:

> Let no priest tell you of any home
> Unseen above the sky's blue dome :
> To have played in childhood by the sea,
> Or to have been young in Italy,
> Or anywhere in the sun or rain ;
> To have loved and been beloved again,
> Is nearer Heaven than he can come

The amended stanza was inferior to this, but the drastic alterations probably began with the omitting of the reference to the priest. Rossetti brooded over poems and designs for years, in some cases for half his lifetime, and although his poetic alterations are usually marvels of tactful recovery of an original inspiration, the habit showed that he never properly extended his mind. He took infinite pains in revising the final drafts and the proofs in the light of the criticisms invited and received from his friends. Because he could ' see ' a poem better in print than in manuscript, he made a habit of issuing his poems in privately printed *Trial Books* before they were actually published. Anyone who has examined Mr. Thomas J. Wise's famous *Catalogue of the Ashley Library* will realize how much revision work this meant for the poet, for Mr. Wise quotes some of his alterations and also reproduces specimens of the manuscripts. Sometimes a single word became the subject of thoughtful correspondence. In ' Love's Nocturne ' he hesitated between ' dreamland ' and ' dreamworld ', and in a long letter to his brother, when he comes to this point he says: ' " Dreamland " is a rather hackneyed phrase I don't like, but it is so valuable for clearing up that I adopted it '. In the collected edition one finds ' dreamworld '. Just before this remark he says: ' I have been worrying about what you said of the obscurity of this poem, and have now put it thus ', and quotes the first two stanzas of the poem as published. ' Now there is another question ', he continues. ' The first conception of this poem was of a man not yet in love who dreams vaguely of a woman who he thinks must exist for him. This is not very plainly expressed, and not I think very valuable, and it might be better to refer the love to a known woman he wished to approach.' This is sufficient proof of the danger of attributing his poems to particular women, because ' Love's Nocturne ' was written in 1854 when, according to all the biographical evidence, he was happily in love with Lizzie Siddal, who may have been the cause of the mood of this poem, though her personality did not interfere with his artistic (and egoistic) purpose.

Because Rossetti could not develop freely away from his self-regarding emotion or maintain a hold of mystical certainty, his work in maturity begins to show the division of his personality. It was all very well for him to write a beautiful piece of paganism like ' Troy Town ' (which is one of his most successful poems) and then a sort of super-ballad like ' Rose Mary ', in which he falls back, too intently, on romantic ideas again; but for complete fulfilment he needed to combine in one work sensuous feeling, spiritual passion, and intellectual contemplation. He does it fitfully in *The House of Life*, but he needed a different framework, more like the Shakespearean drama, perhaps, than Dante's in the *Divine Comedy*. This may be putting the cart before the horse. If he did not find a setting which could hold all his greatness without constraint, the reason must have been in himself. His mind did not move out from its emotional centre far enough. It might have done so but for untoward events like the bad state of health he got into and the injurious attacks upon his reputation. How much energy he could employ is shown by the rapidity of his laborious production. Really it is an astonishing thing that besides ' Rose Mary ',

' The Stream's Secret ', and several other fine poems, not
to mention any painting, he should have written sixty-
four of the *House of Life* sonnets between 1869 and 1871.
In *The House of Life* he made his greatest effort to reconcile
conflicting elements in himself, and he nearly succeeded
in doing the impossible, and making a single poem out of
102 sonnets. Another effort to attain spiritual harmony
through aesthetic expression is represented by the late
pictures, ' Proserpine ', ' Mnemosyne ', ' Astarte Syriaca ',
where the creative artist again—and more surely—breaks
into mystical illumination through the passionate fusion
of pleasure and pain, or sensual and spiritual beauty—

> Betwixt the sun and moon a mystery,

as he wrote in the sonnet for ' Astarte Syriaca '. He could
travel from the ' Venus Verticordia ' (and ' Troy Town ')
as far as ' Beata Beatrix ' and a mystical Astarte (in poetry
' Soul's Beauty ' and ' Insomnia ') but he never safely
passes through the valley of the shadow. His *House of
Life* appropriately ends with ' The One Hope '; but this
shows that the mystery of death is for him a fear. A hope
is a denial of mystical faith. In his youthful ' Ave ' he
had asked:

> Soul, is it Faith, or Love, or Hope,
> That lets me see her standing up
> Where the light of the Throne is bright?

The answer is that it was Love, and in a less inharmonious
personality that Love when it grew into wisdom would
have seen the sibylline Beauty with the eyes of Faith.
Hope is the offspring of a fear of fear. That is just what
Rossetti's ' One Hope ' was. After the subsidence of his
erotic climax he was terribly lonely, like a child in the
dark. He had expended his powers so exhaustively in
portraying and singing that Beauty which was attainment
and peace. In his marvellous youth it was enough to
create, and the joy of it made the spiritual content find its
concrete expression without the distractions of sensuality
or of fear which divided his dream in maturity. While he

was young he could pursue mystery and make romantic pictures and poems of Mary-Beatrice and Paradise. He could still ride buoyantly above the gulfs that went down through the half-remembered darkness of the soul. But all the latent conditions for a disaster were there, should external events clash like converging winds and rouse a tempest.

A mind so powerfully self-centred as Rossetti's needed as many links as possible with the external world, to prevent its very vitality turning inward and consuming it. Rossetti balanced the introversion of his mind by his personal attractiveness which enabled him to be rich in friendship, and in his creative work he achieved the same object by his intuitive sympathy with individuals. This was largely involved in a fine dramatic sense. The remote and dreamlike imagery of his best romantic poems is generally charged with dramatic sympathy. The same is true of the best of the early water-colours. He realizes the human heart. This is why the pictures are often so much like poems, and why other poets were stimulated by them. A third means of externalizing the mind is in intellectual contemplation, which, as we have seen, colours his poetry. This synthetical process of the mind is closely united with his visionary view of human destiny, some-times tinged with satire, as in the sonnet ' On Refusal of Aid Between Nations '. Here there is no irony, but in ' The Burden of Nineveh ' and ' Jenny ' the satire is slightly ironical. The early version of ' Jenny ', which lacked the dramatic sympathy of the mature version, was probably inspired by Alfred de Musset who, in ' Rolla ' and ' Souvenir ', and even in lighter pieces like ' Mimi Pinson ' has affinities with Rossetti. It would be easier to argue from Rossetti's work that he was French than that he was Italian.

A more instructive comparison is with Browning, whose immature and anonymous ' Pauline ' was admired so much by Rossetti. ' Pauline ' is not typical of Browning's poetry, but it is a naive self-revelation. It is not like Rossetti's more artistic early poetry either, but it reveals a youthful self very like Rossetti's. The difference between the career and work of the two men is largely due to the fact that whereas Rossetti ultimately became too introverted, Browning succeeded in getting out of himself rather too thoroughly for the greatest creative work. We can see how a passage like the following in 'Pauline' has a personal reference to Rossetti even though he would never have described himself in so egotistical and analytical a fashion:

> I am made up of an intensest life,
> Of a most clear idea of consciousness
> Of self, distinct from all its qualities,
> From all affections, passions, feelings, powers;
> And thus far it exists, if tracked, in all:
> But linked, in me, to self-supremacy,
> Existing as a centre to all things,
> Most potent to create and rule and call
> Upon all things to minister to it. . . .

But the continuation of the passage hints of the rapid development in Browning of an extroverted mental habit which Rossetti, a more reclusive spirit, approached only for a few years—the years of his ' women and flowers ' phase—and by approaching sensually instead of intellectually, brought about a violent reaction to introversion. A passage further on in 'Pauline' emphasizes the intellectual and moral attitude in Browning which made his life so different from Rossetti's; incidentally it affords a sidelight on the prevalence of certain ideas adopted by the Pre-Raphaelites:

> 'Twas in my plan to look on real life,
> The life all new to me; my theories
> Were firm, so then I left, to look and learn
> Mankind, its cares, hopes, fears, its woes and joys;
> And as I pondered on their ways, I sought
> How best life's end might be attained—an end
> Comprising every joy. I deeply mused.
>
> And suddenly without heart-wreck I awoke
> As from a dream: I said: ''Twas beautiful,
> Yet but a dream, and so adieu to it!'

[309]

DANTE GABRIEL ROSSETTI

Rossetti was an incorrigible dreamer who could not awaken thoroughly to the external world without ' heart-wreck ', and to whom violent intrusion of catastrophic events is an irremediable disaster. His partial movement in the same direction as Browning is shown not only in a poem like ' A Last Confession ', where the manner recalls Browning as well as the dramatic imagination, but in much of the romantic work with a deep human sympathy. And in the picture ' Found ' was a revelation of what his genius might accomplish during an excursion into the external world. But it is a significant fact that ' Found ', although said to be one of the greatest works of the painter, was never finished despite repeated attempts. William Rossetti offered the explanation that his brother might have been discouraged by finding that Holman Hunt had done a picture on a similar theme after ' Found ' had reached its first stage. But Rossetti was not discouraged by another translation of Dante's *Vita Nuova*, and he would not have been prevented from painting ' Beata Beatrix ' or ' Dante's Dream ' for any such reason. His dreaming mind had identified itself with certain feelings and images expressed by Dante. ' Found ' was akin to the story of a poem by W. B. Scott, a friend whose mind was antipathetic to Rossetti's; also its theme was more than outside his dream, it was positively antagonistic; the model for the woman, who was a cast-off mistress, was Fanny Cornforth, who when she married was Rossetti's mistress. Rossetti found out too late what a virago a sensual, greedy, and unfaithful woman can be, but by a no doubt generous use of money Mrs. Schott was temporarily banished when he married Lizzie Siddal. Extremely personal complications of this kind strengthened all his innate inclination to keep within the limits of a closely personal dream world. Very early in adolescence he was entering his lifelong haven of dream, ' As,' in Browning's words,

some world-wanderer sees in a far meadow
Strange towers and high-walled gardens thick with trees,

> Where song takes shelter and delicious mirth
> From laughing fairy creatures peeping over,
> And on the morrow when he comes to lie
> For ever 'neath those garden-trees fruit-flushed
> Sung round by fairies, all his search is vain.

The reader of ' Pauline ', following the path of the fervent youth who read it in the British Museum with growing excitement, will find how Browning traces the growth of his powers, and how he was seized by intellectual pride. Intellectual pride and sloth are his two enemies, he says. So in ' Hand and Soul ' (with a reversal of the order of importance) sloth and intellectual pride are Chiaro's enemies. The pride is treated by Rossetti as a misdirection of energy, the artist exhausts himself in a futile effort to elevate the world by scornful disdain of its affections and the expression of austere abstractions, instead of merely showing it his concrete vision of beauty. In ' Pauline ' (a more immature work, of course) the artist's ' selfishness ' is due to overproud self-dependence, a sort of intellectual Byronism. His powers knelt to him and said ' Thyself, thou art our King! ' The second phase of Chiaro's experience is again reflected in a later passage of ' Pauline ':

> And when all's done, how vain seems e'en success—
> The vaunted influence poets have o'er men! . . .

But the poet learns to ' trust some love is true ' in the delight of his own hero-worship and contented lowness. So when he meets Pauline—his soul's divinity—he is again full of the pride of living, in old delights of fantasy and in the acquisition of knowledge for the pleasure of possession; but she causes him to search inwardly, and then he finds that he lacks her faith and love, and that his proud elation was a false dawn, though now, in their mutual love, he cannot despair. Yet his ' selfishness ' (*i.e.*, desire for pleasures) is a consuming flame, and he envies

> him whose soul
> Turns its whole energies to some one end,
> To elevate an aim, pursue success

[311]

However mean! So, still my baffled hope
Seeks out abstractions.

Chiaro really reaches an experience like that of the lover
of 'Pauline', the only difference being that 'Pauline' is
shown in her true character in 'Hand and Soul' as the
artist's other self. In Pauline's lover his 'restlessness of
passion' meets the 'craving after knowledge'. This
power of passion is ' the sleepless harpy with just-budding
wings ' which he beheld earlier in life,

And I considered whether to forego
All happy ignorant hopes and fears, to live,
Finding a recompense in its wild eyes.
And when I found that I should perish so,
I bade its wild eyes close from me for ever,
And I am left alone with old delights;
See! it lies in me a charmed thing, still prompt
To save me if I loose its slightest bond:
I cannot but be proud of my bright slave.

The theme of intellectual conquest is covered again in
'Paracelsus', and the dying confession of his faith by
Paracelsus is as relevant to Browning's extroverted
development as Rossetti's dream of 'The Orchard Pit'[1]
is to his powerful introversion.

Nearly all Rossetti's creative work may be resumed as
the expression of mingled fear and desire, and its two main
themes are Love and Death. The imagery of the most
romantic poetry is closely connected with the inward-
turning hunger of his mind, but the more personal later
poems show best the autobiographical strain of all his
work. One ought to take seriously the fragment among the
scraps printed by his brother under the title 'To Art':

I loved thee ere I loved a woman love.

His scraps, usually jotted down in pocket notebooks, are
like diary jottings and of uncommon interest. The fragment just quoted is dated 1870 by his brother, which is
in the mid period of his erotic phase in poetry. This is

[1] See chapter xiv.

the year the sonnet 'Death's Songsters'[1] was written,
of which the concluding couplet is:

> Say, soul—are songs of Death no heaven to thee,
> Nor shames her lip the cheek of Victory ?

The sonnet is strangely haphazard for Rossetti. His
brother's note on it says: 'The application of this
sonnet is not entirely clear to me. It will be observed
that, except for its last two lines, the sonnet consists
entirely of a reference to two acts of heroic self-discipline
recorded of Ulysses. Then in the last two lines comes the
application. This application, as I apprehend it, is an
appeal of the poet to his own moral conscience, and relates
to the question of a noble or a degrading tone in the poetry
which he affects, as writer or reader. Will he, like Ulysses,
disregard and disdain the blandishment of the song of the
Sirens, and the wiles of Helen ?' William is clearly
troubled, but perhaps he would have been franker to have
included erotic experience along with poetry as the subject
of his brother's contemplation. A further comment on the
line ' Nor shames her lip the cheek of victory ' justly notes
that ' her lip ' might mean, grammatically, either ' the lip
of Death ' or ' the lip of Victory '. He thinks ' with some
dubiety, that the former is intended '. Rossetti certainly
does personify Death as a woman, and the reading of this
ambiguous line as ' the lip of Death ' would complete the
argument of the sonnet, though very abruptly. If it were
the lip of Victory which shamed the cheek of Victory, the
argument from Ulysses would be contradicted, but with
a point of view which Rossetti elsewhere expresses, viz.,
that the turmoil and effort of the world are made to seem
insignificant and trifling by comparison with the fullness
of love. The truth is that Rossetti could not remain
consistent, because no woman could satisfy him after the
rapturous period of first love, and his poetry about love
tended to break free from the object of love and to enshrine
the ideal Love instead. The title ' To Art ' was probably

---

[1] *House of Life* (87).

given to the fragment by William Rossetti when editing
the *Works*. Without the title, how would that line read?

> I loved thee ere I loved a woman, *Love*.

Now if the first sonnet of *The House of Life* is re-read, it
will be found to throne Love above lovers as well as above
' all kindred powers the heart finds fair ':

> Truth, with awed lips; and Hope, with eyes upcast;
> And Fame, whose loud wings fan the ashen Past
> To signal-fires—

for Youth

> with still some single golden hair
> Unto his shoulder clinging—

and Life

> Still wreathing flowers for Death to wear.

are also those with whom ' Love's throne was not ' . . . .
All the images in this sonnet are important.

> far above
> All passionate wind of welcome and farewell
> He sat in breathless bowers they dream not of.

The Shakespearean[1] imagery is beautifully adapted to
the poet's own needs. Rossetti's pursuit of love was the old
pursuit of ' imperishable peace ', that state of Nirvana
which Francis Thompson described as 'passionless passion'.
Rossetti's first disaster in life was to find a Beatrice whom
he could take as a lover. The next phase was a pursuit of
the quest in the ephemeral forms of other women. He was
going the road that many men have trodden which leads
to an even more urgent hunger for an unattainable satisfaction. The mind delves into dream, or into its emotional
past. The memory of his dead wife provided him with a
symbol of his aspiration, when the Don Juan phase had
led him to the contemplation of death. Venus and Death
are sisters. Then came the new passion in his life, and his
fantasy strove, and succeeded for a time, in identifying
the new love with the old. Both the new love and the
remembered ideal were shadows of the unremembered

[1] *Twelfth Night.*

ideal which lives in every individual and is a buried
memory of the womb; for there is the primordial prototype
of man's earthly paradise as of his heavenly paradise, the
'breathless bowers' that the lovers have forgotten. In
Rossetti the primitive and repressed hunger was strengthened by the affectionate ties of his home during the early
years, and the spiritual companionship of his sister Christina, as well as his mother, remained in life as a reminder
of a former state from which, as from an Eden, he had
been turned out.

The pursuit of love becomes first an unconscious and
then a conscious pursuit of death when the mind fails to
externalize itself sufficiently to maintain a balance between
life and the dream. Rossetti's tremendous energy broke
away from the Siren voices again and again, by expressing
his deepest desires in creative art. There is no essential
contradiction between his recognition of himself, ' I loved
thee ere I loved a woman, Love ', without the title ' To
Art ' and with it, for art is ultimately the embodiment of a
man's alter-ego, whose most fundamental desire is an
ideal Love. The amazing group of sonnets entitled *The
House of Life* has had a stifling effect on the most careful
and sensitive readers simply because of the terrific energy
of the poet's creative resistance of death, and this is in the
verbal texture as well as the dominant moods.

The raptures of the love recorded in *The House of Life*
began to recede like an ebbing flood of moonlit sea which
discloses a ghastly shore. The pursuit of the fleshly
paradise leads always down to ' devious coverts of dismay ' [1]
they are one with those ' charnel caves ' [2] screened by
flowers, above which sing the sirens. The preoccupation
with death and remorse for lost life which makes yet
heavier the resonant gloom of this great sonnet sequence is
the reflection of the poet's mystical failure. A true mystic
in worshipping beauty would overcome fear and remorse
at last by the illumination which succeeds the shadow of

[1] Sonnet 97, ' The Monochord '.   [2] No. 87, ' Death's Songsters '.

[315]

death. Rossetti could gain no surer foothold on spiritual freedom than 'The One Hope'—of re-union, but that was a straw he clung to with the strength of a drowning man. He had dragged his heaven down to earth, environed himself with the fleshly paradise, and before he could gain his freedom it vanished like that paradisal feast which the oriental ruler gave to the youths before drugging them: when they awoke they believed that they had been in heaven; but they had gone no further than the palace of pleasure.

> Even so the thought that is at length full grown
> Turns back to note the sun-smit paths, all grey
> And marvellous once, where first it walked alone;
> And haply doubts, amid the unblenching day,
> Which most or least impelled its onward way,
> Those unknown things or these things overknown.[1]

After the 'mid-rapture', the attempt to measure the 'Heart's Compass', ending, nevertheless, in a question, although answered confidently:

> Even such Love is; and is not thy name Love?
> Yea, by thy hand the Love-god rends apart
> All gathering clouds of Night's ambiguous art;
> Flings them far down, and sets thine eyes above;
> And simply, as some gage of flower or glove,
> Stakes with a smile the world against thy heart.[2]

That is written in 1871. But the passionate lover who had stormed heaven and realized that he had broken down his own defences:

> O love, my love! if I no more should see
> Thyself, nor on the earth the shadow of thee,
> Nor image of thine eyes in any spring,—
> How then should sound upon Life's darkening slope
> The ground-whirl of the perished leaves of Hope,
> The wind of Death's imperishable wing?

moves back, as we all do, to an earlier memory when the ecstasies of unregenerate life, as all such ecstasies must do, subside and leave the self alone with the self and with the darkness.

[1] No. 80, 'From Dawn to Noon'.   [2] No. 27.

APPENDIXES

APPENDIX A

BIBLIOGRAPHICAL LIST OF THE CHIEF SOURCES OF INFORMATION DRAWN UPON IN THIS BOOK

Those which the Author regards as indispensable are marked with an asterisk.

1861 *The Early Italian Poets from Ciullo d'Alcamo to Dante Alighieri* (1100-1200-1300) *in the Original Metres. Together with Dante's* Vita Nuova. Translated by D. G. Rossetti. Part I, Poets chiefly before Dante. Part II, Dante and his Circle. (Smith, Elder & Co.)

1870 *Poems by Dante Gabriel Rossetti.* (F. S. Ellis.)

1874 *Dante and His Circle, with the Italian Poets preceding him.* . . . Revised and rearranged edition. Part I, Dante's *Vita Nuova*, etc., Poets of Dante's Circle. Part II, Poets chiefly before Dante. (Ellis & White.)

1881 *Poems by Dante Gabriel Rossetti.* A new edition. (Ellis & White.)

1881 *Ballads and Sonnets by Dante Gabriel Rossetti.* (Ellis & White.)

1904 *The Poems of Dante Gabriel Rossetti.* With illustrations from his own pictures and designs. Edited, with an Introduction and Notes, by William Michael Rossetti, 2 vols. (Ellis & Elvey.)

1911 *The Works of Dante Gabriel Rossetti.* Edited, with Preface and Notes, by William M. Rossetti. Revised and enlarged edition. (Ellis.)*

1882 *Dante Gabriel Rossetti: a Record and a Study*, by William Sharp. (Macmillan.)

DANTE GABRIEL ROSSETTI

1882 *Recollections of Dante Gabriel Rossetti*, by T. Hall
Caine. (Elliot Stock.)*

1883 *The Truth about Rossetti*, by Theodore Watts
[-Dunton] (*Nineteenth Century*, March.)*

1889 *Rossetti as Designer and Writer*, by W. M. Rossetti.

1892 *Autobiographical Notes of the Life of William Bell
Scott*, edited by W. Minto, 2 vols. (J. R. Osgood,
McIlvaine & Co.) (Especially vol. 2.)

1895 *Dante Gabriel Rossetti. His Family Letters.* With a
Memoir by W. M. Rossetti, 2 vols. (Ellis & Elvey.)*

1895 *The Table Talk of Shirley*, by Sir John Skelton.
(Blackwood & Sons.)

1895-6 *Literary Anecdotes of the 19th Century.* Sir W. R.
Nicoll and Thomas J. Wise.

1897 *Letters of D. G. Rossetti to W. Allingham*, 1854-1876.
Edited by G. B. Hill. (T. F. Unwin.)

1898 *Christina Rossetti: a Biographical and Critical Study*,
by Mackenzie Bell. (Hurst and Blackett.)

1899 *Dante Gabriel Rossetti: an Illustrated Memorial of his
Art and Life*, by H. C. Marillier. (Geo. Bell &
Sons.)*

1899 *Ruskin; Rossetti; Preraphaelitism.* Papers 1854 to
1862 edited by W. M. Rossetti. (George Allen.)*

1899 *The Life of William Morris* (2 vols.), by J. W.
Mackail. (Longmans, Green.)

1900 *Preraphaelite Diaries and Letters*, etc., edited by
W. M. Rossetti.*

1901 *Gabriel Rossetti: a versified autobiography.* Translated and supplemented by W. M. Rossetti.
(Sands & Co.)

1902 *Poetical Works of Christina Rossetti.* With an Introductory Memoir by W. M. Rossetti. (Mac-
millan.)*

1904 *Recollections of D. G. Rossetti and his Circle*, by
H. Treffry Dunn.

1911 *The Life of John Ruskin* (2 vols.), by E. T. Cook.
(George Allen & Co.)

1912 *Memorials of Edward Burne-Jones*, by G. B.-J. (Macmillan.)

1912 *Chronological List, with notes, of paintings and drawings from Dante by Dante Gabriel Rossetti*, by Paget J. Toynbee. (Privately printed as a reprint from ' Scritti Varü di Erudizione e di Critica in onore di Rodolfo Remer '. Torino, 1912.)

1914 *The Theory of Poetry in England*, by R. P. Cowl, M.A. (Macmillan.)

1919-20 *A Bibliography of . . . A. C. Swinburne* (2 vols.), by Thomas J. Wise.

1921 *Un Italien d'Angleterre : le poète-peintre Dante Gabriel Rossetti*, par Henri Dupré. (J. M. Dent & Fils, Paris.)

1927 *The Haunted Castle. A Study of the Elements of English Romanticism*, by Eino Railo. (Routledge.)

1928 *Catalogue of the Ashley Library*, 9 vols. (especially vols. 3, 8, and 9), by Thomas J. Wise. *

1928 *Letters of Dante Gabriel Rossetti to His Publisher F. S. Ellis*, edited by Oswald Doughty. (Scholartis Press.)

APPENDIX B

NOTES ON PICTURES REPRODUCED

(*a*) Mary Magdalene at the Door of Simon the Pharisee

The fine autographed photograph from which the reproduction was made is in the possession of Professor R. Pape Cowl. The original pen-and-ink was done in 1858 and is the best of the versions of this subject by Rossetti. Rossetti's sonnet for the picture:

> Why wilt thou cast the roses from thine hair?
>   Nay, be thou all a rose,—wreath, lips, and cheek.
>   Nay, not this house,—that banquet-house we seek;
> See how they kiss and enter; come thou there.
> This delicate day of love we two will share
>   Till at our ear love's whispering night shall speak.
>   What, sweet one,—hold'st thou still the foolish freak?
> Nay, when I kiss thy feet they'll leave the stair.
>
> Oh, loose me! See'st thou not my Bridegroom's face
>   That draws me to Him? For His feet my kiss,
>   My hair, my tears He craves to-day;—and oh!
> What words can tell what other day and place
>   Shall see me clasp those blood-stained feet of His?
>   He needs me, calls me, loves me: let me go!

Note on the Picture.—The face of Christ in the drawing is a portrait-study of Burne-Jones, not, as often stated, of Meredith, whom also it resembles. 'At a later date' than the first complete version of the picture (which is 1858), that is 1864, 'Mr. Meredith was for a time co-tenant with Rossetti of his Chelsea house, and it is this relationship which may have suggested the theory that he sat for the head. But the date of the pen-and-ink drawing, apart from all other considerations, makes it certain that this

[322]

could not be; and the likeness to Burne-Jones, at the time in question, is said to be sufficiently striking'.—MARILLIER.

H. C. Marillier is the most painstaking of all Rossetti's biographers, but against his argument of the dates it may be suggested that Rossetti might have seen Meredith before 1853, when the picture was first sketched, as Meredith was known to two early friends of Rossetti, Millais and Frederick Sandys. But the weight of the evidence remains in favour of the theory that the model was Burne-Jones, an intimate of the Pre-Raphaelites long before Meredith. The earliest reference to Meredith in Rossetti's correspondence is 1861, when Rossetti, married to Elizabeth Siddal, was living at Chatham Place, by Blackfriars. Rossetti promises his correspondent that Meredith will be among the visitors on a certain day.

(b) THE GIRLHOOD OF MARY VIRGIN

Although the Virgin was painted from Christina, who had brown hair, she has golden hair. Above her head, in the golden circlet, are the letters ' S. Maria S.M. '. Her dress is a soft grey, with sage-green sleeves. Behind her is a harpsichord. The robe of Anna, who was painted from the artist's mother, is umber; her mantle, myrtle-green, her head-cloth brick-red. ' S. Anna ' is inscribed in the golden circlet above her head. The big bound volumes, which were hoisted up to Hunt's studio from Gabriele Rossetti's house, bear the titles of the cardinal virtues: Caritas (golden); Fides (blue); Spes (pale green); Prudentia (grey); Temperantia (white); Fortitudo (light umber). On the floor, in foreground, the slips of thorn are emblems of the future passion, and so are the cross-shaped ivy-grown sticks above the balustrade where St. Joachim is pruning the vine, to paint the leaves of which the young artist took his canvas into the country. The accurate drawing of the vine-leaves and the dove were among the distinctively unconventional signs that this was a ' Pre-Raphaelite ' picture.

DANTE GABRIEL ROSSETTI

Rossetti wrote two sonnets for this picture:

I

This is that blessed Mary, pre-elect
  God's Virgin. Gone is a great while, and she
    Dwelt young in Nazareth of Galilee.
Unto God's will she brought devout respect,
Profound simplicity of intellect,
  And supreme patience. From her mother's knee
    Faithful and hopeful; wise in charity;
Strong in grave peace; in pity circumspect.

So held she through her girlhood; as it were
  An angel-watered lily, that near God
    Grows and is quiet. Till, one dawn at home
She woke in her white bed, and had no fear
  At all,—yet wept till sunshine, and felt awed:
    Because the fulness of the time was come.

II

These are the symbols. On that cloth of red
  I' the centre is the Tripoint: perfect each,
    Except the second of its points, to teach
That Christ is not yet born. The books—whose head
Is golden Charity, as Paul hath said—
  Those virtues are wherein the soul is rich:
    Therefore on them the lily standeth, which
In Innocence, being interpreted.

The seven-thorn'd briar and the palm seven-leaved
  Are her great sorrow and her great reward.
    Until the end be full, the Holy One
Abides without. She soon shall have achieved
  Her perfect purity: yea, God the Lord
    Shall soon vouchsafe His Son to be her Son.

The *Athenaeum's* review of the Free Exhibition at Hyde Park Corner in April-May 1849, from which an extract follows, gave no warning of the storm of abuse about to break over the ' P.R.B.'s ':

' It is pleasant to turn from the mass of commonplace to a manifestation of true mental power in which art is made the exponent of some high aim; and what is of the earth, earthy, and of the art material, is lost sight of in a dignified and intellectual purpose. Such a work will be found here, not from a long-practised hand, but from one young in experience, new to fame, Mr. D. G. Rossetti. He has painted " The Girlhood of the Virgin Mary ", a work which, for its invention and for many parts of its design, would be creditable to any exhibition. In idea it forms a fitting pendant to Mr. Herbert's " Christ subject to his Parents at Nazareth ". A legend may possibly have suggested to Mr. Rossetti also the subject of his present work. The Virgin is in this picture represented as living amongst her family, and engaged in the task of embroidering drapery to supply possibly some future sacred vestment. The picture, which is full of allegory, has much of that sacred mysticism inseparable from the works of the early masters, and much of the tone of the poets of the same time. While immature practice is visible in the executive department of the work, every allusion gives evidence of maturity of thought, every detail that might enrich or amplify the subject has found a place in it. The personification of the Virgin is an achievement worthy of an older hand. Its spiritualized attributes, and the great sensibility with which it is wrought, inspire the expectation that Mr. Rossetti will continue to pursue the lofty career which he has here so successfully begun. The sincerity and earnestness of the picture remind us forcibly of the feeling with which the early Florentine monastic painters wrought; and the form and face of the Virgin recall the words employed by Savonarola in one of his powerful sermons: " Or pensa quanta bellezza avea la Vergine, che avea tanta santita, che risplendeva in quella faccia della quale dice San Tommaso che nessuno che la vedesse mai la guardo per concupiscenza, tanta era la santita che rilustrava in lei ". Mr. Rossetti has perhaps unknowingly entered into the feelings of the renowned Dominican who in his day wrought as much reform in art as in morals. The coincidence is of high value to the picture.'

DANTE GABRIEL ROSSETTI

(c) MRS. ROSSETTI AND CHRISTINA ROSSETTI

'The tinted-chalk head of Christina, along with our mother, now in the National Portrait Gallery, was drawn by Dante Rossetti at Hunter's Forestal, Herne Bay, as he was recovering from an illness in the autumn of 1877. This profile is markedly like a certain aspect of Christina's face which was not exactly unwonted, but still was exceptional; there is a rather inscrutable sphinx-like look about it whenever I set eyes upon it, the lines from her poem, " From House to Home ", come into my mind:

> Therefore in patience I possess my soul;
> Yea therefore as a flint I set my face.'

—(William Rossetti's ' Memoir ' in the *Poetical Works* of Christina Rossetti.)

APPENDIX C

ROSSETTI'S CHLORAL POISONING

In the spring of 1870 Rossetti, whose health had been ailing for over a year, went down to Scalands, near Roberts-bridge, Sussex, the estate of Mrs. Bodichon, an old friend of the Rossettis (formerly Miss Barbara Smith). During the following twelve months he was joined by William J. Stillman, an American literary man who had been a land-scape painter. Rossetti, whose insomnia had begun to trouble him as much as the worry about his eyesight, was recommended by Stillman to try chloral, a new and supposedly harmless soporific. Rossetti used the drug without moderation, intent upon securing the repose without which he could not work. He rapidly increased the doses; but as the chloral was much diluted without his knowledge, by the friendly conspiracy of his doctor and chemist, and assistants in the house, he never consumed doses anything like as large as those of which he foolishly boasted. But the mere boasting about them was a sign of the poisoning of the drug, to which must be added the injurious effect upon him of alcohol. He was normally temperate, but acquired the habit of drinking neat whisky after the chloral to take away the taste, and perhaps to hasten the soporific phase. Both the drug and the alcohol were especially dangerous to a sanguine, choleric constitu-tion and temperament like Rossetti's, and their evil influence followed close upon an emotional crisis in his life. The alcohol made him violently impulsive, and the chloral brought out and intensified the hesitancy of pur-pose which underlay his decisive exterior. A less im-moderate use of chloral than Rossetti's might have sufficed to produce the state of morbid suspicion of the world, and finally of his friends, which culminated in his attempted suicide in the summer of 1872, for other events, such as the public attacks upon his very personal poems, conspired to give a concrete shape to his fears.

There is no scientific reason for the supposition which has been advanced that chloral affected Rossetti's colour-sense, and that it explains in some way his preference for greens and yellows. But it is in any case doubtful if his pictures do show a preference for harmonies of green and yellow tones after he began the use of chloral. Blue is at least as prominent as golden yellows in the great painting period of the sixties; this period leads up to the portrait of Mrs. Morris in a blue dress, done in 1868. But reds became rather less frequent after the sixties, a sufficient explanation for which would be the prevalence of twilight atmospheres in the chief pictures of the seventies.

The following are definite facts, supplied by a physician, concerning chloral:

A. Pharmocological action: (i) It is a gastric irritant; (ii) it depresses the heart, lowers blood pressure, and dilates the blood-vessels; (iii) it lowers the blood temperature; (iv) it acts as a hypnotic on the brain cells; at first it causes a slight mental excitement, then quiescence, then sleep; large doses produce deep coma, then death.

(The initial phase of slight mental excitement was probably that in which Rossetti would begin composing. He told his sister Christina that 'sonnets mean insomnia', meaning that he wrote many of them at night before getting to sleep. He might often have tried to avoid this period by over-dosing.)

B. Acute poisoning by chloral: Shortly after taking a poisonous dose the patient without preliminary excitement becomes drowsy, gradually passes into coma from which he cannot be roused. Respiration slow and laboured, pulse 'thready' and then slow.

APPENDIX C

Pupils contracted, face sunken. Surface of body and limbs noticeably cold. Reflexes abolished and complete absence of sensibility. Perspiration marked.

C. Chronic poisoning in those who form the chloral habit: (i) Craving for it easily established; (ii) gastro-intestinal irritation symptoms; (iii) spots on skin; (iv) noisy breathing; (v) a 'facile mentality', as in certain types of high-grade imbeciles.

INDEX

(NOTE.—*The grouped titles on pp. 294-295 are not indexed.*)

[331]

INDEX

INDEX

DANTE GABRIEL ROSSETTI

CHISWICK PRESS: CHARLES WHITTINGHAM AND GRIGGS (PRINTERS), LTD.
TOOKS COURT, CHANCERY LANE, LONDON.